JOSEPHUS AND FAITH

ARBEITEN ZUR GESCHICHTE DES ANTIKEN JUDENTUMS UND DES URCHRISTENTUMS

HERAUSGEGEBEN VON

Martin Hengel (Tübingen), Peter Schäfer (Berlin),
Pieter W. van der Horst (Utrecht), Martin Goodman (Oxford),
Daniël R. Schwartz (Jerusalem)

XIX

JOSEPHUS AND FAITH

Πίστις and Πιστεύειν as Faith Terminology
in the Writings of Flavius Josephus
and in the New Testament

BY

DENNIS R. LINDSAY

E.J. BRILL
LEIDEN · NEW YORK · KÖLN
1993

The paper in this book meets the guidelines for permanence and durability of the Committee on Production Guidelines for Book Longevity of the Council on Library Resources.

BT
771.2
.L5513
1993

Library of Congress Cataloging-in-Publication Data

Lindsay, Dennis R.
[Pistis] und [pisteuein] als Glaubensbegriffe in den Schriften des Flavius Josephus und im Neuen Testament. English]
Josephus and faith : [pistis] and [pisteuein] as faith terminology in the writings of Flavius Josephus and in the New Testament / by Dennis R. Lindsay.
    p. cm. — (Arbeiten zur Geschichte des antiken Judentums und des Urchristentums, ISSN 0169-734X ; Bd. 19)
Includes bibliographical references and index.
ISBN 9004098585
    1. Faith—History of doctrines—Early church, ca. 30-600.
2. Josephus, Flavius. 3. Pistis (The Greek word) 4. Bible. N.T.–
–Criticism, interpretation, etc. 5. Greek language, Hellenistic
(300 B.C. - 600 A.D.)—Semantics. I. Title. II. Series.
BT771.2.L5513   1993
234'.2—dc20
                                                       93-29156
                                                          CIP

ISSN   0169-734X
ISBN   90 04 09858 5

PRINTED IN THE NETHERLANDS

To my Parents,
Andrew & Esther Lindsay

TABLE OF CONTENTS

PREFACE

From the very early days of the Church the writings of Flavius Josephus have been highly regarded by Christian scholars. The Church of the early Christian centuries was primarily responsible for preserving the works of Josephus for posterity. The historical—and somewhat apologetic—discourses of Josephus provided a quite useful resource for those Christians who found themselves in a position of defending the historicity of their own faith. Josephus' partiality toward Rome over against his Palestinian-Jewish compatriots—a partiality evident throughout the *Bellum Judaicum*—was a position with which the developing Christian community could increasingly identify as tensions mounted between Church and Synagogue.

Probably the strongest witness of the importance of Josephus' writings for early Christian scholars is the so-called *Testimonium Flavianum* in *Ant.* 18,63-64, where Jesus is identified as "the Christ". Of course, the authenticity of this passage is heavily disputed, and most modern scholars regard it as a later Christian gloss. Whatever our conclusion about its genuineness, however, the *Testimonium Flavianum* clearly shows that Josephus' writings were held in high esteem by the Christians who preserved them. Through the centuries Church scholars have returned time and again to the writings of Josephus as a historical reference point for New Testament studies and for the origins of their own faith.

Josephus' use of the Greek πιστ- word group as faith terminology is an area which has, up to this point, been largely unexplored. The present work deals with the broad spectrum of the use of this word group in order: 1) to locate the proper perspective for Josephus' understanding of the πιστ- words as faith terminology, and 2) to clarify the NT understanding of the word group through comparison with Josephus' use.

Josephus and Faith is the English version of my doctoral dissertation, *Πίστις und Πιστεύειν als Glaubensbegriffe in den Schriften des Flavius Josephus und im Neuen Testament*, submitted to the Protestant Faculty of the Eberhard-Karls-Universität, Tübingen, 1990. With the exception of a few minor changes and additions, the English version does not deviate from the original German work.

I am indebted a number of people for their help in producing this work. My dear, dear mentor and doctoral supervisor in Tübingen, Prof. Dr. Otto Betz, planted in my mind the seeds for this project several years prior to the beginning of my formal doctoral studies. The guidance and advice he gave during my research work continue to serve me, and I find that I am still learning from him, even though we are no longer working together. The Institut zur Erforschung des Urchristentums in Tübingen, along with its directors—Dr. William D. Howden and Dr. Ronald E. Heine, respectively—, provided a forum for me to present my ongoing research and to receive critical feed-back. I am deeply in debted to my colleague at Springdale College, Dr. Donn A. Leach, for his meticulous help in proof-reading my English manuscript to prepare it for publication.   I am likewise indebted to Mr. Brian Wicks for his help in producing the camera ready copy. I am grateful to Prof. Dr. Martin Hengel for his willingness to include my work in this series and to the editors at E. J. Brill for their technical help and guidance.   Finally, I express a special word of appreciation to my lovely wife, Karen.   Without Karen's unwavering support and encouragement this book would never have been written.

Dennis R. Lindsay
Springdale College
Birmingham, 19 April 1993

INTRODUCTION

With regard to the question whether the New Testament should be interpreted in light of Old Testament Judaism or of secular Hellenism, the
central theological concept of 'faith, to believe', expressed by the Greek
words πίστις and πιστεύειν, must be given serious consideration. There
have been attempts to show that the use of the πιστ‑ word group as religious faith terminology in the New Testament is itself an important
point of departure from OT Hebrew and Jewish backgrounds. In a
monograph entitled *Two Types of Faith,*[1] for example, Martin Buber
argues that the NT (Christian) concept of faith, particularly as derived
from the Pauline and Johannine writings, is primarily a Hellenistic concept. As such, Buber maintains, Christian faith is radically different from
the OT (Jewish) concept of faith.

Dieter Lührmann has, on the other hand, convincingly demonstrated the influence of the Jewish use of this word group (especially
influence from the LXX) upon the NT.[2] According to Lührmann, the
LXX translators rejected the normal Greek categories for referring to faith
in God[3] in their translation of the Hebrew substantives אֱמֶת and אֱמוּנָה and
selected rather the πιστ‑ word group, which otherwise in Hellenism was
not employed in this context.

Lührmann maintains that the LXX translators employed the words
πίστις and πιστεύειν as what he calls *Bedeutungslehnwörter* in their
rendering of the Hebrew אֱמֶת and אֱמוּנָה. According to Lührmann, this development is comparable to a similar development in the Christian tradition, where the Latin words *fides/credere* or the the German words
Glaube/glauben (or we might well add the English faith/believe) received
their (semantic) content from a foreign language tradition at a later point
in time within the context of Christianity. Using these *Bedeutungslehnwörter*, the LXX translators purposefully by-passed the terms
for religious belief which were normal for that time and in their place introduced a new term into this context. Lührmann writes:

---

[1] See the discussion of Buber's *Two Types of Faith* (New York: Macmillan Publishing Co., 1951)
below, Chapter 8.

[2] Dieter Lührmann, *"Pistis* im Judentum", *Zeitschrift für die Neutestamentliche Wissenschaft* 64
(1973), pp. 19-38.

[3] I.e., νομίζειν θεοὺς εἶναι.

Die LXX-Übersetzer greifen also weder auf das griechische νομίζειν θεοὺς εἶναι noch auf die Wortgruppe σεβ- zurück zur Wiedergabe der alttestamentlichen Stellen, an denen [אמן] die Beziehung des Menschen zu Gott bezeichnet, sondern mit πιστ- auf Wörter, die in der griechischen Sprachtradition gerade nicht in diesem Umkreis verwendet werden.[4]

In support of this argument Lührmann cites the remark by Georg Bertram that at the time of the LXX translation πιστεύειν (= אמן) was not felt to be a religious term.[5]

More recently, in an article entitled "Pistis in hellenistischer Religiosität",[6] G. Barth challenges the thesis of Lührmann that there is no secular Hellenistic religious usage of πίστις and πιστεύειν which influenced the NT authors. Drawing upon passages cited by W. Bauer in his *Wörterbuch zum Neuen Testament* and R. Bultmann in his article on πίστις in the *Theological Dictionary of the New Testament*, and adding a few findings of his own, Barth argues that there may indeed have been a religious use of πίστις in pagan Hellenism which had some degree of influence upon the NT use and understanding of 'faith, to believe'.[7]

On the one hand, it must be admitted that the expression νομίζειν θεοὺς εἶναι, although clearly religious terminology, is far too lacking to be able to express the relationship between humankind and God signified in the OT by the root אמן. For this reason the LXX translators had to find some other term to more fully express this concept. On the other hand, it is particularly noteworthy that the LXX translators entirely avoid the word νομίζειν. Not once is any Hebrew root in the OT translated by the verb νομίζειν.[8]

It would not, however, be accurate to say that the LXX translators or the NT writers replaced the Greek religious belief formula νομίζειν θεοὺς εἶναι with the πιστ- group. This can hardly be the case since πίστις and πιστεύειν signify much more the idea of trust and faithfulness than simply opinion or intellectual persuasion. But it is also clear that

---

[4] Lührmann, "*Pistis* in Judentum", pp. 24-25.

[5] Cf. R. Bultmann, "πιστεύω, κτλ"., *Theological Dictionary of the New Testament (TDNT)* Vol. 6, p. 198, note 149.

[6] In *Zeitschrift für die Neutestamentliche Wissenschaft* 73 (1982), pp. 110-126.

[7] Ibid., p. 126.

[8] A possible exception is Sir. 29,4; see below, Chapter 3. In the OT Apocrypha the verb νομίζειν is used fifteen times. Only twice, however, is it used in the stricter sense of a religious belief formula: 1) Wisd. 13,2: "...but [they] deemed either fire, or wind or the swift air, or the circle of the stars, or the violent water, or the lights of heaven, to be the gods which govern the world"; 2) 4 Macc. 5,18: "...if we wrongly think [our law] to be divine".

the LXX translators had no use for the verb νομίζειν as a religious *terminus technicus*—indeed, no use for the verb νομίζειν at all.[9]

Lührmann's thesis that πίστις and πιστεύειν are *Bedeutungslehnwörter,* receiving their semantic content from a language tradition other than Greek, raises some interesting questions and problems. Perhaps the most crucial question is whether mere *Bedeutungslehnwörter* could be of any significant use to the LXX translators, later to the NT writers or even to Josephus to describe in any meaningful way to a Hellenistic audience the proper human relationship and response toward God,[10] or to carry on mission work among the Greek-speaking populace in any meaningful way. Why indeed was the πιστ- word group selected by the LXX translators to represent the Hebrew אמן stem if this word group was not recognized as religious terminology?

In the arena of this debate, the use of πίστις and πιστεύειν as faith terminology in the writings of Flavius Josephus must be given more detailed attention. With the exception of a brief section in Lührmann's (1973) article on "Pistis in Judentum", the use of this word group by Josephus has been largely neglected.[11] Adolf Schlatter in *Der Glaube im Neuen Testament* provides a three page register of parallels in Josephus to the New Testament use of πίστις and πιστεύειν, but with little commentary or application. Thus Schlatter leaves the impression of comparable use in the two sources.[12] With the help of the recently published concordance to the writings of Josephus by K. H. Rengstorf,[13] it is now much more feasible to undertake a comprehensive study of Josephus' use of πίστις and πιστεύειν as faith terminology.

The first part of this book will address the development of the πιστ- word group as religious faith terminology, partly in comparison with and in contrast to the more normative religious belief terminology found in the formula νομίζειν θεοὺς εἶναι. We shall begin by examining the religious use of the πιστ- word group in Classical and in secular

---

[9] This is not the case with Josephus. Josephus indeed knew and used the verb νομίζειν as a term for religious faith, although primarily in the context of pagan religion. His religious use of the πιστ- word group, by contrast, occurs primarily in the context of Jewish religion.

[10] I.e., πιστεύειν as the equivalent of the Hebrew אמן.

[11] Lührmann, "*Pistis* in Judentum", pp. 26-29; cf. also the more recent article by David M. Hay, "Pistis as 'Ground for Faith' in Hellenized Judaism and Paul", *Journal of Biblical Literature* 108,3 (Fall 1989), esp. pp. 468-470. It is significant that R. Bultmann in his article on πιστεύειν in *TDNT* does not address Josephus' use of the πιστ- group and his concept of faith.

[12] Adolf Schlatter, *Der Glaube im Neuen Testament*, 6th ed. with an introduction by Peter Stuhlmacher (Stuttgart: Calwer Verlag, 1927 = 1982), pp. 582-85.

[13] Karl H. Rengstorf, *A Complete Concordance to Flavius Josephus* (Leiden: Brill, 1973).

Hellenistic Greek literature, and then turn to the use of the word group in the LXX, in Sirach and in Philo of Alexandria.

In the second part of the book we shall turn to Josephus' use and understanding of the πιστ- group as faith terminology—particularly in comparison to the use and understanding of the word group in the NT. Through this contrast and comparison we shall show that Josephus was influenced by two traditions—that of Hellenism and that of the OT—in his (religious) use of the πιστ- group. The NT, however, knows only the OT concept of faith.

PART I:

THE DEVELOPMENT OF THE ΠΙΣΤ- WORDS AS FAITH TERMINOLOGY

CHAPTER ONE

ΠΙΣΤΙΣ AND ΠΙΣΤΕΥΕΙΝ IN SECULAR GREEK

1 THE RELIGIOUS USE OF ΠΙΣΤΙΣ IN THE CLASSICAL PERIOD

Πίστις does not commonly occur in the Classical Greek period as a term for religious faith. When the noun appears in the sense of 'trust, trustworthiness', it is almost exclusively in the context of purely secular [human] relationships. It is therefore accurate to say that πίστις in Classical Greek is a profane term. In one significant passage in Sophocles' *Oedipus Rex*, line 1445, however, πίστις appears in the sense of faith which is directed toward [the] God. This line records the words of Creon to Oedipus concerning actions which must be taken once Oedipus had realized his fatal mistake:

καὶ γὰρ σὺ νῦν τἂν τῷ θεῷ πίστιν φέροις.[1]

It is important to note that this admonition to put trust in [the] God finds its context with other admonitions of Kreon to enquire of the God what must be done in this situation:

ἔδρασ᾽ ἂν εὖ τοῦτ᾽ ἴσθι ἄν, εἰ μὴ τοῦ θεοῦ
πρώτιστ᾽ ἔχρῃζον ἐκμαθεῖν τί πρακτέον.[2]

ὅμως δ᾽ ἵν᾽ ἔσταμεν
χρείας ἄμεινον ἐκμαθεῖν τί δραστέον.[3]

From the context it is very clear that τῷ θεῷ πίστιν φέρειν in line 1445 should be understood as an active faith in [the] God which is demonstrated through obedience to the divine oracle. This religious understanding of πίστις combines elements of intellectual belief and obedient action.[4] It is important that this use of πίστις is at least partially parallel to the under-standing of πίστις as the equivalent of אֱמוּנָה in the OT and LXX.

While this occurrence of πίστις as religious faith in *Oed. Tyr.* is certainly an important forerunner of a religious understanding of πίστις in

---

[1] "For even you would now put trust in [the] God".
[2] Lines 1438-39; "I would gladly have done [what you ask], know this well, if I did not want to first consult the God to learn what must be done".
[3] Lines 1442-43; "Where we now stand [in this matter] it is better to find out what must be done".
[4] I.e., faith is not only an intellectual belief in God, but also a trust in God which naturally implies faithfulness to God.

later writings, this isolated instance is not conclusive. A technical religious understanding of πίστις appears to be a later development[5] than for the verb πιστεύειν. For this reason the religious use of πιστεύειν in the Classical period lends a clearer picture of the development of the πιστ-word group as religious faith terminology.

2 THE RELIGIOUS USE OF ΠΙΣΤΕΥΕΙΝ IN THE CLASSICAL PERIOD

2.1 Νομίζειν Θεοὺς Εἶναι as Belief in the Gods

Νομίζειν θεοὺς εἶναι is the normal expression in Classical Greek for belief in the gods.[6] In the strictest sense this formula refers to belief in the existence of the gods, denoting intellectual theism as opposed to atheism. In this respect νομίζειν θεοὺς εἶναι is synonymous with ἡγεῖσθαι θεοὺς εἶναι,[7] also a religious expression, but not as frequent in occurrence as the formula with νομίζειν. There is possibly another sense in which νομίζειν θεούς is used without εἶναι referring to the idea of *paying honor to* the gods through the performance of the 'customary rites',[8] i.e., in the sense of *worshiping* the gods.

This latter interpretation of νομίζειν θεούς, however, has for some time been a point of contention among Classical scholars. One clear example of the dispute centers around the charge against Socrates by the Athenians in Plato's *Apology* 24,b. The passage reads:

> The charge is as follows: They say that Socrates is guilty of wrongdoing in that he is corrupting the youth and that he is not 'νομίζοντα' the gods which the city 'νομίζει', but instead other new 'δαιμόνια'.[9]

The disputed issue is whether Socrates was accused of pure intellectual atheism or whether the charge had to do with impious conduct—the failure to participate in the customary rites due the gods.

Each side of this debate has been argued to the extreme. J. Tate maintains that νομίζειν θεούς is exactly the same as νομίζειν θεούς

---

[5] Note, for example, the (relatively low) frequency of the use of πίστις in the LXX as compared with Philo or the NT.

[6] In the NT the verb νομίζειν appears fifteen times, but only in Acts 17,29 as a religious *terminus technicus*: οὐκ ὀφείλομεν νομίζειν χρυσῷ ἢ ἀργύρῳ ἢ λίθῳ ... τὸ θεῖον εἶναι ὅμοιον; "We should not think that the Deity is like unto gold or silver or stone". A secular religious usage of νομίζειν is quite appropriate here within the context of Paul's address at the Areopagus in Athens.

[7] As, for example, in Plato, *Laws* 10,885b,4. 7: οὐχ ἡγούμενος θεοὺς εἶναι.

[8] τὰ νομισμένα.

[9] Ἔχει δέ πως ὧδε· Σωκράτη φησὶν ἀδικεῖν τούς τε νέους διαφθείροντα καὶ θεοὺς οὓς ἡ πόλις νομίζει οὐ νομίζοντα, ἕτερα δὲ δαιμόνια καινά.

εἶναι, both referring to a purely intellectual belief in the existence of the gods.[10] Still others have argued that there are a number of instances where νομίζειν θεούς cannot simply refer to an intellectual theism (or atheism) but can only carry the idea of honoring the gods (i.e., by performing the customary religious rites).

A moderate view is more likely correct, as Wilhelm Fahr points out in his 1969 Tübingen dissertation. Fahr has shown that the verb νομίζειν from the earliest usage carried a *double meaning*.

> Die Akkusativobjekte, die dort von νομίζειν abhängen ... bezeichnen einer-seits den Bereich der bloßen Meinung (Gegensatz: εἰδέναι), der Unverbindlichkeit, und andererseits den des richtigen Handelns, der Verbindlichkeit. Diese doppelte Ausrichtung der Bedeutung von νομίζειν wird in den ersten Belegen des Verbums bei den Lyrikern und Vorsokratikern bestätigt....[11]

Fahr charts the development of the general and religious use of νομίζειν. He demonstrates that on a religious level as well as on a secular level the underlying ideas of *Verbindlichkeit* and *Unverbindlichkeit* are integrally related, and perhaps even inseparable, in the meaning of νομίζειν.[12] In any case it is obvious, particularly in light of Fahr's overview of the usage of νομίζειν,[13] that the verb is an important religious *terminus technicus* in Classical Greek. It refers simultaneously to belief in the existence of the gods[14] and also to a certain personal commitment with respect to the gods.[15]

2.2 Πιστεύειν as a Religious Term

2.21 The Πιστ- Words as Non-Religious Terminology

It is normally maintained that the πιστ- words were not viewed as religious terms in Classical Greek. Bultmann summarizes as follows:

> The words in πιστ- did not become religious terms in Classical Greek. It is true that faithfulness to a compact is a religious duty, and fidelity and

---

[10] See J. Tate, "Greek for Atheism", *Classical Review* 50(1936), pp. 3-5; and "More Greek for Atheism", *Classical Review* 51(1937), pp. 3-6. In the case of Plato, *Apology* 24,b.c, Tate is probably correct in his interpretation.

[11] Wilhelm Fahr, "ΘΕΟΥΣ ΝΟΜΙΖΕΙΝ: zum Problem der Anfänge des Atheismus bei den Griechen", *Spudasmata* 26(1969) (Hildesheim: Georg Olms Verlag), p. 158.

[12] Ibid., esp. pp. 164-67.

[13] Ibid., pp. 190-93.

[14] "Unverbindliche Meinung".

[15] "Verbindliches Handeln".

piety are closely related. πίσυνος, which means the same as πιστός in the sense of 'trusting', can have the deity as object, Aesch. Sept. c. Theb., 211f; ἄπιστος = 'unbelieving' can also carry a reference to deity. But in no sense is πιστός used for the true religious relationship to God or for the basic religious attitude of man. Nor did πίστις become a religious term. At most one can only say that the possibility of its so doing is intimated by the fact that it can refer to reliance on a god and that in the sense of 'conviction' it can take the existence of the deity as its object.[16]

Regarding the verb πιστεύειν[17] Bultmann remarks that "there are only the first beginnings of religious use".

In the sense of 'to trust' πιστεύειν can refer to τύχη and also to deity. When it means 'to put faith' the object can be, not only human words, but also divine sayings and even divinity itself.[18]

2.22 The "First Beginings of Religious Use"

In my opinion it is precisely at these "first beginnings of religious use" where we can begin to trace a very important development in the use of πιστεύειν[19] as a theological term. Kurt Latte in a review of the "Inscriptiones Epidauri"[20] sees the use of ἀπιστεῖν in one of the Epidaurian *Heilsinschriften*[21] as an ultimate root of the later Christian concept of πίστις. Latte claims for the first time in 4th century B.C. Epidaurus ἀπιστεῖν in the sense of 'to doubt' occurs with reference to religious guilt. He writes: "Das Fürwahrhalten bestimmter Wunder ist eine geforderte individuelle Leistung, ein *sacrifizio dell' intelleto*, dessen Weigerung gestraft wird".[22] And so, according to Latte, this understanding of faith in connection with a divine wonder in 4th century B.C.E. Epidaurus is the *very first step* within the Greek world toward the Christian understanding of πίστις.

---

[16]   Bultmann, *TDNT* 6, p. 179.
[17]   Also ἀπιστεῖν.
[18]   Bultmann, *TDNT* 6, p. 179.
[19]   And then perhaps only later the noun πίστις, through a process of assimilation.
[20]   Kurt Latte, Review of *I. G. IV: Inscriptiones Epidauri*, Ed. Hiller de Gaertringen, *Gnomon* 7(1931), p. 120.
[21]   Inscriptiones Graecae IV: Inscriptiones Epidauri 121,22.
[22]   Latte, *Gnomon* 7, p. 120. Indeed, in both the OT and NT traditions, miracles and wonders play a very important role in relationship to πίστις and πιστεύειν; cf. for example, Mk. 6,5. 6, where Jesus was not able to perform any wonders in his home town because of the unbelief (ἀπιστία) of the people; cf. also the important relationship between πιστεύειν and the signs and wonders of Moses in Ex. 4,8. 9. 31. Otto Betz suggests that even the faith of Abraham in Gen. 15,6 is connected with a miracle—i.e., the miracle of Abraham and Sarah having a child in their old age!

Just a few lines earlier in his review, however, Latte mentions four instances of the phrase πιστεύειν θεοῖς which seem to me to indicate that the beginnings of a religious understanding of πιστεύειν, such as we find in the LXX and later in Christian writings, go back even earlier than 4th century Epidaurus.

In Aeschylus' (525-456 B.C.E.) *Persians*, line 800,[23] is a reference to belief in the oracles of the gods:

εἴ τι πιστεῦσαι θεῶν
χρὴ θεσφάτοισιν ἐς τὰ νῦν πεπραγμένα
βλέψαντα·[24]

In Sophocles' (496?-406 B.C.E.) *Philoctetes* 1373-75 the gods themselves are the object of πιστεύειν:

λέγεις μὲν εἰκότ', ἀλλ' ὅμως σε βούλομαι
θεοῖς τε πιστεύσαντα τοῖς τ' ἐμοῖς λόγοις
φίλου μετ' ἀνδρὸς τοῦδε τῆσδ' ἐκπλεῖν χθονός.[25]

Thirdly, Latte cites Plato's (427?-347 B.C.E.) *Epinomis* 980,c:

ἀλλ', ὦ δαιμόνιε, πιστεύσας τοῖς θεοῖς εὔχου τε καὶ λέγε τὸν ἐπιόντα
σοι λόγον τῶν καλῶν περὶ τοὺς θεούς τε καὶ τὰς θεάς.[26]

And finally, Latte cites Xenophon's (434?-355 B.C.E.) *Apomnemoneumata* I,1,5:

δῆλον οὖν ὅτι οὐκ ἂν προέλεγεν, εἰ μὴ ἐπίστευεν ἀληθεύσειν. ταῦτα
δὲ τίς ἂν ἄλλῳ πιστεύσειεν ἢ θεῷ; πιστεύων δὲ θεοῖς πῶς οὐκ εἶναι
θεοὺς ἐνόμιζεν;[27]

The last of these passages we will take up again at a later point. What is interesting here, however, is the comparison drawn by Latte between νομίζειν θεούς and πιστεύειν θεοῖς. Latte writes:

---

[23] Latte cites line 786, which is obviously a mistake.
[24] "If one can trust the oracles of the gods, having seen the things which have just now happened..."
[25] "What you say may be true; nevertheless I desire that you trust the gods and my words and set sail from this land with this man, a friend".
[26] "Therefore, my good sir (ironic!), trusting the gods, pray and speak the word which comes to you concerning the lovely things about the gods and the goddesses!"
[27] "It is therefore clear that [Socrates] would not have spoken earlier if he did not believe he was speaking the truth. But who would believe [that he could do] these things (i.e., ἀληθεύσειν) by anyone other than God? If he trusted in the gods therefore, how could he not believe in the existence of the gods?!" Note in this passage the important relationship between faith/belief and truth—between πιστεύειν and ἀληθεύειν. This suggests that the LXX equation of the πιστ- group with the Hebrew root אמן was a fairly precise translation.

Für alt-hellenistischen Glauben sind die Götter κρείττονες, daß man ihnen ein von irdischen Schranken befreites Wirken zutraut, ist mit der Anerkennung ihrer Göttlichkeit ohne weiteres gegeben; sie verlangen tätige Verehrung in den überkommenen Formen (das ist νομίζειν θεούς); von einem πιστεύειν θεοῖς kann man nur sprechen, *soweit das Vertrauen auf ihre Hilfe oder ihre Orakel das eigene Handeln veranlaßt.*[28]

If, as Latte here indicates, we have in the above-mentioned instances a use of πιστεύειν θεοῖς (θεῷ) referring to a trust in the gods resulting in an active personal commitment which corresponds to this trust in the gods or in the oracle of a god, and not simply indicating the performance of customary religious rites,[29] then we indeed have an important parallel for πιστεύειν = אמן as we find it, for example, in Gen. 15,6 or in Isa. 53,1.[30]

2.23 Additional Instances of Religious Use of Πιστεύειν

To these passages cited by Latte I would add three passages in which πιστεύειν θεῷ/θεοῖς represents a trust in God/in the gods which further implies an active response on the part of the believer.

1) Thucydides (471?-?400 B.C.E.), *Historia* 4,92,7:

πιστεύσαντας δὲ τῷ θεῷ πρὸς ἡμῶν ἔσεσθαι ... καὶ τοῖς ἱεροῖς ἃ ἡμῖν θυσαμένοις καλὰ φαίνεται, ὁμόσε χωρῆσαι τοῖσδε....[31]

A very similar statement appears in Josephus' *Ant.* 3,309, where Joshua and Caleb urge the Israelites to place their faith in God as their leader and to go up and take possession of the promised land.[32]

2) Xenophon, *Apology of Socrates* 15:

ὅμως δὲ ὑμεῖς μηδὲ ταῦτ᾽ εἰκῇ πιστεύσητε τῷ θεῷ, ἀλλὰ καθ᾽ ἓν ἕκαστον ἐπισκοπεῖτε ὧν εἶπεν ὁ θεός.[33]

---

[28] Latte, *Gnomon* 7, p. 120; italics mine.

[29] τὰ νομισμένα.

[30] Cf. also Isa. 7,9; 28,16.

[31] "But having attained trust (aorist tense) in God, that he will be with us, and in the sacrifices which seem good to us who offer them, let us go up against them in battle...".

[32] "ἴωμεν οὖν," ἔφασαν, "ἐπὶ τοὺς πολεμίους μηδὲν ἔχοντες δι᾽ ὑποψίας ἡγεμόνι τε τῷ θεῷ πεπιστευκότες". Cf. also *Ant.* 2,333; 3,44; 4,5; 9,12.

[33] "Nevertheless, you yourselves would never rashly believe (in) God with respect to these things (i.e., the χρησμοῖς), but rather you pay regard to every single detail of the things God has spoken".

3) Aeschines (389-314 B.C.E.), *Ctesiphont* 1:

> ἐγὼ δὲ πεπιστευκὼς ἥκω πρῶτον μὲν τοῖς θεοῖς, ἔπειτα τοῖς νόμοις καὶ ὑμῖν....[34]

These instances of πιστεύειν θεῷ/θεοῖς[35] do not, of course, prove that πιστεύειν is a religious concept in Classical Greek. Indeed, it is not our purpose here to argue such a point; rather it is our purpose to show that there is already precedent in Classical Greek for the use of πιστεύειν within a religious context. This is a precedent by which πιστεύειν, indicating a trust which has direct implications upon personal action, was later 1) capable of being understood by a Greek audience in reference to God,[36] and 2) capable of being developed into a religious *terminus technicus* for 'faith, belief', expressing (in Bultmann's words) "the true religious relationship [of mankind] to God".[37]

2.24 Hindrances to a Religious Understanding of Πιστεύειν

Let us pause at this point and ask the obvious question: If the roots were already present in Classical Greek for the understanding of πιστεύειν as an important theological concept, why then did this word and this word group not develop into such in the Classical period? On the one hand, it should be noted that the πιστ- word group was indeed in a process of development throughout the Classical period. Bultmann sketches this development, pointing out: "[The] first attested of the words with πιστ- is the (verbal) adjective πιστός, with the privative ἄπιστος".[38] The noun πίστις appears at a later point, and the verb πιστεύειν only from the 7th Cent. B.C.[39] With the appearance of new forms of verbs and substantives, the meaning of the word group developed accordingly,[40] so that in one sense one could say that the πιστ- word group in Classical

---

[34] "I have come, having trusted first in the gods, and then also in the laws and in you". The descending order of faith in this passage is quite interesting, with a divine object at the highest point of the spectrum and a human object at the lowest. Here also we see an important example in secular Greek literature for πιστεύειν νόμοις/νόμῳ—a key concept for pietism in Hellenistic Judaism!

[35] For other related uses of πιστεύειν in a religious context, see Eurip. *Ion* 557; Plat. *Tim.* 40,d. e.

[36] As, for example, in the LXX translation of the Hebrew אמן, or in the NT use of the verb.

[37] Cf. Bultmann, *TDNT* 6, p. 179.

[38] Ibid., p. 175.

[39] Ibid., pp. 176-78; cf. also Ernst Fraenkel, *Griechische Denominativa in ihrer geschichtlichen Entwicklung und Verbreitung* (Göttingen: Vandenhoeck und Ruprecht, 1906), pp. 177-180.

[40] Fraenkel, *Griechische Denominativa*, p. 177.

times simply had *not yet* reached the stage of development to be
recognized as a central theological concept.

On the other hand, it is significant that the nature of Greek religion
itself may have prohibited this concept of πιστεύειν as 'action-motivating trust' from becoming a central theological concept. The Greeks,
as we have seen, were primarily concerned in their religion with νομίζειν
θεοὺς [εἶναι] as the expression for believing in the existence of the gods
and honoring the gods with the customary cultic rituals. Bruno Snell
points out in a chapter entitled: "Der Glaube an die olympischen Götter"
that there is a basic qualitative difference between the 'Glaube' of the
Homeric religion and that of the Christian religion; i.e., 'belief' in the
Christian sense has as a prerequisite the possibility of unbelief.

> Der 'Glaube', das *credo*, bedingt einen falschen, einen ketzerischen
> Glauben, gegen den er sich abhebt, und daher ist der Glaube gebunden an
> ein Dogma, für oder wider das man kämpft. Das hat es im Griechischen
> nicht gegeben; dem Griechen sind seine Götter so natürlich und selbstver-
> ständlich, daß er nicht einmal auf den Gedanken kommt, andere Völker
> könnten einen anderen Glauben oder andere Götter haben.[41]

Karl Kerényi takes the comparison an important step further back to the
OT concept of faith versus the Greek concept. Kerényi points out that
there is no specific command to belief or faith in the OT—faith was a
Selbstverständlichkeit for the Israelites due to their intimate relationship
with Jahwe.

> Es gab da die Verheißung Jahves und das Vertrauen auf ihn—*solche*
> *Verheißung hatten aber die Griechen nicht.* Es ist kein Wunder, daß die
> πίστις erst in Christentum zu einem grundlegenden religiösen Begriff
> wurde.[42]

In Classical Greek religion the gods themselves are subject to the natural
order of the universe. The signs given by the gods are quite natural signs:
a lightning bolt, a bird flying overhead, a sneeze, etc.[43] In Greek
religion, then, πίστις and πιστεύειν could only stand for faith or trust in
the reality of the world.[44] Only in the context of another theological
system could πιστεύειν fully develop into a central theological concept.

---

[41] Bruno Snell, *Die Entdeckung des Geistes* 4. Auflage (Göttingen: Vandenhoeck u. Ruprecht, 1975), pp. 30ff.

[42] Karl Kerényi, *Die Antike Religion* 2. Auflage (Düsseldorf: Eugen Diederichs Verlag, 1952), pp. 77-78 (italics mine).

[43] Snell, *Entdeckung,* p. 34.

[44] Kerényi, *Antike Religion,* pp. 77-78.

2.25 Πιστεύειν in Xenophon, *Apomn*. I,1,5

Perhaps one point where πιστεύειν comes very near to representing a religious concept in Classical Greek is the above-mentioned passage from Xenophon, *Apomn*. I,1,5: πιστεύων δὲ θεοῖς πῶς οὐκ εἶναι θεοὺς ἐνόμιζεν; Xenophon here defends Socrates against the charge of atheism[45] and cites as evidence against this charge the fact that Socrates indeed *trusted* in the gods.[46] What is meant by πιστεύειν θεοῖς in this instance must be understood from the preceding context.

According to Socrates, the 'god' gave him direct instructions[47] instead of speaking indirectly through birds or other omens. Upon the basis of these divine instructions Socrates advised many of his friends what they should do or what they should not do. Those who paid heed to him prospered; those who did not pay heed suffered because of it. But this very action of Socrates was, according to Xenophon, sufficient proof that Socrates was πιστεύων θεοῖς. This was in turn proof for him that Socrates ἐνόμιζεν θεοὺς εἶναι. Πιστεύειν θεοῖς and νομίζειν θεοὺς εἶναι are certainly not synonymous in this context; and it is further not clear that νομίζειν θεοὺς εἶναι even implies πιστεύειν θεοῖς. On the other hand, it is clear that πιστεύειν θεοῖς does imply νομίζειν θεοὺς εἶναι. The very linking of these terms together in this context already begins to give religious significance to the verb πιστεύειν.

3 THE RELIGIOUS USE OF ΠΙΣΤΙΣ AND ΠΙΣΤΕΥΕΙΝ IN THE HELLENISTIC PERIOD

Not until the Hellenistic period and the Christian era do πίστις and πιστεύειν come into full bloom as faith terminology. But precisely here is where the question arises as to how πίστις and πιστεύειν developed into key theological concepts, and, more specifically, as to what relationship exists between the use of the πιστ- word group in the OT-NT tradition and its use in secular Hellenistic literature.

This is one of the foci of the debate presented above in the Introduction. Reitzenstein, on the one hand, argues from (much later) Egyptian and Persian texts that Christianity did not have a 'corner on the market', so to speak, with regard to πίστις and πιστεύειν as faith termi-

---

45 οὓς μὲν ἡ πόλις νομίζει θεοὺς οὐ νομίζων; *Apomn*. I,1,1.

46 πιστεύων δὲ θεοῖς.

47 τὸ δαιμόνιον γὰρ ἔφη σημαίνειν; *Apomn*. I,1,4.

nology.[48] Bultmann takes up this argument and develops it further.[49] D.
Lührmann, on the other hand, skillfully refutes the conclusions of
Reitzenstein and Bultmann and maintains that πίστις and πιστεύειν are
Bedeutungslehnwörter which take on a *new meaning*[50] within the
context of OT and NT usage—a meaning not normally found in Greek.[51]
G. Barth takes up the argument, on the one hand affirming many of
Lührmann's objections to Reitzenstein and Bultmann regarding their use
of later proof texts, but on the other hand adding his own examples of
πίστις and πιστεύειν as religious terms in Hellenistic religion, and thus
challenging Lührmann's strict conclusions.[52]

3.1 Development of Πιστ- as Religious Terminology Within and Without the OT—Hellenistic Jewish—NT Tradition

In light of the evidence, there is actually little doubt that πίστις and
πιστεύειν developed into religious concepts without as well as within the
OT—Hellenistic Jewish—NT tradition. It is clear, for example, from
writings such as the Greek Sirach that the πιστ- word group in
Hellenistic Judaism was developing beyond the earlier pattern of LXX
usage into a central theological concept. Other developments can be seen
elsewhere in Hellenistic Judaism, e.g., in Philo and, of course, in the
NT.[53] But, as G. Barth points out, there are also clear developments of
the πιστ- word group as religious terminology particularly in the
writings of Plutarch[54] and by Lucian of Samosata.[55]

3.2 Two Trends of Development

It is not necessary, however, to view the development of the πιστ- word
group outside the OT—Hellenistic Jewish—NT tradition as the result of
such a development within this tradition,[56] nor is it necessary to maintain

---

[48]   R. Reitzenstein, *Die hellenistischen Mysterienreligionen nach ihren Grundgedanken und Wirkungen* 3. Auflage (Leipzig, 1927), pp. 234-36. The "decisive" texts cited by Reitzenstein, as well as by Bultmann (see below), are later writings. Obviously their use of the πιστ- word group was influenced by Christian use and not vice versa.

[49]   Bultmann, *TDNT* 6, pp. 181-82.

[50]   I.e., the meaning of the Hebrew אמן.

[51]   D. Lührmann, "*Pistis* in Judentum".

[52]   G. Barth, "*Pistis* in hellen. Religiosität".

[53]   We shall explore in the following chapters the more important developments in the use of this word group in the LXX, Sirach and Philo.

[54]   Cf. Barth, "*Pistis* in hellen. Religiösität", pp. 115-18.

[55]   Cf. ibid., pp. 118-120. Dr. David Balch has further indicated to me that instances of πιστεύειν as religious terminology are to be found throughout the writings of Dionysius of Halicarnassus.

[56]   I.e., Lührmann's position.

the opposite view.[57] But if indeed the potential for this development already existed in the Classical period, then these developments in the
Hellenistic period can be viewed as general, logical trends, 'growing up'
perhaps side by side in various religions using a common language. It
does seem important, however, to differentiate between *two basic trends*
in the development of the verb πιστεύειν into a religious *terminus*
technicus in the Hellenistic Greek period.

One trend is the use of πιστεύειν with the dative case form, referring to a faith/trust in God/the gods or in a divine oracle. This faith has a
direct impact upon the actions of the believer. We have noted above that
this understanding of πιστεύειν was present in Classical Greek. It was
developed further by the LXX translators who translated the Hebrew אמן
with the verb πιστεύειν. This use is also found in non-Jewish
Hellenism.[58]

The second tendency in the Hellenistic period is to employ
πιστεύειν theologically as 'to believe', in the purely intellectual sense;
i.e., to believe *that* something is or is not the case. This is most clearly
seen in the use of πιστεύειν as a synonym for νομίζειν in the formula
νομίζειν θεοὺς εἶναι. For example, Lucian's *Philopseudes* 10 reads: σύ
μοι δοκεῖς ... τὰ τοιαῦτα λέγων οὐδὲ θεοὺς εἶναι πιστεύειν.[59] Or
again in Porphyrius of Tyre in *ad Marcellam* 22: οἱ δὲ μήτε εἶναι
θεοὺς πιστεύσαντες.[60]

Bultmann comments:

> Whereas in the older [Greek] world the idea that there are gods used to be
> expressed by νομίζειν, πιστεύειν can be used in a later period. In keeping
> is the fact that πιστεύειν can take on the sense of 'to believe'.[61]

For Bultmann, however, this seems to be the main trend in the development of πιστεύειν as a theological *terminus technicus*. He does not take
into account the use, already present in Classical Greek, of πιστεύειν
θεοῖς as an action-modifying trust in the gods. Or if he does take this
into account, he sees no significant distinction.[62]

---

[57] I.e., Reitzenstein and Bultmann.
[58] E.g., Polybius 10,7,3: οὐ τῇ τύχῃ πιστεύων; cf. Barth, "*Pistis* in hellen. Religiösität", pp. 114-
15.
[59] "It seems to me that you, speaking thus, do not believe in the existence of the gods".
[60] "For they do not believe in the existence of the gods".
[61] Bultmann, *TDNT* 6, p. 179.
[62] Ibid., pp. 180f.

3.3 The Distinction Between the Two Trends

Yet there *is* an important distinction. Once again in Xenophon's statement about Socrates in *Apomn.* I,1,5 the distinction becomes obvious:
πιστεύων δὲ θεοῖς πῶς οὐκ εἶναι θεοὺς ἐνόμιζεν; Here the fact that
Socrates trusted in the gods was proof that he believed in the existence of
the gods. But the converse of this, as noted above, is not necessarily
true. Although the two terms πιστεύειν and νομίζειν are brought together in this same context in a conditional relationship to one another,
and although πιστεύειν in later Greek could be substituted for νομίζειν in
the apodosis even of this sentence, it is clear here that πιστεύειν θεοῖς
and νομίζειν (πιστεύειν) θεοὺς εἶναι must be distinguished from one
another in meaning. The distinction between these two trends in the development of πιστεύειν as a theological term must be carefully observed
in relationship to the development of the word group within and without
the OT—Hellenistic Jewish—NT tradition.

4 SUMMARY

We have shown in this chapter that there is a clear precedent in Classical
Greek for the use of the πιστ- word group in the religious sense of trusting and relying upon God or upon God's promises. That is, there is a
precedent for the use of πίστις and πιστεύειν as an accurate translation of
the Hebrew root אמן. Thus, it is not necessary to maintain with
Reitzenstein and Bultmann that the OT and NT traditions necessarily bor-
rowed the terminology from pagan Hellenistic religion. Neither is it necessary to maintain with Lührmann that the πιστ- words were adopted by
the LXX translators purely as *Bedeutungslehnwörter*, having never been
used in Greek literature to mean what they mean in their translation of the
Hebrew stem אמן.

Nevertheless, we must agree in part with Lührmann's
Bedeutungslehnwörter theory, for it is obvious that the אמן root in the
OT is not restricted to the sense of an action-motivating faith/trust in
God. The idea of truth[63] is one important nuance of the Hebrew אמן; also
the idea of 'standing firm', particularly in the passage Isa. 7,9 . Especially
in this passage it is apparent that the LXX translators had difficulty
giving a consistent literal translation of אמן and πιστεύειν. Instead of
translating both occurrences of the root אמן in this passage with

---

[63] ἀλήθεια.

πιστεύειν, the LXX substituted   the verb συνῆτε for the second occurrence: ἐὰν μὴ πιστεύσητε, οὐδὲ μὴ συνῆτε. There is, therefore, clearly a development in the LXX whereby the πιστ- word group evolves into the central theological faith terminology that we find in the NT and in later Christian writings. This development arises out of and goes beyond previous religious uses of the word group. We shall address this development further in the following chapters.

CHAPTER TWO

ΠΙΣΤΙΣ AND ΠΙΣΤΕΥΕΙΝ IN THE SEPTUAGINT

1 INTRODUCTION

We have shown in the previous chapter that the πιστ- word group, though not originally theological terminology, was already appearing in secular Classical and early Hellenistic Greek in religious contexts. The important use of the word group as central theological concepts in NT and also in later Hellenistic Greek should be seen as the result of a process of development—a process having roots even in Classical Greek. A significant contributor to this development of the πιστ- word group was the Greek translation of the Hebrew scriptures.

The πιστ- word group in the LXX consistently represents the Hebrew root אמן of the MT. Bultmann describes the striking regularity of this pattern in the LXX:

> [The hiphil האמין of the OT is rendered πιστεύειν in the LXX] 45 times; ἐμπιστεύειν five times, and once each καταπιστεύειν and πεισθῆναι.... Similarly, πιστεύειν is used almost exclusively for האמין, once for the niphal and aphel of אמן, once for שמע (Jer. 25,8, though obviously only for the sake of variety; in vs. 7 שמע is rendered ἀκούειν). The other constructs of πιστ- are almost without exception used for constructs of the stem אמן. It may be noted that πιστός is almost always (29 times) used for the niphal of אמן, and that πίστις is used 6 times for אמת, 20 for אמונה, but that ἀλήθεια is used 87 times for אמת and 22 (esp. Ps.) for אמונה.[1]

It is obvious that the πιστ- word group in the LXX (especially the verb πιστεύειν) was meant to be understood in light of the Hebrew אמן. The contribution of the LXX to the development of the πιστ- word group as faith terminology, therefore, cannot be fully appreciated apart from the Hebrew root אמן.

---

[1] Bultmann, *TDNT* 6, p. 197, n. 149.

2 THE HEBREW ROOT אמן

2.1 General Observations

אמן is actually only one of several Hebrew roots in the OT referring to an
attitude of faith in the sense of humankind's relationship to and attitude
toward God. Weiser[2] lists, in addition to אמן, the verbal stems: בטח;[3]
חסה;[4] and the verbs of hope, חכה, יחל, קוה.[5] Among these verbal stems,
אמן (= πιστεύειν) ranks only fourth in frequency of occurrence.
Nevertheless, Weiser intimates that this was a "term in which the profun-
dity of the OT concept of faith was really brought to full and comprehensive expression".[6]

The use of אמן in a religious context and as a religious term appears
to be a later development beyond the purely secular understanding of the
term. Indeed, as Weiser points out, "none of the stems mentioned [above]
is specifically religious in origin".[7] Hans Wildberger drives home this
point in commenting upon the basic meaning of אמן and its development
as religious terminology:

> Die אמן entsprechenden Vokabeln in den anderen semitischen Sprachen
> lassen zusammen mit dem alttestamentlichen Befund keinen Zweifel
> darüber bestehen, daß die Grundbedeutung der Wurzel 'fest, sicher,
> zuverlässig' ist. Ebenso gewiß ist die Sonderbedeutung, die das hiphil in
> der religiösen Sprache des Alten Testaments gewonnen hat, eine
> Sonderentwicklung innerhalb des Hebräischen.[8]

In this sense the development of אמן itself as faith terminology is not
unlike the development of the πιστ- word group as noted in the previous
chapter. Nonetheless, as Jepsen indicates, it is difficult—even misleading—to examine the root אמן in light of its 'original meaning'.[9] It is
therefore necessary for us to briefly survey the use and meaning of אמן and
its derivatives in the OT.

---

2 Weiser, "πιστεύειν, κτλ." *TDNT* 6, p. 183.
3 'To trust'; cf. ibid., pp. 191f.
4 'To seek refuge'; cf. ibid., pp. 192f.
5 Ibid., pp. 193-96.
6 Ibid., p. 183.
7 Ibid.
8 H. Wildberger, "Glauben, Erwägungen zu האמין", *Hebräische Wortforschung, Festschrift für Walter Baumgartner*, Suppl. *Vetus Testamentum* 16 (Leiden, 1967), p. 373.
9 "The meaning of a word cannot be inferred from the (more or less certain) etymology, but only by a careful study of the way it is used in the language". Jepsen, "אמן", *Theological Dictionary of the Old Testament (TDOT)* 1, p. 293.

2.2 The Substantives of the אמן Stem

2.21 The Substantive אֱמֶת[10]

The substantive אֱמֶת occurs much more frequently than אֲמָנָה[11] but is translated as πίστις in the LXX only six times. In 99 instances the substantive is translated ἀλήθεια or ἀληθινός and in ten instances δικαιοσύνη or δίκαιος. The normal meaning of אֱמֶת is therefore: 'truth, truthfulness'. 'Faith, faithfulness', as understood in the Greek πίστις, is at best a secondary meaning of אֱמֶת.

Nevertheless, the point of contact between אֱמֶת = ἀλήθεια = 'truth' and אֱמֶת = πίστις = 'faithfulness' should not be underestimated. Also for the substantive אֱמוּנָה, which Schlatter sees as a later substantival construction than אֱמֶת,[12] ἀλήθεια[13] stands together with πίστις[14] as the normal translation in the LXX. This apparent inability to translate either of the Hebrew substantives exclusively with πίστις or ἀλήθεια demonstrates that there is much more being expressed by the Hebrew terms than can be interpreted by either of the Greek words alone. The Greek terms must therefore be interpreted in light of the Hebrew.

It would be an injustice to the substantive אֱמֶת to understand the term simply in light of ἀλήθεια. Rather the Hebrew substantive must be interpreted in its own right; and in its own right it is made up of *many components*, of which ἀλήθεια (or πίστις) is only one.[15] Schlatter writes:

---

[10] Cf. ibid., pp. 309-316.

[11] 126 times in contrast to 42 times.

[12] Schlatter, *Glaube im NT*, p. 551. The relationship between אֱמֶת and אֱמוּנָה in their historical development is not easy to determine. Jepsen (*TDOT* 1, pp. 316-320) shows that אֱמוּנָה is used primarily in later texts whereas אֱמֶת is used throughout the Hebrew scriptures, and that in some of these passages (e.g., Ps. 98,3; 143,1; 119,75) אֱמוּנָה has become the equivalent of אֱמֶת. Nevertheless, Jepsen maintains a fundamental distinction between the two substantives: "While *'emeth* describes the character of a person on whose words and deeds one can rely, *'emunah* denotes the conduct of a person corresponding to his own inner being. *'emeth* is used of God's words or deeds on which man can rely; *'emunah* is used of God's conduct which corresponds to the nature of his deity" (p. 320). Jepsen suggests that the historical development is theological rather than profane: "Israel's poets now attempted to see the nature of Israel's God in his *'emunah*" (i.e., in contrast to his אֱמֶת!). The question which substantive is earlier, is—at least for Jepsen—an open question, if not an irrelevant one.

[13] 22 times.

[14] 20 times.

[15] Brown, Driver & Briggs (*Hebrew and English Lexicon of the Old Testament* (Oxford: Clarendon Press, 1906)) list the following meanings of אֱמֶת: 1) reliability, sureness; 2) stability, continuance; 3) faithfulness, reliableness; 4) truth; 5) adv. in truth, truly. Cf. Jepsen, *TDOT* 1, p. 310.

Ebensowenig wird die Vielheit der Vorgänge, die zusammen die Zuverlässigkeit ergeben, in ihre einzelnen Bestandteile aufgelöst. Das Wohlwollen, das für Haß und Neid verschlossen ist, die Wahrhaftigkeit, die nichts verheimlicht und nicht betrügt, das Vertrauen, das gegen den Genossen keinen Verdacht hegt, die Beständigkeit, die im Glück und Unglück bei ihm ausharrt, der Mut und die Geschicklichkeit, die den Dienst auch zu verrichten und die Hilfe zu leisten versteht, nicht dies oder jenes, sondern all dies zusammen ist die אֱמֶת.[16]

If πιστ- in the LXX is to be interpreted in light of אמן, then it is important to keep in mind all of the above components when considering the significance of πίστις as a term for faith in the LXX.

2.22 The Substantive אֱמוּנָה

אֱמוּנָה is the substantival form of אמן most frequently and most proportionately rendered πίστις in the LXX. But even the translation of אֱמוּנָה with πίστις accounts for less than half of the total occurrences,[17] and is in itself no solid reason for understanding the substantive as 'faith' in the religious sense. Indeed there are a number of lexicographers who would deny that a Hebrew substantive with the meaning 'faith' exists at all![18] This latter position is certainly extreme and overlooks some very important, even if very few, occurrences of אֱמֻנָה in the OT.

The most decisive passage is Hab. 2,4: "but the righteous shall live by his faith/faithfulness".[19] Otto Betz comments on this verse: "Der Text ist schwierig, aber die Aussage über den Glauben ist klar und lapidar, wie in Gen. 15,6 und vor allem wie in Jes. 28,16: 'Der Glaubende wird nicht weichen'".[20] Wildberger unterscores the parallelism of אֱמֻנָה in this passage to הֶאֱמִין in Isaiah, particularly Isa. 7,9.[21] Hab. 2,1-4 is without a doubt a Heilsorakel, similar in both structure and content to Isa. 7. With regard to the use of the substantive אֱמֻנָה here versus the hiphil הֶאֱמִין there, Wildberger concludes: "Sachlich bedeutet die Variation keine wesentliche Veränderung. Damit ist aber auch klar, daß אֱמוּנָה mit 'Glaube' zu übersetzen ist".[22] Wildberger is quick to warn against an understanding of אֱמֻנָה in this passage as πίστις = 'faith' in the full spectrum of the NT

---

16   Schlatter, *Glaube im NT*, p. 553.
17   Otherwise it is translated ἀλήθεια, as noted above.
18   See Wildberger, "Glauben im Alten Testament", *Zeitschrift für Theologie und Kirche* 65 (1968), pp. 129f., esp. note 6.
19   וְצַדִּיק בֶּאֱמוּנָתוֹ יִחְיֶה; cf. also Jer. 5,3; Dt. 32,20.
20   Otto Betz, "Die Gestalt des Glaubens im AT und im frühen Judentum" (an unpublished lecture).
21   Wildberger, "Glauben im AT", pp. 139f.
22   Ibid.

understanding, but points out that if הֶאֱמִין = πιστεύειν = 'believe, have faith', then there is no reason why in this passage אֱמוּנָה should not be interpreted as πίστις = 'faith'.[23]

According to Jepsen, the substantive אֱמוּנָה finds its primary use in later texts of the OT.[24] This, along with the fact that its use in the sense of religious faith is strongly connected with the parallel use of the hiphil verbal stem, indicates that the employment of אֱמוּנָה as faith terminology is most likely subsequent to and determined by the similar understanding of הֶאֱמִין.[25] Likewise, the substantive אֱמֶת was also retained as the corresponding substantival form for the the hiphil of אמן.[26] Therefore we must examine the verbal stems of אמן[27] to to determine the proper understanding of this Hebrew root as faith terminology.

2.3 אמן in the Verbal Stems

2.31 The Qal Stem[28]

In the qal stem אמן occurs only in the active participle and has a limited range of meaning.[29] Jepsen concludes: "[The qal stem of אמן] is used of men and women who are entrusted with the care of, or who take it upon themselves to care for dependent children".[30] In 2 Ki. 10,1. 5 הָאֹמְנִים refers to an official commission—those who are entrusted with the responsibility of leadership and education. In Est. 2,20 the abstract feminine substantival אָמְנָה refers to 'education, upbringing'[31] or 'care'.[32] In all eight instances, where אמן appears in the qal stem, the term carries this limited technical meaning of *sustenare, educare; tutor et altor*.[33] In none of these instances is the qal participle of אמן in any sense a *terminus*

---

23 Ibid, p. 140.
24 Jepsen, *TDOT* 1, p. 320.
25 This is not unlike the development we have already seen in Classical Greek with πίστις and πιστεύειν (see above, Chapter One).
26 Schlatter, *Glaube im NT*, p. 558.
27 The verbal stems are much more regularly translated with πιστ- than is the substantive אֱמוּנָה!
28 Cf. Weiser, *TDNT* 6, pp. 183f.; Jepsen, *TDOT* 1, p. 294. It is a debatable whether the qal forms really belong to the Hebrew root in question here; cf. Jepsen, p. 293.
29 Weiser, *TDNT* 6, p. 183.
30 Jepsen, *TDOT* 1, p. 294.
31 Weiser.
32 Jepsen.
33 Cf. S. Mandelkern, *Veteris Testamenti Concordantiae*, Reprint (Graz, Austria: Akademische Druck- und Verlaganstalt, 1955), p. 108.

technicus for faith, nor does the LXX ever translate it with a πιστ-
word.[34]

2.32 The Niphal Stem[35]

The niphal of אמן has a broader range of usage and meaning than the qal
stem. This stem occurs also mainly as a participle,[36] the perfect and the
imperfect appearing only five and eight times, respectively.[37] The LXX
translates the niphal of אמן with πιστός 29 times, with πιστοῦν nine
times, and one time each with ἀξιόπιστος, ἐμπιστεύειν, πίστιν ἔχειν,
and θαυμαστός. In secular use the niphal participle and perfect occur in
connection with either persons or things. Regarding the latter, נֶאֱמָן means
'lasting, continual, firm'; e.g., unceasing afflictions,[38] water which will
flow continually,[39] or a firm place into which a peg may be driven so that
it will hold.[40]

In connection with persons נֶאֱמָן carries the idea of 'reliability'; i.e.,
a reliable messenger,[41] a reliable witness,[42] reliable priests,[43] and David is
referred to in 1 Sam. 22,14 as reliable. Jepsen notes: "In these passages
the emphasis seems to be that such reliability is not obvious; it must be
pointed out in particular".[44] Jepsen also cites a few passages in the
Wisdom literature referring to the נֶאֱמָנִים in a general, profane sense.[45]

In a theological sense, the niphal participle of אמן can in some instances apply to God or to the relationship of individuals to God, but
more often appears in connection with the promises concerning David's
dynasty or with regard to the conduct of Israel.[46] When applied to God

---

[34] Rather with θρεπτός one time; τιθηνός six times and τιθηνεῖν one time; (cf. Elmar Camilo Dos
Santos, *An Expanded Hebrew Index for the Hatch-Redpath Concordance to the LXX* (Jerusalem:
Dugith Pub., Baptist House), p. 12). Nonetheless, it is interesting that the idea of 'entrusting'
which seems to be present in the qal forms of אמן is basic to the understanding of πιστεύειν ,
particularly in non-religious usage.

[35] Cf. Weiser, *TDNT* 6, pp. 184-86; Jepsen, *TDOT* 1, pp. 294-98.

[36] 32 times.

[37] Jepsen, *TDOT* 1, p. 294. Jepsen dismisses the passages Hos. 5,9; 12,1; 1 Chr. 17,24 as un-
intelligible or corrupt.

[38] Dt. 28,59.

[39] Isa. 33,16; cf. Jer. 15,18.

[40] Isa. 22,23. 25. Cf. Jepsen, *TDOT* 1, p. 295.

[41] Prov. 25,13.

[42] Isa. 8,2; cf. Jer. 42,5.

[43] Neh. 13,13.

[44] Jepsen, *TDOT* 1, p. 295.

[45] E.g., Prov. 11,13; 27,6; Ps. 101,6; Job 12,20.

[46] Jepsen, *TDOT* 1, pp. 295-97.

personally, נֶאֱמָן means 'faithful, reliable'.[47] In reference to the precepts and commandments of God, נֶאֱמָן denotes "surety; as precepts on whose validity one can rely because they partake of God's reliability".[48]

When referring to the relationship of individuals to God the niphal participle again carries the meaning 'faithful, loyal, reliable'. But the fact that נֶאֱמָן is used only a few times in this context, along with the fact that when it is used in this context it is referring to central figures of Israel's history,[49] suggests that "a unique relationship to the deity, indeed a special divine evaluation" of these individuals is being expressed by נֶאֱמָן.[50] Likewise, when referring to the conduct of Israel, the sense is also 'faithful, steadfast'.[51] With regard to the promise of God concerning the dynasty of David[52] the sense is 'continuous, enduring, lasting'.[53]

In the LXX the adjective πιστός is employed consistently to translate the niphal participle נֶאֱמָן. This is no surprise since πιστός normally means 'faithful, reliable, loyal'. However, whereas in secular Greek πιστός generally appears in a profane sense,[54] in the LXX it gains a new religious significance in connection with נֶאֱמָן, as well as with other forms of the root אמן. This religious use of πιστός in connection with אמן is the major contributor to the NT understanding of πιστός.

In the imperfect tense the niphal of אמן is connected almost exclusively with דָּבָר, 'word'.[55] In one instance the niphal imperfect refers to the word of Joseph's brothers[56] and in four instances to the word of God.[57] Jepsen suggests the best rendering of this formula is 'to prove to be reliable'.[58] In searching out a translation which would embrace the different meanings of the niphal stem of אמן, Jepsen proposes the translation: "'Constant', which can include the permanency of things and the stability

---

47   Cf. Isa. 49,7; Dt. 7,9; Jer. 42,5.
48   Jepsen, *TDOT* 1, p. 295.
49   Abraham, Neh. 9,8; Moses, Num. 12,7; Samuel, 1 Sam. 3,20; cf. 1 Sam. 2,35.
50   Jepsen, *TDOT* 1, p. 296.
51   Ps. 78,8. 37; cf. Isa. 1,21. 26.
52   1 Sam. 25,28; 2 Sam. 7,16; Ps. 89,29. 38; Isa. 55,3; cf. 1 Sam. 2,35; 1 Ki. 11,38.
53   Jepsen, *TDOT* 1, p. 296.
54   In Josephus, for example, the adjective πιστός appears *only* in a profane sense. (Cf. below Chapter Seven)
55   Isa 7,9 and its reproduction in 2 Chr. 20,20 are exceptions. In these instances, however, the niphal imperfect represents the attempt at a play on words and is best interpreted in light of the hiphil forms.
56   Gen. 42,20.
57   1 Ki. 8,26; 1 Chr. 17,23; 2 Chr. 1,9; 6,17; cf. 1 Ki. 3,6; 2 Sam. 7,25.
58   Jepsen, *TDOT* 1, p. 297.

of persons. The result is that one may build or rely upon the thing or person giving proof of constancy".[59]

2.33 The Hiphil Stem

In all but one of the 52 occurrences of the hiphil stem of אמן, the LXX translates with the verb πιστεύειν or one of its compounds.[60] Rudolf Smend locates instances of the use of האמין from every period of ancient Israelite literary history, although he views the religious use of the verb as a later development in the OT writings and not to be dated before the writings of Isaiah.[61] Jepsen outlines the distribution of האמין in its varying syntactical constructions and its use in various literary types as follows: With the preposition ־ב = 'in, on', 23 times; with the preposition ־ל = 'in', 14 times; with an infinitive clause, two times; with a כי clause, four times; and absolutely, seven times;[62] literary types: narrative contexts, 24 times plus four Psalms passages; prophetic oracles, seven times; other Psalms, four times; wisdom literature, eleven times.[63] Jepsen explains: "This (very rough) distribution shows that [האמין] is not used very often in the Prophets and the Psalms, but does appear frequently in the narratives of Israel's early history and in the Wisdom Literature".[64]

The hiphil is the most important of the verbal stems of אמן for the OT concept of faith, but the possible interpretations of האמין are also widely varied.[65] Weiser presupposes an original transitive sense for האמין and proposes this general definition: "to say Amen with all the consequences for both obj[ect] and subj[ect]".[66] In the secular use this implies first of all 'believing' in the sense of recognizing and accepting that a word or account or matter is true. But it also implies a "corresponding relation to the matter".[67] In other words, האמין implies the aspect of *Verbindlichkeit* as well as *Unverbindlichkeit,* as we have also seen with the religious use of πιστεύειν in Classical Greek. Similarly, when the

---

[59]   Ibid., p. 298.
[60]   ἐμ-, κατα- πιστεύειν.
[61]   Rudolf Smend, "Zur Geschichte von האמין", *Hebräische Wortforschung, Festschrift für Walter Baumgartner,* Suppl. *Vetus Testamentum* 16 (Leiden, 1967), pp. 285 - 87.
[62]   Jepsen excludes Jud. 11,20 and Isa. 30,21 from the discussion as texts requiring emendation; cf. also Wildberger, "Erwägungen zu האמין", p. 375.
[63]   Jepsen, *TDOT* 1, p. 300.
[64]   Ibid.
[65]   For a brief sketch of the most popular interpretations, see Jepsen, *TDOT* 1, p. 298.
[66]   Weiser, *TDNT* 6, pp. 186ff.
[67]   Ibid.

secular 'object' of האמין is a person, it is the reciprocal relation of trust or confidence which is being expressed.[68]

This reciprocal relation is also present when האמין expresses humankind's relationship to God. In this context האמין means "to declare God אמן, to say Amen to God".[69] God is personally the author of this relationship either by divine requirement,[70] order or command, or by divine promise.[71] האמין implies in the former instance "acknowledgement of the requirement and man's obedience", and in the latter case, the "acknowledgement of the promise and of God's power to fulfill it, and ... the implied worship of God as the almighty Lord (Num. 20,12)".[72] Both requirement and promise are expressed by האמין in Ex. 4,1 and Ps. 106,24.

Weiser points out further that האמין undergoes a deepening and extension when applied to a person's relationship with God: "It denotes a relation to God which embraces the whole man in the totality of his external conduct and inner life".[73] האמין can emphasize the aspect of knowledge (Isa. 43,10); the aspect of feeling (cf. דעת in Hos. 4,1); the element of will; and even the element of fear (Ex. 14,31; Jos. 24,14; 2 Chr. 19,9; Ps. 86,11). There is an "exclusiveness of the reciprocal relation between God and man" which is to be found in the religious use of האמין.[74]

Weiser maintains that the absolute use of האמין in Isaiah is the "most significant extension and deepening" of the religious understanding of the verb.

> The differentiation of faith from political considerations (7,1ff), from security in face of perils (28,14ff) and from trust in human might (30,15ff), shows, along with the absolute use of הֶאֱמִין, that faith is for Isaiah a particular form of existence of those who are bound to God alone—a form which works itself out as heroic strength (גְּבוּרָה, 30,15) and which is the divinely established basis of the community of God (28,16).[75]

---

68 Weiser: "The OT uses האמין only for the personal relation, for behind the word which is believed is the man [sic] whom one trusts"; ibid., p. 187.
69 Ibid.
70 E.g., Dt. 9,23; Ps. 119,66.
71 E.g., Gen. 15,6.
72 Weiser, *TDNT* 6, p. 187.
73 Ibid., p. 188.
74 Ibid. It is significant here that האמין is never used for the relationship to other gods and idols. בטח (= 'to trust') and חסה (= 'to seek refuge'), on the other hand, can be used freely to apply to idols.
75 Ibid., p. 189.

Faith and existence are identical in Isaiah, for faith is the only possible mode of existence. "Hence", concludes Weiser, "there can be no further deepening of the usage in this direction".[76]

With this basic understanding of האמין, let us turn our attention to the most important OT passages where האמין acquires its theological content and thereby gains its importance as faith terminology.

One of the most important occurrences of האמין in absolute usage is Isa. 7,9:

[77]אִם לֹא תַאֲמִינוּ כִּי לֹא תֵאָמֵנוּ

In this familiar passage it is the political threat from without—from Israel and Syria—which, having brought Judah and her King to their knees in fear, sets the stage for the present *Heilsorakel* and the call to faith. The traditional interpretation of this passage, particularly in light of the similar situation in 2 Chr. 20,20, assumes an ellipsis in the text and proposes that Isaiah was calling for faith in God or faith in the prophetic message.

Hans Wildberger challenges this traditional interpretation. In contrast to Weiser, he presupposes that האמין originally carried an intransitive, absolute sense, due to the lack of clear evidence of the verb followed by an accusative object.[78] According to Wildberger, the syntactical constructions of the verb with the prepositions בְּ and לְ must therefore be interpreted in a secondary relational sense to an intransitive האמין.[79] In Isa. 7,9 Wildberger denies any ellipsis and interprets האמין in a purely intransitive sense:

> 'Glaube' bei Jesaja ist, um es zugespitzt zu sagen, nicht Glaube an Gott und auch nicht Glaube an das prophetische Wort, sondern eine aus dem Wissen um Gott und seine Verheißungen sich ergebende Haltung der Festigkeit, der Zuversicht und des Vertrauens angesichts der Bedrohlichkeit der konkreten Situation. Jesaja kämpft in 7,9 nicht darum, daß der 'Glaube' sich auf Jahwe richte oder ein Fürwahrhalten des prophetischen Wortes sei, sondern daß er sich existentiell als Zuversicht bewahrende Lebenshaltung zeige.[80]

---

[76] Ibid.
[77] "If you do not believe, you shall not remain". Luther's translation is particularly enlightening: "Glaubt ihr nicht, so bleibt ihr nicht".
[78] Wildberger, "Erwägungen", pp. 373-76.
[79] Cf. ibid., pp. 379, 381.
[80] Ibid., pp. 377f.

This observation, however, cannot account for the use of the niphal of אמן in Isa. 7,9. At least it cannot account for any difference in interpretation between the niphal and the hiphil forms of אמן in this passage. In the most basic sense of the stems the hiphil of אמן must carry the idea 'to make firm' and the niphal 'to become firm'. Thus it is the niphal, not the hiphil, which refers to a faith which shows itself existentially as a "Zuversicht bewahrende Lebenshaltung". The hiphil then must be understood in relationship to some syntactical ellipsis—calling for either faith in God or faith in the prophetic message.

Once again in Isa. 28,16 the absolute use of האמין appears in the context of a *Heilsorakel*, denoting an attitude and manner of steadfastness, confidence and trust in the midst of a life-threatening situation. But this time it is elevated even further as a theological term. This oracle of the precious cornerstone in Zion levels a warning against the corrupt leaders of the people (vs. 14). In Zion the only source of security to be found is in faith itself.[81] This is the meaning of the sentence: הַמַּאֲמִין לֹא יָחִישׁ.[82] Wildberger comments:

> Wie in Jes. 7, Gen. 15 und Hab. 2 ist der Glaube auch hier Kriterium wahrer religiöser Haltung und Voraussetzung weiteren Bestandes. Ausdrücklich ist vom Prüfstein die Rede, und dieser Prüfstein ist der Glaube. An ihm entscheidet sich Heil und Unheil, Leben und Tod.[83]

A further important instance of האמין in absolute use is Ex. 4,31. After Aaron had spoken the words which the Lord had given to Moses and had performed the signs in the sight of the people, it is reported that "the people believed".[84] Similarly Hab. 1,5; reads: "For I am doing a work in your days [that] you would not believe if told".[85] Both of these passages find their setting in a *Heilsorakel* and האמין in each instance denotes an attitude and manner of steadfastness, confidence and trust.[86]

Also very important to the development of האמין as faith terminology and perhaps also as background contributors to the Isaianic concept of

---

[81] Wildberger, "Glauben im AT", p. 148.
[82] "He who believes will not be in haste" (RSV); cf. Wildberger's suggested translation: "Wer glaubt, läuft nicht ängstlich davon".
[83] Wildberger, "Glauben im AT", p. 148. Here once again Wildberger does not want to speak of an object of faith. Faith itself is the cornerstone in his interpretation. This faith is a "Zuversicht bewahrende Lebenshaltung" (see above). We have already pointed out the problems with this interpretation.
[84] וַיַּאֲמֵן הָעָם.
[85] לֹא תַאֲמִינוּ.
[86] Cf. also Ps. 116,10.

faith are the passages Gen. 15,6 and Ex. 14,31.[87] Otto Betz refers to
Gen. 15,6 as "die klassische, auch für das NT wichtige Glaubensstelle" in
the OT.[88] The text reads: וְהֶאֱמִן בַּיהוָה וַיַּחְשְׁבֶהָ לּוֹ צְדָקָה:[89] The setting for
this use of הֶאֱמִן is again a *Heilsorakel*.[90] As in Isa. 7, the 'faith' of
Abraham in Gen. 15,6 is his steadfastness, his confidence, his trust over
against the backdrop of an impossible situation; i.e., the promise of God
that his descendants would be numerous as the stars of heaven. "Glaube
ist keine Selbstverständlichkeit" in this situation.[91]   Contrary to the
assumption of Bultmann that the righteous one believes in God on the
basis of God's works which are already seen and experienced, Betz points
out: "Abraham glaubt somit an die Zukunft, eine volkreiche Zukunft, die
angesichts der leeren Gegenwart völlig paradox, 'unglaublich' ist; …Gar
nichts lag für Abraham am Tage, alles sprach gegen die Verheißung".[92]

Wildberger points out that faith in this context is not simply faith
in the reliability of God's promise but must be defined in terms of
Abraham's entire disposition: "Er verhielt sich in dieser höchst undurch-
sichtigen, rational nicht zu bewältigenden Situation so, wie es sich für
einen an Gott Glaubenden geziemt".[93] The fact that הֶאֱמִן is used with the
preposition בְּ signals that Abraham displayed his steadfastness and confidence in that he was founded upon Jahwe.[94]

Ex. 14,31 tells of the faith of the Israelites which resulted from the
Red Sea miracle: וַיַּאֲמִינוּ בַּיהוָה וּבְמֹשֶׁה עַבְדּוֹ:[95] The *Heilsorakel* in this
instance stems back to vs. 13 where, before the parting of the waters and
the salvation of Israel from the Egyptians, Moses had exhorted the people:

---

[87] Rudolf Smend, "Zur Geschichte von הֶאֱמִן", pp. 286ff., argues that הֶאֱמִן in both of these pas-
      sages is a post-Pentateuchal source addition. He affirms that the Isaianic period is the
      "Geburtsstunde des Glaubens" and that these two passages are molded and determined by Isaiah's
      use of הֶאֱמִן. I am inclined rather to follow Wildberger in his interpretation of these passages,
      who in turn follows Noth in attributing both passages to the Jahwist (cf. Wildberger, "Glauben
      im AT", p. 146). While it may be argued that the Jahwist is later than the Isaiah tradition,
      Wildberger has shown that this particular type of *Heilsorakel* goes back to a very early period in
      the ancient Orient and, therefore, that Gen. 15,6, while indeed very similar to Isa. 7,9, is not
      necessarily dependent upon Isaianic use. Nevertheless, Wildberger concedes that the question of
      the source of Gen. 15,6 is a difficult question to which there are not yet any decisive answers (cf.
      Wildberger, "Erwägungen zur הֶאֱמִן", p. 380).

[88] Otto Betz, "Die Geschichtsbezogenheit des Glaubens im Alten und Neuen Testament", *Glaube
      und Geschichte*, ed. by Helge Stadelmann (Giessen: Brunnen Verlag, 1986), p. 10.

[89] "And [Abraham] believed Jahwe and he credited it to him as righteousness". The occurrence of
      faith and righteousness together here is particularly important for the NT understanding of faith;
      cf. also Isa. 28,16f and Hab. 2,4.

[90] Cf. Wildberger, "Glauben im AT", p. 142ff; "Erwägungen", p. 379f.

[91] Wildberger, "Glauben im AT", p. 143.

[92] Betz, "Geschichtsbezogenheit des Glaubens", p. 11.

[93] Wildberger, "Glauben im AT", p. 144.

[94] "…indem er in Gott gründete"; ibid.

[95] "And they believed in Jahwe and in Moses his servant".

"Fear not, stand firm,[96] and see the salvation of the Lord. ...You have only to be still".[97] Vs. 31 stands at the end of the narrative emphasizing the fact that Israel came to fear Jahwe (instead of the Egyptians!) and 'gained confidence' in Jahwe and in Moses his servant. Important here is that Moses as Jahwe's servant is introduced, along with Jahwe, as the object of the Israelites' faith.[98] Also important from this context is that the verbs 'to believe', 'to stand firm' and even 'to be still'[99] belong together in this religious context and also tend to mutually define one another.

Isa. 53,1 is one more OT passage with הֶאֱמִין which deserves attention: מִי הֶאֱמִין לִשְׁמֻעָתֵנוּ[100] Not a person but a message is the object of הֶאֱמִין in this passage. Wildberger argues once again for an intransitive meaning of הֶאֱמִין even when the formula הֶאֱמִין לְ- occurs.[101] Nevertheless, he is forced to concede that there is indeed a *Gegenüber* to which this faith is directed.[102] It is significant for the NT that this *Gegenüber* of faith in Isa 53,1 is the gospel message itself.[103] According to Betz, this OT passage forms the basis for the preaching of Jesus: "believe in the gospel" (Mk. 1,15). For, as Betz shows, the term 'gospel' is derived from the Targum of Isa. 53,1.[104]

In this context הֶאֱמִין as an act of faith necessarily implies obedience.[105] To stand firm in the gospel message (as is also the case in standing firm in the Law, in the word of God or in Jahwe himself!) implies nothing less than obedience to the gospel message.[106]

---

[96] הִתְיַצְּבוּ.

[97] Vs. 14b: וְאַתֶּם תַּחֲרִישׁוּן. It is clear from this context that the Israelites were indeed *very much afraid*.

[98] This, according to Wildberger, is the sense of הֶאֱמִין בְּ-; cf. "Erwägungen", p. 380. Wildberger cites other instances of הֶאֱמִין בְּ- where faith in Jahwe is expressed as faith in the divine Word (Ps. 106,12. 24); faith in the commandments (Ps. 119,66) = faith in the Law (vs. 67); and faith in miracles (Ps. 78,32). Although these are later developments, the basic meaning of הֶאֱמִין as 'to remain steadfast (הֶאֱמִין = הִתְיַצֵּב), to be confident, to trust' remains the same.

[99] הֶאֱמִין, הִתְיַצְּבוּ, and תַּחֲרִישׁוּן.

[100] "Who has believed our message?"

[101] I.e., "Festigkeit, Vertrauen gewinnen im Blick auf eine Person oder eine Sache"; Wildberger, "Erwägungen", p. 381f.

[102] Ibid.

[103] Cf. Betz, "Geschichtsbezogenheit des Glaubens", p. 20.

[104] Ibid.; cf. also Wildberger, "Erwägungen", p. 383. שְׁמֻעָתנוּ in the MT, however, means: 'that which we have heard' = 'our message'.

[105] I.e., because the object of הֶאֱמִין is לִשְׁמֻעָתֵנוּ from the root שׁמע, indicating both 'to hear' and 'to obey'.

[106] For later constructions of הֶאֱמִין with כִּי or with an infinitive clause signifying the content of what is believed, cf. Wildberger, "Erwägungen", pp. 383f.

When the hiphil stem הֶאֱמִין occurs in a religious sense it is virtually impossible to pinpoint one particular nuance and to conclude that this
is the absolute meaning of the verb. Weiser notes the tendency of this
verbal stem "to extend into the most comprehensive possible sphere of
application, just as אֱמֻנָה too embraces the whole attitude of a life lived in
faith, Hab. 2,4; 2 Chr. 19,9; Jer. 7,28 (5,3)".[107] Thus the context of Ex.
14 which leads up to the statement about faith in Jahwe and his servant
Moses in vs. 31 is also very important for the understanding of הֶאֱמִין as
faith terminology. As noted above, הֶאֱמִין in this context is closely related
to, as well as mutually defined by the terms to stand firm (vs. 13) and to
be still (vs. 14).

Therefore, when used in connection with the preposition בְּ־, the
hiphil הֶאֱמִין carries the idea 'to stand firm in, to trust in [someone or
something]'. In relationship to Jahwe or divine revelation the meaning of
הֶאֱמִין is 'to believe in'.[108] הֶאֱמִין with the preposition לְ־ means 'to believe
in someone or something', in the sense of an 'act of faith in a particular
situation'.[109]

3 THE ΠΙΣΤ- WORD GROUP AS THE EQUIVALENT OF אמן

3.1 General Observations

It is not necessary to discuss in detail the LXX passages employing
πίστις and πιστεύειν, for the important passages with אמן already
considered are also the important passages for πίστις and πιστεύειν. We
must once again underscore the importance of the *consistency* and *exclusiveness* with which LXX relates the πιστ- stem to the Hebrew אמן.
This is no accident. Rather it is most significant for the proper
understanding of both the אמן root and the πιστ- root as faith
terminology.

According to Wildberger, this relationship with πιστ- implies the
following for the Hebrew root אמן:

> Wenn πιστεύειν mit den ihm zugehörenden nominalen Ableitungen πίστις
> und πιστός eine solch eruptive Gewalt bewiesen hat, kann das

---

[107] Weiser, *TDNT* 6, p. 190.
[108] "...aber nicht im Sinn von 'für existent, wahr, zuverlässig erachten', sondern in der Bedeutung
'sein Vertrauen setzen auf', wobei Zuversicht und Gehorsam mit eingeschlossen sind"; Wildberger,
"Erwägungen", p. 385.
[109] Cf. ibid.

alttestamentliche Grundwort nicht eine theologisch farblose Vokabel neben
vielen anderen sein.[110]

Likewise, Weiser points out the importance of this relationship for the
πιστ- group: "The LXX and NT were right when they related their term
for faith (πιστεύειν) to the OT stem אמן, for in this word is expressed the
most distinctive and profound thing which the OT has to say about
faith".[111] It is therefore correct to interpret the πιστ- root in the LXX in
light of the Hebrew אמן.

The verb πιστεύειν is rarely found with an intransitive meaning.
And where πιστεύειν is used absolutely, it is generally clear from the
immediate context that there is a 'what' or a 'whom' that is (or is not) believed. This is in general agreement with the patterns of behavior for the
hiphil of אמן.[112] As we have shown in the previous chapter, πιστεύειν
in Classical Greek religious use carries the idea of *Verbindlichkeit* as
well as that of *Unverbindlichkeit*. This is also true of האמין.

3.2 Dissimilarities Between ΠΙΣΤ- and אמן

Nevertheless, it is obvious from the 'normal' use of Classical and
Hellenistic Greek that there are some very striking dissimilarities between
πιστ- and אמן. The noun πίστις, for example, could not fully express the
idea of 'truth' which is also inherent in אמונה, and especially in אמת, and so
ἀλήθεια had to be adopted in many instances. And, while the verb
πιστεύειν in Classical religious use does indeed carry both the ideas of
Verbindlichkeit and *Unverbindlichkeit*, it does not necessarily have the
base meaning of 'to stand firm', which is extremely important in האמין.

For the LXX translators the πιστ- root was not a 'perfect match'
for the Hebrew אמן. The usage, as well as the meaning, had to be
modified—particularly in the case of the verb πιστεύειν. The dilemma of
no perfect match is perhaps most clearly seen in the LXX translation of
Isa. 7,9. The word play with the hiphil and niphal forms of אמן was
impossible to reproduce with the verb πιστεύειν, precisely because
πιστεύειν did not carry the basic meaning 'to stand firm'. Here the translators opted for modification and used a completely different Greek verb to
express the niphal תאמנו: καὶ ἐὰν μὴ πιστεύσητε, οὐδὲ μὴ συνῆτε.
With the employment of συνῆτε for תאמנו, the LXX translators not only

---

[110] Wildberger, "Glauben im AT", p. 130.
[111] Weiser, *TDNT* 6, p. 196.
[112] This is in contrast to Wildberger who maintains that האמין is primarily intransitive in meaning!

broke a consistent pattern of rendering forms of אמן with forms of πιστ-, but they also altered the meaning of this passage. Συνῆτε has conceptually nothing to do with אמן; it corresponds rather to the verb בין.[113]

In the related passage 2 Chr. 20,20 there was indeed an attempt to assimilate the verb πιστεύειν into this formula and to reproduce the Hebrew word play in Greek: ἐμπιστεύσατε ἐν κυρίῳ θεῷ ὑμῶν, καὶ ἐμπιστευθήσεσθε. This translation does make sense,[114] but it is not the correct sense. Even this Greek translation of the niphal of אמן cannot be properly interpreted without taking into consideration the Hebrew root אמן.

3.3 LXX Attempts to Bridge the Gaps

2 Chr. 20,20 also provides a good example of how the LXX translators attempted to deal with the relational aspect of the Hebrew construction with האמין ב-. The compound verb ἐμπιστεύειν as an expression of religious faith[115] appears to be an innovation to express the Hebrew preposition ב-.[116] If this were not enough, the preposition ἐν (= ב) is repeated before the dative κυρίῳ θεῷ. This construction ἐμπιστεύειν ἐν is unprecedented (and superfluous!) in Classical and Hellenistic Greek where the simple dative suffices. But here it is important as an attempt to retain the relational idea of the Hebrew preposition ב-.[117] A further innovation of the LXX usage is the construction πιστεύειν ἐπί plus the dative in Isa. 28,16.[118] This is particularly innovative since האמין in the Hebrew text is employed absolutely.

The most common use of πιστεύειν in the LXX, however, is the normal Greek construction of the verb followed by a simple dative,

---

[113] Cf. e.g., Isa. 52,15. It is interesting however that the Greek Sirach uses the verb ἐμπιστεύειν in 33,3a, where the Hebrew fragments employ the verb יבין.

[114] I.e., "...you will be believed".

[115] Cf. also Dt. 1,32; Jon. 3,5.

[116] The verb ἐμπιστεύειν does occur in secular Hellenistic Greek, but practically never in the sense of religious faith or trust. Rather the sense is the profane meaning 'entrust' and the verb is used in the active construction ἐμπιστεύειν τινί τι or in the passive construction ἐμπιστεύεσθαί τι; but never in the active transitive or absolute passive sense as found in 2 Chr. 20,20! Cf. 2 Macc. 10,13; Josephus Bel. 1,262; 3,137; Ant. 10,190.

[117] Cf. Jer. 12,6; Ps. 77(78),22. 32; Dan. 6,24; also Mk. 1,15.

[118] Paul quotes the LXX of this passage in Rom. 9,33; 10,11; cf. also 1 Pet. 2,6. Elsewhere in the NT where πιστεύειν ἐπί occurs, the preposition is followed by an accusative case form; cf. Mt. 27,42.

regardless of whether the preposition following הֶאֱמִן is בְּ or לְ.[119] Also, in keeping with some of the later and more isolated uses of הֶאֱמִן, it is quite natural for πιστεύειν to occur with a ὅτι (= כִּי) clause [120] or with an infinitive clause.[121]

4 SUMMARY

The evidence cited shows that the LXX translators interpreted the πιστ- word group in light of the Hebrew אמן and not vice-versa. And because πιστεύειν was not (in its earlier Classical usage) a perfect match for the אמן word group, the LXX translation represents *a significant development* in the use of the πιστ- group as faith terminology.

Already in Classical Greek πιστεύειν could refer to faith in the gods in the sense of trusting in them or in their word or oracle. This trust was not simply an intellectual assent to the truth of the gods' existence or the validity of their oracles (i.e., *Unverbindlichkeit*), but also an active engagement—i.e., reliance upon and obedeience to the god or the divine oracle.

This is admittedly not a perfect match with the base idea of 'standing firm' which is inherent in אמן, but it is also not a distant step away. In the LXX this step is made. Πίστις and πιστεύειν gain the meaning of 'having firmness, steadfastness' by association with הֶאֱמִן, and the πιστ- word group is expanded in its meaning, enabling it to be employed as faith terminology. Also, by reason of its association with the אמן group, the πιστ- group begins to assimilate some other very important nuances, such as a close relationship with 'truth'[122] and 'righteousness'.[123] The end result is that πίστις and πιστεύειν can now have the tendency, just as אֱמוּנָה and הֶאֱמִין, to "extend into the most comprehensive sphere of application ... [and to embrace] the whole attitude of a life lived in faith".[124]

Likewise, the use of the adjective πιστός to translate adjectival forms of אמן, particularly the niphal participle נֶאֱמָן, displays a new development. Indeed, the basic meaning of πιστός remains the same as in pro-

---

[119] Cf. Gen. 15,6; Ex. 4,1. 5. 8. 9; 14,31; Num. 14,11; Dt. 9,23; Isa. 53,1; Jer. 25,8; Ps. 106(105),24; 119(118),66.
[120] E.g., Isa. 43,10; Lam. 4,12.
[121] Ps. 27(26),13; cf. Num. 20,12.
[122] I.e., אֱמֶת and אֱמוּנָה = πίστις.
[123] Cf. Hab. 2,4; Isa. 28,16f; Gen. 15,6.
[124] Cf. Weiser, *TDNT* 6, p. 190.

fane use, i.e., 'faithful, reliable, loyal', but the sense of *religious* faithfulness or trustworthiness is new. And in the context of God[125] or God's
word,[126] it is clear that πιστός once again borrows from אמן the idea of
'firm, steadfast'.

At work here is, in fact, the *Bedeutungslehnwörter* theory
proposed by Dieter Lührmann:[127] The relative neutral πιστ- word group
is not without important precedent in religious usage and is therefore capable of being understood within a religious context and being developed
further within this context. This word group was adopted and employed
by the LXX translators to express the full breadth of the Hebrew אמן in its
use as faith terminology.

Here we must proceed carefully, however. It would be too much to
say that the πιστ- group actually became and was understood as a perfect
match for אמן. This is not the case, as can be clearly seen in the examples
above where the LXX translators had difficulty 'fitting in' the πιστ-
words for every occurrence of אמן in the Hebrew text. Rather what we see
here is a step in the development of the πιστ- word group as faith terminology—indeed a very important step. The identification of πιστ-
with אמן is a development that is unparalleled in the secular Greek world
of this time. It is a development which stands as the basis for the proper
understanding of the πιστ- group as faith terminology in the NT.

This development of the πιστ- word group does not end with the
LXX. Rather the process continues through the intertestamental period
and into the NT period. In the next chapter we shall see how the word
group in the apocryphal Greek Sirach undergoes further religious
development beyond the normal patterns of translation elsewhere in the
LXX.

---

[125] E.g., Isa. 49,7.
[126] E.g., Ps. 19,7 (18,8).
[127] See above, Introduction.

CHAPTER THREE

ΠΙΣΤΙΣ AND ΠΙΣΤΕΥΕΙΝ IN JESUS BEN SIRACH

In the OT Apocrypha the book of wisdom by Sirach holds a special place. It is the only one of the apocryphal books for which extensive fragments of a Hebrew original exist. Indeed, the majority of the other writings do not claim to have been originally written in Hebrew.

The Greek translation of Sirach from the Hebrew[1] represents a further development of the use of the πιστ- word group as faith terminol-ogy. This development will be illustrated, first of all, by a comparative study of the Hebrew equivalents of the πιστ- words in the LXX and in Sirach and, secondly, by a study of Sirach's own understanding of the word group.

1 HEBREW EQUIVALENTS OF THE ΠΙΣΤ- WORD GROUP IN SIRACH[2]

Greek Sirach employs five cognates of the πιστ- word group in 48 in-stances (not including the more dubious textual variants). The verbs πιστεύειν, ἐμπιστεύειν and πιστοῦν[3] occur eleven times, twelve times and two times respectively. The noun πίστις occurs ten times and the ad-jective πιστός occurs thirteen times, either adjectivally or substantivally. In the Hebrew fragments from Cairo-Geniza (et al.) the Hebrew equiva-lents are lacking in 22 of these 48 instances, leaving us to rely heavily upon the reverse translation into Hebrew by M. Segal[4] in our comparison of the Hebrew equivalents for the πιστ- word group. For this study it will be helpful to keep in mind the trends of the LXX translation in general for each of the words in this Greek word group.

1.1 The Substantive Πίστις

Πίστις appears eleven times in Sirach, but there are only two instances where a recognizable parallel in the Hebrew fragments exists. It is there-fore difficult to speak of a norm for Sirach's use of the substantive. Nevertheless, it is significant that the Hebrew equivalent, where it does

---

[1] Ca. 132 B.C.E.

[2] For an overview see "Appendix One: Hebrew Equivalents for Πιστ- in Jesus ben Sirach".

[3] Πιστοῦν appears only in Sir. 27,17 and 29,3. In neither instance is there textual evidence from the Hebrew fragments of Sirach. In both instances Segal's back-translation represents the Greek pas-sive imperative πιστώθητι with the niphal imperative האמן. This seems to be the normal Hebrew equivalent of the passive of πιστοῦν elsewhere in the LXX (cf. 2 Sam. 7,16; 1 Ki. 8,26; 1 Chr. 17,23. 24; 2 Chr. 1,9; 6,17; Ps. 78,8. 37; 93,5).

[4] M. Z. Segal, *Das vollständige Buch Ben Sira (hebräisch)* (Jerusalem, 1958).

exist in Sir. 15,15 and 45,4, is the substantive אמונה. This is what one would expect from the normal use of πίστις elsewhere in the LXX.[5]

Where there are lacunae in the Hebrew fragments Segal's back-translation also follows the normal LXX pattern and reverts to the Hebrew אמונה as the parallel for πίστις in the Greek. In Sir. 1,27 אמונה is most likely correct, due to the parallelism with 45,4. A similar argument could be made for the use of אמונה at 46,15a and 49,10, also based upon the Cairo-Geniza text of 45,4. Therefore, it is safe to say that Sirach's use of the substantive πίστις in translating the Hebrew root אמן is the same as the normative use elsewhere in the LXX.

1.2 The Verb Πιστεύειν

We have shown in the previous chapter that there is not only a pattern, but also a preference on the part of the LXX translators to represent the hiphil of אמן with the Greek verb πιστεύειν or one of its compounds. Sirach also displays a strong tendency in this same direction, however with some variation from the consistency demonstrated elsewhere in the LXX. When the Greek translation of Sirach uses πιστεύειν to render אמן, the Hebrew verb always occurs in the hiphil stem. Generally the hiphil of אמן is translated πιστεύειν (or a compound of the verb). יאמין in manuscript 'B' of Sir. 37,13a has no recognizable parallel in the LXX[6] which follows the variant found in Mss. B[mg], D:

וגם עצת לבב הבין

Likewise, πιστότερος in vs. 13b follows the Hebrew אמון in Ms. D.[7] So also in 15,15 the Greek follows the older text form:[8] ואמונה לעשות רצון[9] and translates accordingly with πίστιν ποιεῖν. Only in Sir. 45,13 does the (probable) reading הֻא[מ]ן have no corresponding form of πιστεύειν in the Greek.

This is not to say, however, that πιστεύειν in the Greek consistently represents a form of אמן in the Hebrew text. Sirach deviates from the normal LXX equivalency by translating Hebrew roots other than אמן with πιστεύειν. Whereas there is only one instance of such a

5 Πίστις in Sir. 37,26 does not represent כבד in the Hebrew! Cf. J. Ziegler (ed., *Sapientia Iesu Filii Sirach,* in *Vetus Testamentum Graecum* Vol. 12,2 (Göttingen: Vandenhoeck und Ruprecht, 1965)): τιμήν; or Ms. *L:* δόξαν.

6 καὶ βουλὴν καρδίας στῆσον.

7 אמן in Mss. B[mg] and B.

8 Cf. Hans Peter Rüger, *Text und Textform im Hebräischen Sirach* (Berlin: Walter de Gruyter, 1970), p. 78.

9 The later reading is: אם תאמין בו; cf. Prov. 12,22.

deviation from this normal pattern in the LXX, [10] in Sirach there is more variety. In Sir. 32,21 the qal of בטח[11] is rendered πιστεύσης. In 32,23 the Hebrew שמור נפשך[12] becomes πίστευε τῇ ψυχῇ σου.[13] Similarly, 'the one who trusts (or believes) in the law' in the Greek text of 32,24[14] represents the 'keeper of the law' in the Hebrew text.[15] In each of these instances the Greek Sirach is at variance with the normal LXX use of πιστεύειν as the equivalent of the Hebrew אמן.

The Cairo-Geniza fragment Sir. 11,21 shows yet another variation from the norm. Here the Hebrew imperative רוץ ל ייי[16] is translated πίστευε κυρίῳ. It is interesting to note that the Hebrew text of Segal at this point reproduces from the Greek πίστευε the normative hiphil ל ייי האמן, in spite of the precedence he gives to the Cairo-Geniza fragments at other passages. Also interesting to note is that when there is no evidence from the Hebrew fragments for an equivalent for the verb πιστεύειν,[17] Segal translates back into the Hebrew with the hiphil of אמן.

1.3 The Verb 'Εμπιστεύειν

The compound verb ἐμπιστεύειν follows the same pattern as the simple verb πιστεύειν with regard to Hebrew equivalents in Sirach and in the LXX. It appears for the most part to be either an arbitrary deviation from, or a personal stylistic preference over the normal use of πιστεύειν in the LXX translation. The prefix ἐμ (= ἐν) corresponds to the Hebrew preposition -ב.[18] Half of all occurrences of ἐμπιστεύειν in the LXX appear in the Greek text of Sirach. There are both parallels and deviations in Sirach from the normal LXX use of ἐμπιστεύειν as the equivalent for the Hebrew verb אמן. Similar are two instances in Sir. 7,26 and 16,3 where ἐμπιστεύειν represents the hiphil of אמן. In both instances the preposition -ב accompanies the verb האמין. Also similar is the use of a passive form of ἐμπιστεύειν in Sir. 36,15 to translate the niphal of אמן.

Without precedent in the normal LXX pattern, however, the Greek of Sir. 50,24 represents the passive niphal stem of אמן with an active form of ἐμπιστεύειν. Even more striking are the deviations encountered

---

[10] Cf. Jer. 25,8 where the Hebrew root שמע is rendered by the verb πιστεύειν.
[11] 'To trust'.
[12] 'Keep your soul'.
[13] 'Trust in your soul'.
[14] ὁ πιστεύων νόμῳ.
[15] שומר תור[ה].
[16] The lacuna here is puzzling. R. Smend (*Griechisch-Syrisch-Hebräischer Index zur Weisheit des Jesus Sirach* (Berlin: Georg Reimer Verlag, 1907), p. 189) suggests the underlying root קרץ.
[17] E.g., Sir. 2,6. 8. 13 and 19,15.
[18] I.e., in the formula: האמין ב-.

at 4,17; 6,7; 33,3a where ἐμπιστεύειν stands for a Hebrew root other than אמן. In Sir. 6,7 the Hebrew reads: ואל תמהר לבטח עליו.[19] The Greek translates with ἐμπιστεύσῃς,[20] taking the Hebrew לבטח as an infinitive.[21] In this instance ἐμπιστεύειν takes on the (profane) sense of 'to trust': "Do not hurry to trust him".

The verb in Sir. 4,17 is מלא: ועד עת ימלא לבו בי.[22] The Greek changes this into the active expression: ἕως οὗ ἐμπιστεύσῃ τῇ ψυχῇ αὐτοῦ.[23] The use of ἐμπιστεύειν in this instance represents an interpretation by the translator and, thus, a further deviation from the normal pattern in the LXX. In 33,3a ἐμπιστεύειν represents the Hebrew verb בין, 'to observe, to give heed to'. In the Hebrew text there is a word play with the niphal participle and the qal imperfect forms of בין: דבר ייי איש נבון יבין[24] This word play would have been difficult to reproduce in the Greek. What we find instead is another interpretation of the Hebrew: ἄνθρωπος συνετὸς ἐμπιστεύσει λόγῳ. Nowhere else in the LXX is the Hebrew verb בין translated by the Greek (ἐμ)πιστεύειν.[25]

Again, all of the deviations from the normal LXX translation pattern with the verb ἐμπιστεύειν occur in instances where there are existing fragments of the Hebrew text of Sirach. And again the indication is that the deviation in the Greek Sirach from the LXX norm was deliberate. Moreover, as is the case with the verb πιστεύειν, where there are lacunae in the Hebrew text Segal reverts to the normal pattern using the hiphil of אמן for the active ἐμπιστεύειν[26] and the niphal of אמן for the passive of ἐμπιστεύειν.[27]

1.4 The Adjective Πιστός

Πιστός appears approximately forty times in the LXX as the translation of a recognizable Hebrew equivalent. As with the substantive πίστις, there is more variety in the pattern of equivalents for the adjective. The most common Hebrew equivalent for πιστός is the niphal stem of אמן, occurring in 29 instances. Conversely, the niphal of אמן is regularly

---

19 "Do not hasten to trust him [i.e., your new friend]".
20 καὶ μὴ ταχὺ ἐμπιστεύσῃς αὐτῷ; cf. Sir. 32,21.
21 I.e., לִבְטֹחַ instead of לְבֶטַח.
22 "Until his heart is filled with me [i.e., Wisdom]".
23 "Until she [Wisdom] trusts his soul".
24 "A discerning man will discern the word of the Lord".
25 But cf. Isa. 7,9 in the LXX where the Greek verb συνιέναι (= בין) represents the niphal of אמן, rather than the normal πιστεύειν.
26 E.g., Sir. 2,10; 4,16; 19,4.
27 Sir. 1,15.

translated in the LXX by the πιστ- word group, generally by the adjective πιστός.[28]

The pattern of Hebrew equivalents for πιστός in Sirach falls generally in line with the pattern of equivalents elsewhere in the LXX. In Sir. 37,23b there is no recognizable equivalent in the Hebrew text. Πιστός in Sir. 33,3b may represent an assimilation of the word play in 33,3a where the πιστ- words stand for the Hebrew root בין.[29] Otherwise, in the places where Hebrew fragments exist, πιστός in Sirach consistently represents the Hebrew root אמן. In Sir. 37,13 the comparative form of the adjective[30] corresponds to the Hebrew אמון.[31] Three times, in Sir. 6,14. 15. 16, the noun אמונה is translated by the adjective πιστός as elsewhere in the LXX.[32] In all three instances here the expression 'friend of faithfulness'[33] is correctly reproduced in the Greek as φίλοςπιστός.[34] In three instances, Sir. 31,23; 44,20; 46,15b, πιστός represents the niphal stem of אמן.[35]

1.5 Summary

From this overview of Hebrew equivalents for the πιστ- word group in Sirach and in the LXX there is evidence of a new trend appearing in the Greek translation of Sirach. Sirach stands with one foot firmly planted in the normal LXX use of the word group but begins to take a further step with his use of πιστ-, and especially with the verb (ἐμ)πιστεύειν. Sirach employs the Greek word group to represent Hebrew expressions other than ones represented by the root אמן—a use unprecedented elsewhere in the LXX. Sirach represents a development in the use of the πιστ- word group beyond the normal use of the group in the LXX. This development is displayed further by Sirach's understanding of πίστις and πιστεύειν.

---

[28] Another frequent translation of the niphal אמן is the passive form of the verb πιστοῦν.
[29] Cf. Ziegler, ed., *Sirach*, p. 277.
[30] πιστότερος.
[31] Ms. B.
[32] E.g., Dt. 32,4.
[33] אוהב אמונה
[34] 'Faithful friend'.
[35] In three other instances where there are lacunae (Sir. 1,14; 34,8; 48,22) Segal uses the niphal of אמן in his 'back-translation'.

2 SIRACH'S UNDERSTANDING OF THE ΠΙΣΤ- WORD GROUP

2.1 The Substantive Πίστις

2.11 Πίστις in Human Relationships

Πίστις appears twice within the context of friendship. In 22,23 Sirach
admonishes to 'keep faith'[36] with one's neighbor while he is poor. This
keeping faith is obviously an admonition to faithfulness and
steadfastness, and is directly parallel to 'stand by him[37] [in time of
trouble]' in the second part of this verse. The sense of πίστιν κτῆσαι in
this passage is exactly the same as that of πιστώθητι in 27,17 and 29,3,
as is attested by the common Hebrew equivalent האמן.

In 27,16 Sirach warns that one who discloses secrets destroys (a
relationship of) trust.[38] Such a person will never find an intimate friend.
Therefore the admonition in the following verse is to 'keep faith' with a
friend.[39] In 22,23 and 27,16 πίστις appears on the surface to have a
neutral and profane implication; i.e., trustworthiness in relationships with
friends. But when the intensity and passion of Sirach's passages about
friendship are taken into account, it becomes obvious that friendship itself
is a 'sacred' relationship and that πίστις in these contexts cannot be fully
appreciated simply at the profane level.[40]

2.12 Πίστις in a Religious Sense

Elsewhere in Sirach it is fairly clear that πίστις is more a religious than a
secular concept. In 15,15 the idea of keeping faith [with God], upon the
basis of personal desire, is parallel to keeping the commandments.[41] The
substantive πίστις carries the idea of steadfastness, faithfulness and even
obedience in a religious sense,[42] just as the verb πιστεύειν does. Πίστιν
ποιεῖν in this passage is precisely the same as ὁ ποιῶν πίστιν[43] in Prov.
12,22 and is parallel also to Jer. 40(33),6 where the LXX reads: ποιήσω
αὐτοῖς εἰρήνην καὶ πίστιν.[44] This, in turn, is very similar to the
formula ἀλήθειαν ποιεῖν which appears in the NT.[45]

---

[36] πίστιν κτῆσαι.
[37] διάμενε αὐτῷ.
[38] ἀπώλεσεν πίστιν.
[39] στέρξον φίλον καὶ πιστώθητι μετ᾽ αὐτοῦ.
[40] Cf. e.g., Sir. 27,24 regarding the discloser of secrets; Sirach comments about such a one: "There
        are many things I hate, but him above all; *the Lord will hate him too!*"
[41] ἐὰν θέλῃς, συντηρήσεις ἐντολὰς καὶ πίστιν ποιῆσαι εὐδοκίας.
[42] I.e., faithfulness and obedience to God.
[43] Hebrew: עשׂי אמונה; in Qumran this formula appears as עשׂה אמת (cf. 1 QS 1,5; 5,3; 8,2).
[44] Hebrew: עתרת שׁלום ואמת.
[45] Jn. 3,21; 1 Jn. 1,6.

Πίστις in Sirach is also a sort of 'religious virtue'. In 40,12 πίστις is pitted against the vices of bribery and injustice which are temporary and fleeting; in contrast to these, πίστις will endure forever.[46] In 40,17 the virtues of kindness and almsgiving[47] are parallel to πίστις: "But kindness is a luxurious garden, and almsgiving will last forever".[48] Also in the NT πίστις is employed in a very similar way. This especially clear in 1 Cor. 13,13: Νυνὶ δὲ μένει πίστις, ἐλπίς, ἀγάπη, τὰ τρία ταῦτα.

This is also the sense of πίστις in Sir. 41,16. The context speaks of every [kind of] shameful thing which is inconsistent with πίστις: "For it is not good to foster every [kind of] shameful thing, nor are all things acceptable to all people in (or by) faith".[49] Sir. 41,17 through 42,1b follows with a catalog of shameful things which should be avoided. In Sir. 42,1c-8, then, is a catalog of virtuous things. Πίστις in 41,16 must again be viewed in light of this contrast.

Πίστις appears along with πραΰτης[50] in Sir. 1,27 as that which comprises the delight of the Lord.[51] Here πίστις is a virtue by which a person finds approval in the sight of the Lord. This is shown further in 45,4 where Sirach states that Moses was sanctified in faith and humility.[52] This recalls the tradition about Moses found in Num. 12. Moses is described by God in Num. 12,3 as a very humble man[53]—more humble than all the men on earth. In Num. 12,7 the Lord goes on to say that Moses "is faithful in my entire household".[54] It was upon the basis of Moses' humility and faithfulness that he was allowed[55] to speak face to face with Jahwe and to view the glory of the Lord (Num. 12,8). Therefore, πίστις in Sir. 45,4 corresponds to πιστός in Num. 12,7[56] and refers clearly to Moses' faithfulness to God. In the NT Heb. 3,2. 5 also takes up the tradition of Num. 12,7. The Hebrews passage, however, does not introduce the substantive πίστις into the discussion, only the adjective πιστός. Moses' faithfulness is not viewed by the writer of Hebrews as a 'virtue'.

Sir. 46,15 speaks of the prophet Samuel in similar terms as of Moses. "In his faithfulness the prophet was proven accurate, and in his

---

[46] Πᾶν δῶρον καὶ ἀδικία ἐξαλειφθήσεται, καὶ πίστις εἰς τὸν αἰῶνα στήσεται.

[47] χάρις; ἐλεημοσύνη.

[48] The verb here is διαμενεῖν.

[49] οὐ γάρ ἐστιν πᾶσαν αἰσχύνην διαφυλάξαι καλόν, καὶ οὐ πάντα πᾶσιν ἐν πίστει εὐδοκιμεῖται.

[50] 'Gentleness, humility'.

[51] ἡ εὐδοκία αὐτοῦ.

[52] ἐν πίστει καὶ πραΰτητι αὐτὸν ἡγίασεν.

[53] πραΰς σφόδρα.

[54] ἐν ὅλῳ τῷ οἴκῳ μου πιστός ἐστιν.

[55] Sirach: 'sanctified'!

[56] Hebrew: נאמן.

utterances he became known as a faithful/trustworthy seer".[57] The tradition for these statements about Samuel comes from 1 Sam. 3,20: "All of Israel from Dan to Beersheba became aware of the fact that Samuel was trustworthy as a prophet of the Lord".[58] The LXX repeats this idea in vs. 21: "In all of Israel Samuel was believed to be[59] a prophet of the Lord".

Finally, in praise of the 'twelve prophets', Sir. 49,10 relates that "they brought comfort to Jacob and rescued the people ἐν πίστει ἐλπίδος". This relationship between faith/faithfulness and hope recalls the entire context of the NT epistle to the Hebrews and especially Heb. 11,1ff.

Πίστις in Sirach, then, is almost exclusively a religious term describing a relationship of faithfulness and obedience toward God. It is ἐν πίστει that a person is sanctified, approved by God, pleasing to God or even redeemed by God. Πίστις is also a virtue—a virtue which endures forever. And even πίστις in relationships with friends has direct implications for one's relationship to God.

2.2 The Verb ('Εμ)πιστεύειν

The basic meaning of (ἐμ)πιστεύειν in Sirach is 'to trust in, to stand firm in [someone or something]'. This remains true to the meaning of the Hebrew אמן in the hiphil stem which, as shown above, is the Hebrew equivalent in the majority of instances where (ἐμ)πιστεύειν occurs. Upon close examination, two distinct groups of passages involving (ἐμ)πιστεύειν become evident: 1) Passages where, by command or implication, trust is discouraged, and 2) passages where, by command or implication, trust and steadfastness are encouraged.

2.21 Passages Where Trust is Discouraged

In the first group we encounter passages which are typical of the *Erfahrungsweisheit* genre. A good example is Sir. 6,7: "If you would acquire a friend, acquire him by testing and do not trust him too quickly".[60] Similarly, Sir. 19,15 instructs that a friend should be proven and that not every word should be trusted.[61] Also in Sir. 19,4 there is a

---

[57] ἐν πίστει αὐτοῦ ἠκριβάσθη προφήτης καὶ ἐγνώσθη ἐν ῥήμασιν αὐτοῦ πιστὸς ὁράσεως.
[58] πιστὸς (נאמן) Σαμουὴλ εἰς προφήτην τῷ κυρίῳ.
[59] Or 'to become'; ἐπιστεύθη Σαμουὴλ προφήτης γενέσθαι.
[60] εἰ κτᾶσαι φίλον, ἐν πειρασμῷ κτῆσαι αὐτὸν καὶ μὴ ταχὺ ἐμπιστεύσῃς αὐτῷ. Cf. also Mic. 7,5.
[61] ἔλεγξον φίλον, πολλάκις γὰρ γίνεται διαβολή, καὶ μὴ παντὶ λόγῳ πίστευε. Cf. Prov. 14,15.

warning against being too quick to trust: "One who trusts quickly is light of heart".[62]

An untried friend is not the only unworthy object of blind trust. An incompatible wife must not be trusted (Sir. 7,26).[63] The summoning of an influential person or political ruler is not to be shunned (Sir. 13,9-10), but such a person must be dealt with wisely. His lengthy speeches are not to be trusted.[64] The lives of worthless and ungodly children are not worthy of trust, even if the children be numerous (Sir. 16,3),[65] for one child is better than a thousand, and to die childless is better than to have ungodly children. Especially not ever to be trusted is an enemy (Sir. 12,10).[66] Sir. 36,26(31) asks rhetorically: "Who would trust a well-dressed thief?"[67] And Sir. 32,21 warns against putting trust in a path that is seemingly clear and void of offense.[68]

With a different emphasis Sir. 38,33-34 explains that the craftworkers (farmers, carpenters, smiths and potters), because they simply trust in their own hands,[69] are not in a position to discern weightier, more spiritual matters. Ἐμπιστεύειν is particularly significant in this passage since it appears with the preposition εἰς plus accusative case form. This is the only time in the LXX where this syntactical construction occurs and indicates, no doubt, an attempt to reproduce the Hebrew preposition בּ.[70] In the NT the 'hebraism' πιστεύειν εἰς with an accusative appears more frequently.[71]

Conceptually, however, all of these passages in Sirach deal with situations of experiential wisdom, generally with situations of uncertainty and untried motives where a basis for trust has not been firmly estab-lished. (Ἐμ)πιστεύειν is used in these instances in a profane sense rather than a strictly religious sense. Nonetheless, it is important to note that these passages generally discourage the practice of faith or trust under secular circumstances.

2.22 Passages Where Trust is Encouraged

On the other hand, there are situations where trust and steadfastness are certainly in order. Jahwe should always be the object of trust and

---

[62] ὁ ταχὺ ἐμπιστεύων κοῦφος καρδίᾳ.
[63] Cf. Jos. *Bel.* 2,121.
[64] Sir. 13,11: μὴ ἔπεχε ἰσηγορεῖσθαι μετ' αὐτοῦ καὶ μὴ πίστευε τοῖς πλείοσιν λόγοις αὐτοῦ.
[65] μὴ ἐμπιστεύσῃς τῇ ζωῇ αὐτῶν καὶ μὴ ἔπεχε ἐπὶ τὸ πλῆθος αὐτῶν.
[66] μὴ πιστεύσῃς τῷ ἐχθρῷ σου εἰς τὸν αἰῶνα.
[67] τίς γὰρ πιστεύσει εὐζώνῳ λῃστῇ ἀφαλλομένῳ ἐκ πόλεως εἰς πόλιν;
[68] μὴ πιστεύσῃς ἐν ὁδῷ ἀπροσκόπῳ.
[69] Sir. 38,31: Πάντες οὗτοι εἰς χεῖρας αὐτῶν ἐνεπίστευσαν.
[70] Cf. Segal's back-translation into the Hebrew.
[71] E.g., Mt. 16,8; Mk. 9,42; Jn. 1,12; Rom. 10,14.

steadfast faith.[72] It is a 'slack heart' (in contrast to a steadfast heart) which does not trust in Jahwe.[73] Along with Jahwe, the prophets are to be trusted;[74] also Wisdom[75] and the Law.[76] In Sir. 4,17 Wisdom herself is said to trust[77] the soul of the man she has tried, tested and proven. In connection with trusting the Law, Sirach admonishes in 32,23 that one should trust even his own soul in every deed, for this is the keeping of the commandments.[78]

The trust that is encouraged in these instances implies far more than an intellectual belief in Jahwe, the prophets, the Law or Wisdom. It is clear from these passages that (ἐμ)πιστεύειν involves steadfastness, faithfulness, perseverance and, especially with regard to the Law, obedience. Along with the command in Sir. 2,6 to trust in the Lord appears the admonishment to steer straight paths and to hope in the Lord.[79] In Sir. 2,10 trusting in the Lord[80] is directly parallel to remaining steadfast in the fear of the Lord[81] and to calling upon the Lord.[82] In Sir. 11,21 trusting the Lord involves enduring and persevering in one's own toils.[83] The one who trusts the Law also devotes himself to the commandments.[84] And the one who devotes himself to Wisdom and trusts steadfastly in her will eventually inherit her.[85] (Ἐμ)πιστεύειν appears two more times in the sense of 'standing firm'. In Sir. 50,24, along with a psalm of praise to God, there appears the request that God will "make his mercy stand firm with us".[86] In Sir. 1,15 it is the fear of the Lord itself which will stand firm with the offspring of men.[87]

Clearly the use of (ἐμ)πιστεύειν in the LXX underlies Sirach's use of the verb. In both instances the hiphil of אמן provides the basic meaning of (ἐμ)πιστεύειν, and in both instances the religious context plays an important role in the practice of this steadfast faith or trust. But

---

[72] Sir. 2,6. 8. 10; 11,21; cf. Isa. 28,16.
[73] Sir. 2,13: οὐαὶ καρδίᾳ παρειμένῃ, ὅτι οὐ πιστεύει· διὰ τοῦτο οὐ σκεπασθήσεται.
[74] Sir. 36,15(21): οἱ προφῆταί σου ἐμπιστευθήτωσαν.
[75] Sir. 4,16.
[76] Sir. 32,24: ὁ πιστεύων νόμῳ προσέχει ἐντολαῖς, καὶ ὁ πεποιθὼς κυρίῳ οὐκ ἐλαττωθήσεται. Important here is that faith in the law is directly parallel to faith in the Lord. Cf. also Sir. 33,3a.
[77] This is, as noted above, inconsistent with the Hebrew niphal form of מלא found in the fragments.
[78] ἐν παντὶ ἔργῳ πίστευε τῇ ψυχῇ σου· καὶ γὰρ τοῦτό ἐστιν τήρησις ἐντολῶν.
[79] εὔθυνον τὰς ὁδούς σου καὶ ἔλπισον ἐπ' αὐτόν.
[80] ἐμπιστεύειν κυρίῳ.
[81] ἐμμένειν τῷ φόβῳ αὐτοῦ.
[82] ἐπικαλεῖν αὐτόν.
[83] πίστευε δὲ κυρίῳ καὶ ἔμμενε τῷ πόνῳ σου. This idea of steadfastness connected with (ἐμ)πιστεύειν is basic to the meaning of the Hebrew אמן.
[84] Sir. 32,24: ὁ πιστεύων νόμῳ προσέχει ἐντολαῖς.
[85] Sir. 4,16: ἐὰν ἐμπιστεύσῃ, κατακληρονομήσει αὐτήν.
[86] ἐμπιστεῦσαι [aor. inf.] μεθ' ἡμῶν τὸ ἔλεος αὐτοῦ καὶ ἐν ταῖς ἡμέραις ἡμῶν λυτρωσάσθω ἡμᾶς.
[87] μετὰ ἀνθρώπων θεμέλιον αἰῶνος ἐνόσσευσεν καὶ μετὰ τοῦ σπέρματος αὐτῶν ἐμπιστευθήσεται. See also the use of ἐμπιστεύειν for the niphal of אמן in 2 Chron. 20,20 (cf. Isa. 7,9).

Sirach develops the religious concept of (ἐμ)πιστεύειν a bit further in two ways. In the first place, Sirach draws a clear distinction between the proper and the improper objects of trust. He tends to remove the verb from a neutral, profane setting and elevates it to a religious concept by pointing out the improper (secular) objects of trust and by encouraging the proper (sacred) objects of trust within the religious context.

In the second place, whereas the LXX limits the use of (ἐμ)πιστεύειν to correspond to the Hebrew אמן, the Greek Sirach includes additional Hebrew roots and concepts under the umbrella of (ἐμ)πιστεύειν.[88]   In this tendency (ἐμ)πιστεύειν acquires further significance as a religious term.

2.3 The Adjective Πιστός

2.31 Πιστός as a Neutral Term

The Adjective πιστός is generally a neutral term in Sirach. The φίλος πιστός of Sir. 6,14. 15. 16 is simply a trustworthy or true friend in the normal sense of the word. So also the μαρτυρία πιστή of 31,23 is simply a 'trustworthy testimony'. In Sir. 37,13 there is nothing more trustworthy[89] than the counsel of the heart. In Sir. 37,22-23 the fruits of the wise man's understanding are described as 'enduring'.[90]

2.32 Πιστός in a Religious Context

Within a sacred context, the trustworthy character of the Law is only hinted at in Sir. 34,8,[91] but expressed directly in 33,3b: ὁ νόμος ... πιστός. In Sir. 1,14 the plural μετὰ πιστῶν refers substantivally to 'the faithful ones'; i.e., they are the ones in whom the fear of the Lord dwells. This displays once again the important relationship between faith and the fear of the Lord in Sirach.

The most important instances, where πιστός appears denoting trustworthiness or faithfulness on the sacred level, are Sir. 44,20; 46,15 and 48,22. In Sir. 46,15b the prophet Samuel is described as "trustworthy in his visions".[92] Parallel to this is the description of Isaiah in Sir. 48,22. Here Isaiah is called "the great [prophet] and trustworthy in his visions [as a seer]".[93] Nowhere else in the OT is Isaiah explicitly described as πιστός.

---

88 E.g., בטח in Sir. 6,7 and 32,21; שמר in Sir. 32,23; בין in Sir. 33,3a.
89 πιστότερος.
90 πιστοί.
91 ἄνευ ψεύδους συντελεσθήσεται νόμος, καὶ σοφία στόματι πιστῷ τελείωσις.
92 πιστὸς ὁράσεως.
93 ... Ἡσαΐας ὁ προφήτης ὁ μέγας καὶ πιστὸς ἐν ὁράσει αὐτοῦ.

In Sir. 44,20 is the important assertion about Abraham, that he "kept the law of the Most High and entered into a covenant with Him; he confirmed this covenant in his own flesh and in the test he was found faithful".[94] From Gen. 15,6 comes the tradition that Abraham believed God when God promised him innumerable descendants, but the reference in Sirach to the test brings rather to mind the context of Gen. 22 and the offering of Isaac. Gen. 22,1 states plainly that God tested[95] Abraham. The implication throughout the chapter is that Abraham was faithful to God and proved himself trustworthy in the test. It is not explicitly stated, however, that Abraham "was found faithful". In the book of Jubilees, on the other hand, there is a direct parallel to this idea of Abraham's faithfulness in the time of testing:

> And the Lord was aware that Abraham was faithful in all of his afflictions because he tested him with his land, and with famine. And he tested him with the wealth of kings. And he tested him again with his wife, when she was taken (from him), and with circumcision. And he tested him with Ishmael and with Hagar, his maidservant when he sent them away.
>
> And in everything in which he tested him, he was found faithful. And his soul was not impatient. And he was not slow to act because he was faithful and a lover of the Lord.[96]

In Jubilees 18,16, after recounting the story of the binding of Isaac according to Gen. 22,1-19, Jubilees adds the following line in the Lord's response to Abraham: "And I have made known to all that you are faithful to me in everything which I say to you. Go in peace". The fact that Abraham's obedience in this 'test' signified his faith in God and his faithfulness toward God is a key component of the later LXX and NT concept of πίστις. It is quite possible that the Jubilees passage borrows the terminology from Sirach 44,20 and even more probable that this is the case in 1 Mac. 2,52.[97]

3 SUMMARY

The use of the πιστ- word group in Sirach is demonstrative of a development of the use and understanding of this word group in Hellenistic Judaism beyond that of the LXX. This development in Sirach is a process of both specialization and generalization. The specialization is evident in Sirach's elevation of πίστις and πιστεύειν as primarily religious

---

[94] ['Αβραὰμ] συνετήρησεν νόμον ὑψίστου καὶ ἐγένετο ἐν διαθήκῃ μετ' αὐτοῦ· ἐν σαρκὶ αὐτοῦ ἔστησεν διαθήκην καὶ ἐν πειρασμῷ εὑρέθη πιστός. (Hebrew: ובנסיוי נמצא נאמן)

[95] ἐπείραζεν = נסה.

[96] Jubilees 17,17-18.

[97] In the NT, cf. Heb. 11,17; Jas. 2,21f.

terms. The generalization occurs in Sirach's use of the word group to translate additional Hebrew expressions in the religious sphere. The frequency of occurrence of the πιστ- word group in Sirach is itself demonstrative of this development. Sirach uses the terms πίστις and πιστεύειν more frequently than any other book in the LXX. Sirach is representative of one trend, perhaps even of one attempt, to create a key theological concept from the πιστ- word group.

CHAPTER FOUR

ΠΙΣΤΙΣ AND ΠΙΣΤΕΥΕΙΝ IN THE WRITINGS OF PHILO OF
ALEXANDRIA

1 INTRODUCTION

1.1 General Remarks

A further development of the religious use of the πιστ- word group is
found in Philo of Alexandria (ca. 25 B.C.E. to 40+ C.E.). Philo's
importance as theologian and philosopher and the significance of his
attempt to harmonize Judaism and Hellenism can hardly be over-
emphasized.[1] With one foot firmly planted in his Jewish heritage and the
other in his Greek education Philo emerged in the first century C.E. as "a
pioneer in a number of important fields of human thought".[2] The Jewish
scholar Hans Lewy comments further:

> [Philo] was not only the first theologian, i.e., the first who tried to bring
> into harmony the teachings of a supernatural revelation and the conclusions
> of speculative thought, but also the first psychologist of faith, the first
> mystic among professors of monotheism, and—last but not least—the first
> systematizer of Biblical allegory.[3]

1.2 Philo's Jewish Heritage

Lewy indicates that Philo lived in a locale and at an age which had become ripe for a synthesis of Jewish creed and Greek thought.[4] Philo had
the good fortune to be in the right place at the right time. From his
Jewish heritage Philo drew the foundational material for his writings.
"Seine ganze Weltanschauung", writes Bousset, "scheint er aus dem

---

[1] Cf. D. Wilhelm Bousset, *Die Religion des Judentums im neutestamentlichen Zeitalter* 1.
Auflage (Berlin: Verlag von Reuther u. Reichard, 1903), p. 411.

[2] Hans Lewy, ed., "Philo: Selections" in the collection, *Three Jewish Philosophers* (New York:
Atheneum Press, 1977), p. 7.

[3] Ibid.

[4] Ibid., p. 8: "Judaism had for long been slowly, but steadily, developing the universalistic
tendencies of its great prophets, the rational trend of its moral legislation and the consciousness of
individual piety; while Hellenism had similarly been developing the idea of a cosmopolitan
community united by the bond of Greek education and a rigid canon of rules for ethical conduct,
along with a strong bent towards the theological side of philosophical speculation. These two
spiritual movements met in Alexandria, at once the chief centre of Hellenistic culture; and their
conjuncture provided the material ... for a new presentment of religious and philosophical
problems".

Pentateuch zu entwickeln".[5]   The vast majority of his writings are
expositions of the Mosaic writings or summaries of Mosaic legislation.[6]
Moses is of particular importance for Philo, serving in the role of high
priest, prophet, king and lawgiver. As a Jew, Philo remained ever true to
the Mosaic Law.[7] In spite of his allegorization and spiritualization of the
Law, Philo always held fast to a literal fulfillment and interpretation of
the Law as well. Bousset explains:

> Das mosaische Gesetz hat nicht nur eine Seele, welche durch die geistige
> Deutung enthüllt wird, sondern auch einen Leib. Wenn man die Seele
> will, muß man auch den Leib wollen. Man muß nicht nur innerlich der
> Weise sein wollen, sondern auch äußerlich als solcher erscheinen.[8]

1.3 Philo's Greek Heritage

From his Hellenistic education Philo drew a number of elements
important to his methodology and synthesis. His method of allegory he
owed above all to the Stoics. The allegorical method was actually first
introduced by pre-Platonic philosophers and was later more fully
developed by the Stoics, "who employed it in order to reconcile the
grossness of Greek mythological theology hallowed by long tradition and
glorified by poetic treatment, with the principles of their philosophy".[9]
Philo was well-versed in Greek philosophy and quotes in his writings
from some of the greatest philosophers. "Vor allem weist er wieder und
wieder ... auf den einen großen Meister, den heiligen Plato hin, als den
starken und unübertrefflichen Bundesgenossen Moses".[10]

Alongside the Platonic school, the neo-Pythagorean school with its
technique and terminology were highly influential upon the thought and
writing of Philo.[11] It is little wonder in light of such factors that
Hellenistic dualism became a key element in the theosophic system of
Philonic pietism. Bousset writes:

---

5 Bousset, *Religion des Judentums,* p. 142.
6 It should be noted that Philo made use of the LXX translation of the Pentateuch. He may have been familiar with the Hebrew language but did not make use of the MT in his writings. Nevertheless, he would have considered the LXX translation to be inspired, as would all Hellenistic Jews. See Lewy, "Philo", p. 20.
7 "...nicht gerade in dem palästinensischen Sinn, aber doch soweit einem Diasporajuden dies möglich war"; Bousset, *Religion des Judentums,* pp. 412-13.
8 Ibid., p. 413; cf. also Lewy, "Philo", pp. 11f.
9 Lewy, "Philo", p. 13. Lewy indicates that there was earlier Jewish precedent for the use of the allegorical method: "A considerable period before Philo there arose a special school of Jewish expositors who used allegory to defend Biblical imagery against the mockery of rationalists and to bring Jewish religion into line with the thought of the Greek world. These Jewish allegorists were the teachers of Philo". (Lewy does not state his source for this information.)
10 Bousset, *Religion des Judentums,* p. 114.
11 Cf. ibid., p. 114; Lewy, "Philo", p. 16.

Der Grundgedanke, auf dem die Lebensanschauung und Frömmigkeit des
Philosophen Philo ganz und gar ruht, ist demgemäß ein hellenistischer.
Es ist der Gegensatz von Geist und Materie, ideellem und materiellem
Sein, oder in Philos eigenstem Sinn zu reden, von Gott und Welt.[12]

1.4 Philo's Synthesis of Jewish and Greek

Philo's efforts to synthesize Jewish and Hellenistic thought were neither
coincidental nor aimless. According to Lewy, Philo's twofold aim in his
commentaries on the Pentateuch is "...to show his co-religionists the
identity of their holy tradition with Hellenistic wisdom, and to prove to
the Greeks the conformity of all that was best in their philosophy with
the teachings of the Bible".[13] Philo ultimately understood this synthesis
as a 'mission'.[14] He took seriously the prophetic charge to Israel to be a
light unto the nations and wrote proudly of the success of proselytism in
his time—of the constant spread of Jewish rites among the Gentiles. The
Judaism of Alexandria in the first century B.C.E. to the first century C.E.
was in touch with the culture of the Greeks and well aware of affinities
between the enlightened theism of the Greeks and the monotheistic creed
of the Jews, between Hellenistic morality and Mosaic law, between philo-
sophic interpretation of cultic ceremonies as symbols of philosophical
truths and the Jewish-Hellenistic attitude toward its own ritual tradition.

> In this spiritual atmosphere, in which the differences, real as they were,
> faded into insignificance, the vision of a universal Judaism embracing the
> sum of human wisdom arose. This idea was fostered in the circles of
> Hellenistic Jews and ... received its fullest expression in the exoteric
> writings of Philo.[15]

1.5 Summary

As a result of the mixture of Jewish and Hellenistic tendencies in Philo it
is most difficult, if not impossible, to identify a unified system of
theology in his writings. "Seine geistige Gesamtpersönlichkeit macht
also keinen einheitlichen Eindruck, und von einem eigentlichem
Lehrsystem Philos kann nicht gesprochen werden; es mischen und
kreuzen sich darin die verschiedenartigsten Einflüsse".[16]

Nonetheless, Philo in his role as mediator between Judaism and
Hellenism had an enormous effect especially upon later exegetes and apol-

---

[12] Bousset, *Religion des Judentums,* p. 144; cf. Lewy, "Philo", p. 18.
[13] Lewy, "Philo", p. 14.
[14] Cf. ibid., pp. 16-17.
[15] Ibid., p. 17.
[16] L. Baur, "Philo v. Alexandrien", *Lexikon für Theologie und Kirche,* Vol. 8 (Freiburg: Herder &
Co., 1936), col. 243.

ogists in the Christian Church, thanks to whom the majority of his writings were saved for posterity.

The immediate question here concerns Philo's concept of faith. Is
it primarily a Jewish concept, primarily Hellenistic or a synthesis of the
two influences? To answer this question we move now to an
examination of Philo's use of πίστις and πιστεύειν as faith terminology.

2 PHILO'S USE OF ΠΙΣΤΙΣ AND ΠΙΣΤΕΥΕΙΝ

It is necessary to examine Philo's use and development of the πιστ- word
group as faith terminology in light of his mission of synthesis. Philo's
use of the πιστ- word group is the subject of a number of in-depth
studies.[17] We shall concern ourselves here with an overview of the
important features of πίστις and πιστεύειν in Philo. The basis for this
overview is the summary provided by A. Schlatter in "Erläuterung 4" of
Der Glaube im NT, pp. 575-81. In this summary Schlatter collects and
organizes the important representative occurrences of πιστ- words in
Philo's writings.[18]

2.1 The Substantive Πίστις

2.11 Πίστις as Pledge, Security, Proof

Schlatter identifies four basic understandings of the substantive πίστις as
used by Philo: A) Gewähr, Garantie, Beweis (pledge, security, proof); B)
Zuverlässigkeit in der Ausübung einer Pflicht (trustworthiness or faithfulness in the execution of a charge or duty); C) Vertrauen (trust, faith);
and D) Überzeugung (conviction, belief). The first of these uses, πίστις
as a pledge, security or proof, is a purely non-religious use and is, as
Schlatter notes, quite common in the writings of Philo.[19]

In *de Iosepho* 242, for example, Joseph explains to his brothers in
Egypt how God had actually worked through their evil intentions and
deeds to bring about salvation for the family.[20] The clear proof of this

---

[17] See esp. A. Schlatter, *Glaube im NT*, pp. 60-80; 575-581; also R. Bultmann, *TDNT* 6, pp. 201-
202; E. Grässer, *Der Glaube im Hebräerbrief* (Marburg: N. G. Elwert Verlag, 1965), esp. pp.
95-146; Bousset, *Religion des Judentums*, pp. 411-431 (esp. pp. 421ff.); R. Williamson, *Philo
and the Epistle to the Hebrews* (Leiden: E. J. Brill, 1970), pp. 331-372; H. Windisch, *Die
Frömmigkeit Philos und ihre Bedeutung für das Christentum* (Leipzig: J. C. Hinrichs'sche
Buchhandlung, 1909), pp. 23-29; Spicq, *L' Epistle á Hebreaux*, Vol. 2 (Paris, 1952).

[18] The index in Cohn-Wendland's edition of Philo's works is also very important. I have chosen to
use Schlatter's summary because of its arrangement of the πιστ- words according to similar
context and usage.

[19] Schlatter, *Glaube im NT*, p. 576. Cf. also David M. Hay, "*Pistis* as 'Ground for Faith'", *JBL*
108,3 (Fall 1989), pp. 463-68.

[20] Cf. Gen. 50,20.

fact was to be obtained in the things now visible to them[21]—i.e., in the high position of Joseph in the land of Egypt. Similarly, in *de vita Mosis* 2,288, Philo reflects upon the prophecies of Moses to the tribes of Israel prior to his death (cf. Dt. 33 - 34) and states: "Some of these have already taken place, while others are still being awaited; the pledge of things to come is the fulfillment of things in the past".[22] Likewise, something which is already said (τὴν λεχθεῖσαν ἤδη) can be offered by Philo as 'clear proof' (ἐμφανεστάτην πίστιν).[23]

Πίστις, as pledge, security, proof, appears also quite frequently in the plural in Philo. Schlatter cites the following instances:

> Plural: τὸ μὲν κεφάλαιον εἴρηται, τὰς δὲ πίστεις ὑφηγήσεται 1,594,31. 2,59,34. 1,566,1; πίστεων τοῖς οὕτως ἐμφανέσιν πρὸς μαρτυρίαν ὡς ἀδηλουμένοις οὐδεμία χρεία 2,507,13. 506,6; ἀληθείας βάσανος αἱ συνλόγῳ π. 2,362,16. 564,45; ἐὰν πᾶσαι αἱ ψευδεῖς πιθανότητες διελεγχθῶσιν ὑπὸ τῶν ἀληθῶν πίστεων 1,517,17; ὁμολογοῦσιν τἀληθές, ἅμα καὶ τὰς διὰ τῶν ἔργων π. ἐφαρμόζοντες 2,537,38; τὰς τούτων π. οἱ ἀναγραφέντες δηλοῦσι χρησμοί 1,573,1. 351,46. 384,10.[24]

It is particularly clear from the plural use of πίστις that this understand-ing of the substantive is purely secular and typical of Hellenistic Greek.

2.12 Πίστις as Faithfulness in the Execution of a Charge

Also the second category identified by Schlatter, where πίστις means trustworthiness or faithfulness in the execution of a duty or charge, is primarily a non-religious use of the substantive by Philo. A typical example is Philo's description of the faithfulness and trustworthiness of Joseph as second in command to Pharaoh in Egypt:

> Now the young man's trustworthiness was exceedingly great,[25] so much so that, though the times and state of affairs gave him very numerous opportunities for gaining wealth, and he might have soon become the richest of his contemporaries, his reverence for the truly genuine riches rather than the spurious, the seeing rather than the blind, led him to store up in the king's treasuries all the silver and gold which he collected from

---

21 ἐναργῆ δὲ πίστιν δύνασθε λαβεῖν ἐξ ὧν ὁρᾶτε.

22 διότι πίστις τῶν μελλόντων ἡ τῶν προγεγονότων τελείωσις. Cf. also *vit. Mos.* 1,280: πίστις γάρ, ὡς ὁ παλαιὸς λόγος, τῶν ἀδήλων τὰ ἐμφανῆ: "as the old saying goes, the things which are certain are proof of things uncertain". (Cf. *de sacr. Ab. et Cain.* 34; *vit. Mos.* 1, 274.) The idea that things which are visible provide πίστις (= proof, pledge, security) is quite common in Josephus' use of the substantive; cf. Hay, "*Pistis* as 'Ground for Faith'", pp. 468-470.

23 *De opficio mundi* 57.

24 Schlatter, *Glaube im NT,* p. 576. N.B. Schlatter cites passages in Philo according to the edition of Mangey.

25 ὁ δὲ νεανίας τοσαύτῃ πίστεως ἐχρήσατο ὑπερβολῇ.

the sale of corn and refuse to appropriate to himself a single drachma, contented with nothing more than the gifts with which the king repaid his services.[26]

Likewise of Moses, who was tending the flocks of his father-in-law in Midian (cf. Ex. 3,1ff), Philo reports that he maintained a pure and guileless 'πίστις' in the conduct of his office.[27] In this instance πίστις is a purely ethical, moral category; Moses was 'above board' in his dealings with his father-in-law.

To say that someone possesses πίστις (i.e., that someone possesses faithfulness or trustworthiness in the execution of a task or charge) is simply another way of saying that someone is πιστός, 'faithful, trustworthy'. The adjective πιστός also occurs in a non-religious sense,[28] but its religious usage is of greater interest to us here. Πιστός in Philo can refer to the faithfulness or trustworthiness of persons in relationship to God. Abraham is called the 'faithful one' in *de post. Caini* 173. Likewise Moses is often described as faithful or trustworthy. In *de sacr. Abel et Caini* 17 Moses is called the faithful witness.[29] Num. 12,7, where Moses is called faithful by God,[30] provides the OT precedent for Philo's designation of Moses as πιστός.[31]

Πιστός also denotes the faithfulness and trustworthiness of God in relationship to humankind. In *leg. alleg.* 3,204, for example, we read that God alone is faithful;[32] likewise *de sacr. Abel et Caini* 93: ὁ δὲ θεὸς καὶ λέγων πιστός ἐστιν; and further in the same section: οὐ γὰρ δι᾽ ὅρκον πιστὸς ὁ θεός, ἀλλὰ δι᾽ αὐτὸν καὶ ὁ ὅρκος βέβαιος.[33]

Philo's religious use of πιστός stands as a basis for his religious understanding of πίστις as faithfulness or trustworthiness in the execution of a charge or task. The clearest proof of this is found in *de mut. nom.*

---

[26] *De Iosepho* 258 (cf. 148); Josephus also uses πίστις in the context of Joseph in Egypt; cf. *Ant.* 2,57.

[27] μετὰ καθαρᾶς καὶ ἀδόλου πίστεως ηὔξησε τὰς ἀγέλας, *de vit. Mos.* 1,63; cf. *de virt.* 66; *de plantatione* 101; *quod deus sit immut.* 101.

[28] E.g., *quod deus sit immut.* 113: with reference to the figurative 'governor' of the prison of human passions, Philo comments that some people "become right joyfully his courtiers and satellites, in the hope that having judged them to be faithful (πιστοί) he may make them his subalterns and lieutenants to keep guard over the sins which are committed with the will or without it". Cf. also *de ebrietate* 82; *de aetern. mundi* 16; *quod deterius potiori insidiari soleat* 65.

[29] πιστὸς δὲ τούτου μάρτυς ὁ νομοθέτης αὐτός.

[30] LXX: ἐν ὅλῳ τῷ οἴκῳ μου πιστός ἐστιν; cf. Heb. 3,2. 5.

[31] Cf. *leg. alleg.* 3,103. 204. 228; 2,67.

[32] πιστὸς δὲ μόνος ὁ θεός. Cf. *quis rer. div. heres* 93.

[33] In this passage βέβαιος is virtually synonymous with πιστός; see E. Grässer, *Glaube im Hebr. Brief*, pp. 99, 144ff. In addition, by virtue of their special relationship to God, the following things are regarded as πιστός: the altar of God (*de sacr. Abel et Caini* 137); the third sign given to Moses to display before the king of Egypt (*de vit. Mos.* 1,82); the friend of God = Moses (*leg. alleg.* 3,204).

182. Here Philo quotes Dt. 32,4, θεὸς πιστός, καὶ οὐκ ἔστιν ἀδικία ἐν αὐτῷ, as the basis for understanding the noun πίστις a couple of lines earlier. The text reads:

> τὴν γὰρ πίστιν, ἧς ἔλαχεν ἄνθρωπος, οὕτω βέβαιόν φησι δεῖν εἶναι, ὡς μηδὲν διαφέρειν τῆς περὶ τὸ ὄν, [τῆς ἀρτίου καὶ περὶ πάντα πλήρους].[34]

One further example from *de vit. Mos.* 2,177 shows that Philo's religious understanding of πίστις as the faithfulness or trustworthiness of humankind is firmly rooted in the fact that God is faithful. Upon the occasion of Korah's rebellion (cf. Num. 16,1-3),

> [Moses] was naturally pained at this, not merely that he was distrusted (ἀπιστεῖν) when he had shown his [πίστις] by so many proofs, but that this distrust extended to actions which concerned the honoring of God, actions which by themselves would necessarily ensure truthfulness even in one whose character was false in everything else, for truth is God's attendant.[35]

Schlatter indicates that there is common ground between his first two cat- egories of the use of πίστις in Philo. This should not be surprising since the quality of faithfulness or trustworthiness possessed by a person or ob- ject can itself be considered a pledge or guarantee or even a proof. A good example of this 'common ground' usage is *de Abr.* 273:

> ὃς τῆς πρὸς αὐτὸν πίστεως ἀγάμενος τὸν ἄνδρα πίστιν ἀντιδίδωσιν αὐτῷ, τὴν δι' ὅρκου βεβαίωσιν ὧν ὑπέσχετο δωρεῶν.[36]

The first instance of πίστις in this passage represents more the idea of faithfulness in the execution of a trust or charge and the second instance represents a pledge or guarantee or proof. But it is difficult to classify these instances exclusively under either of Schlatter's categories 'A' or 'B'. Πίστις in the second instance, by connection with the firm oath of God, also represents God's faithfulness in the execution of a task, i.e., the fulfillment of the promises made to Abraham, and in the first instance Abraham's proved faithfulness also represents a guarantee or pledge of his

---

[34] "For, he says, the faithfulness, of which man partakes, must be so firm/steadfast, that it does not differentiate itself in the least from the faithfulness of the One who Is—i.e., the perfect faithfulness and in all things fully complete". Cf. *de migr. Abr.* 44; *de plantatione* 82: διὰ τοῦθ' ὅρκος ὠνομάσθη προσφυέστατα τὸ πίστεως βεβαιοτάτης σύμβολον μαρτυρίαν θεοῦ περιεχούσης. Cf. also *de spec. leg.* 2,8.

[35] This passage also displays in Philo's thinking an important connection between faith(fulness) and truth—between πίστις and ἀλήθεια. This would indicate some inheritance, at least, of the Hebrew root אמן, even if Philo was in fact not literate in Hebrew.

[36] "[God] marvelled at [Abraham's] faithfulness towards him and repaid him with faithfulness, i.e., the confirming by an oath of the gifts which he had promised".

faithfulness in the future. Here the first two categories melt into one another.[37]

2.13 Πίστις as Faith, Trust

The most prominent religious use of πίστις by Philo is classified by Schlatter as *Vertrauen*. Πίστις as religious faith or trust is exclusively πίστις which is directed toward God. The necessary corollary to faith in God is a mistrust or disbelief in creation, in things which have come into being—τὴν πρὸς τὸ γενητὸν ἀπιστίαν.[38] The idea that faith might be placed in some object other than in God, however, is not a part of the OT-Hebrew understanding of faith. Philo is using Greek ethical categories when he sets up this contrast between faith in God and faith in material, created things.

The construction ἡ πρὸς θεὸν πίστις appears often in Philo.[39] This πίστις which is confidence or trust in God is often described as βέβαιος—firm, steadfast, sure.[40] Indeed, as noted above, πίστις in Philo is regarded by some as synonymous with βεβαιότης (= firmness, steadfastness, safety).[41] In praise of this kind of πίστις Philo writes in *de Abr.* 268:

> μόνον οὖν ἀψευδὲς καὶ βέβαιον ἀγαθὸν ἡ πρὸς θεὸν πίστις,
> παρηγόρημα βίου, πλήρωμα χρηστῶν ἐλπίδων, ἀφορία μὲν κακῶν,
> ἀγαθῶν δὲ φορά, κακοδαιμονίας ἀπόγνωσις, γνῶσις εὐσεβείας,
> κλῆρος εὐδαιμονίας, ψυχῆς ἐν ἅπασι βελτίωσις ἐπερηρεισμένης καὶ
> ἐφιδρυμένης τῷ πάντων αἰτίῳ καὶ δυναμένῳ μὲν πάντα, βουλομένῳ
> δὲ τὰ ἄριστα.[42]

This definition of faith, or paeon of faith, is exactly the opposite of the faith described in Hebrews 11. It is not 'the good life', as Philo describes here, which the author of Hebrews views in connection with faith; rather

---

[37] For further instances of Schlatter's category B "im Übergang zu A", see *Glaube im NT*, p. 577.

[38] *De mut. nom.* 201. Πίστις as trust, confidence is also used of 'menschliche Verhältnisse' in a non-religious sense. See, e.g., *de Iosepho* 149; *leg. ad Gaium* 37; *de cherub.* 14; *quod omnis probus* 35.

[39] E.g., *de Abr.* 268. 270. 271; *de mut. nom.* 201; *de praem. et poen.* 27; *de somniis* 1,68; *quis rer. div. heres* 94; cf. *de mut. nom.* 182. The formula ἡ πρὸς θεὸν πίστις also occurs in Josephus and in the NT; see below, Chapter Five.

[40] Cf. *de conf. ling.* 31; *de post. Caini* 13; *de migr. Abr.* 43; also *de mut. nom.* 182; *de plant.* 70; *de praem. et poen.* 30.

[41] Actually, πιστός and βέβαιος are not precisely the same. An obvious difference is that πιστός is primarily a personal adjective for Philo, while βέβαιος is commonly used as a modifier of impersonal nouns; e.g., with the noun πίστις itself. Nevertheless, the important similarity between πίστις and the Hebrew root אמן is reflected in the affinity between πιστός and βέβαιος.

[42] "Faith in God, then is the one sure and infallible good, consolation of life, fulfillment of bright hopes, dearth of ills, harvest of goods, inacquaintance with misery, acquaintance with piety, heritage of happiness, all-round betterment of the soul which is firmly stayed on Him Who is the cause of all things and can do all things yet only wills the best".

the hardships of life. This is particularly obvious from the catalog of martyrs in Heb. 11,32-40. For Philo, faith in this passage is a *utilitarian* faith. That is, faith serves to bring about the good life.[43]

Faith (in God) is the "surest and most certain quality".[44] But above all, faith is a virtue—ἀρετή. She is "the most perfect of the virtues";[45] indeed, faith in God is the "queen of the virtues".[46] As such, the one who obtains or possesses faith in God obtains or possesses a prize.[47] Πίστις is therefore not only a given, but also a goal; indeed a goal which must be actively and painstakingly sought after. Philo writes the following about Moses:

> But so unceasingly does he himself yearn to see God and to be seen by Him, that he implores Him to reveal clearly His own nature (Ex. 33,13), which is so hard to divine, hoping thus to obtain at length a view free from falsehood, and a most assured confidence.[48]

The faith of Abraham in Gen. 15,6 is very important for Philo's use of πίστις as faith in God, and Abraham becomes the great example of faith, employing many of the elements associated with πίστις already noted above. Philo writes in *de migr. Abr.* 43-44:

> There is deliberate intention when his words take the form of a promise and define the time of fulfillment not as present but future. He says not "which I am shewing" but "which I shall shew thee" (Gen. 12,1). Thus he testifies to the trust which the soul reposed in God,[49] exhibiting its thankfulness not as called out by accomplished facts, but by expectation of what was to be. For the soul, clinging in utter dependence on a good hope, and deeming that things not present are beyond question already present by reason of the sure steadfastness of Him that promised them,[50] has won as its meed faith, a perfect good;[51] for we read a little later [ἐπίστευσεν Ἀβραὰμ τῷ θεῷ] (Gen. 15,6).[52]

---

43   We will return to this theme at a later point in this chapter.
44   τὴν ὀχυρωτάτην καὶ βεβαιοτάτην διάθεσιν; *de conf. ling.* 31.
45   τὴν τελειοτάτην ἀρετῶν; *quis rer. div. heres* 91.
46   τὴν βασιλίδα τῶν ἀρετῶν; *de Abr.* 270.
47   ἆθλον; *de praem. et poen.* 27. 30.
48   βεβαιοτάτην πίστιν; *de post. Caini* 13. Again this is clearly the opposite of faith in Hebrews 11, where πίστις is the prerequisite for being pleasing to God (Heb. 11,6). Faith is not the goal but the starting point! In Heb. 11,1 faith is directed toward 'things unseen'—faith and sight are opposites in Heb. 11.
49   εἰς μαρτυρίαν πίστεως ἣν ἐπίστευσεν ἡ ψυχὴ θεῷ.
50   διὰ τὴν τοῦ ὑποσχομένου βεβαιότητα πίστιν.
51   ἀγαθὸν τέλειον, ἆθλον εὕρηται.
52   For other instances where Philo quotes directly or indirectly from Gen. 15,6, cf. Schlatter, *Glaube im NT*, p. 579.

It is significant also that Abraham is called righteous because of his faith; for, as Philo says in *quis rer. div. heres* 94, nothing is more righteous [53] than to put in God alone a trust which is pure and unalloyed. [54]

2.14 Πίστις as Conviction, Belief

For πίστις as *Überzeugung* (conviction, belief) Schlatter lists relatively few instances in Philo. It would seem that a religious use of πίστις in this sense plays a secondary role. In a purely non-religious use of the word, Philo recounts how Joseph in Egypt commanded his brothers (who did not yet recognize him) to send for their youngest brother to come to Egypt so that Joseph would personally be convinced (πρὸς πίστιν τὴν ἐμήν) that they were not spies. [55]

Employed on a religious level, this kind of πίστις represents a creedal faith, a 'belief that...' (i.e., a belief that something is or is not the case). In *de decalogo* 15, for instance, Philo says the belief [56] must be implanted in the minds [57] that the laws are not human inventions; rather they are the most clear oracles of God. Here it is clear that πίστις now refers to the *content* of what is believed rather than a personal stance of faith or trust in God. [58] This concept is even more prominent in *de ebrietate* 40, where Philo spiritualizes the words of Jethro to Moses in Num. 10,30: "For we read that he said to Moses, 'I will not go, but I will go to my land and my generation'; that is, to the unfaith (ἀπιστίαν) of false opinion which is his kinsman, since he has not learnt the true faith, so dear to real men". [59]

There is no doubt from this that Philo knew and used πίστις in the religious sense of 'faith' as the content of what is believed. This sense is more typically Greek than Hebrew for it indicates an intellectual (philosophical!) and *unverbindliche* relationship to God rather than a combination of intellectual belief and personal commitment. [60]

---

[53] δίκαιον.

[54] ἀκράτῳ καὶ ἀμιγεῖ τῇ πρὸς θεὸν μόνον πίστει κεχρῆσθαι. Hab. 2,4 and its linking of the concepts faith and righteousness is also very important in this context.

[55] *De Iosepho* 168; cf. *de ebrietate* 188.

[56] πίστιν.

[57] ταῖς διανοίαις.

[58] Cf. *de vit. Mos.* 1,90, a passage which Schlatter includes under category C, but labels as "mehr intellektuell".

[59] ἐπειδὴ τὴν ἀληθεύουσαν ἀνδράσι φίλην πίστιν οὐκ ἔμαθε.

[60] This intellectual, philosophical kind of faith is lacking in the Hebrews Epistle.

2.2 The Verb Πιστεύειν

2.21 Πιστεύειν in Creedal Formulas

According to Schlatter's list, the frequency of the use of πιστεύειν in the
sense of 'to believe that...'[61] corresponds to the frequency of the noun
πίστις as 'content of faith' in the writings of Philo.   This use of
πιστεύειν occurs relatively seldom.   However, πιστεύειν in a creedal
formula does appear in a few important passages in Philo; e.g., in *de
migr. Abr.* 122:

> And it is by reason of this that Abraham, the wise, when he had made trial
> of God's unvarying lovingkindness, believed that,[62] even if all else be done
> away, but some small relic of virtue be preserved as a live coal to kindle
> with, for the sake of this little piece [God] looks with pity on the rest also,
> so as to raise up fallen things and to quicken dead things (Gen. 18,24ff.).[63]

It is interesting here that the resurrection of the dead is, in an indirect
way, a part of the creedal statement. In *de spec. leg.* 1,242 forgiveness of
sins is also the point of a similar creedal statement.[64]   This type of
creedal statement appears also with πιστεύειν and the indirect discourse in
leg. alleg. 3,164: ἄπιστος δὲ [γίνεται], εἰ μὴ πεπίστευκε καὶ νῦν καὶ
ἀεὶ τὰς τοῦ θεοῦ χάριτας ἀφθόνως τοῖς ἀξίοις προσνέμεσθαι ....[65]
Again this is typically Hellenistic faith, where personal commitment is
practically divorced from the more important intellectual belief in a fact.
Faith for Philo in this sense depends not so much upon the relationship
of a person to God.   Rather faith is the 'proper belief' (orthodoxy!) by
which a person may expect to prosper in the present life.

2.22 The Formula πιστεύειν θεῷ

The above examples show that Philo recognized and used the Hellenistic
creedal formula πιστεύειν ὅτι. But more important for us here is his use
of the formula πιστεύειν θεῷ. This verbal formula is directly parallel to
and synonymous with the substantival formula ἡ πρὸς θεὸν πίστις al-

---

61   πιστεύειν ὅτι ...; πιστεύειν with indirect discourse.
62   πεπίστευκεν ὅτι ...
63   Abraham's belief in the resurrection is also a theme found in the NT; cf. Rom. 4,17; Heb. 11,19.
     Cf. also Josephus and the belief of the Pharisees in the immortality of the soul; *Ant.* 18,14.
64   ἵνα βεβαιότητα πιστεύσωσιν, ὅτι οἷς ἁμαρτημάτων εἰσέρχεται μεταμέλεια ἵλεω τὸν θεὸν
     ἔχουσιν. For further instances of πιστεύειν ὅτι as a creedal formula, cf. *de migr. Abr.* 18; *quis
     rer. div. heres* 101; *legatio ad Gaium* 367.
65   "He lacks faith, if he has no belief that both in the present and always the good gifts of God are
     lavishly bestowed on those worthy of them...".

ready discussed. The verbal formula, however, is more frequent in appearance.

This formula indicates (as does πίστις, category 'C') a faith or trust whose object is God. In a number of instances Philo's use of πιστεύειν θεῷ is either in a direct quotation of or in an indirect reference to the faith of Abraham in Gen. 15,6.[66] Indeed, the faith of Abraham is an important starting point for much of what Philo has to say about faith in God. And with this use of the verb, much more so than with the noun, one begins to grasp the religio-philosophical dimensions of Philo's understanding of faith in God. To trust in God is the 'true doctrine',[67] but to trust in vain reasonings[68] is false doctrine. Likewise, the one who puts trust in bodily and external things[69] actually disbelieves in God,[70] and the one who disbelieves the former things puts trust in God.[71]

These references provide evidence of the dualism of Philo's philosophical presuppositions. Nonetheless, it is important to note the exclusiveness with which faith is directed toward God alone.

> τίνι γὰρ ἄλλῳ πιστευτέον; ἀρά γε ἡγεμονίαις ἢ δόξαις καὶ τιμαῖς ἢ περιουσίᾳ πλούτου καὶ εὐγενείᾳ ἢ ὑγείᾳ καὶ εὐαισθησίᾳ ἢ ῥώμῃ καὶ κάλλει σώματος;[72]

This passage displays Philo's employment of πιστεύειν as an ethical, moral term. This kind of faith is more closely related to the Hebrew בטח ('to trust') than to אמן. It is exactly the same kind of moral teaching that we find, for example, in Jesus' Sermon on the Mount, Mt. 6,24: "You cannot serve (δουλεύειν] God and mammon". In this context of serving, Jesus makes the contrast between love and hate: to love God is to hate mammon; to hate mammon is to love God.[73] In Philo the corresponding moral categories are πίστις and ἀπιστία; πιστεύειν and ἀπιστεῖν.

---

[66] E.g., de virt. 216; de mut. nom. 177-78. 186; quis rer. div. heres 90; for further instances, see Schlatter, Glaube im NT, p. 579.

[67] ἀληθὲς δόγμα, leg. alleg. 3,229; cf. Martin Buber, Two Types of Faith, pp. 33-34.

[68] τοῖς κενοῖς λογισμοῖς; leg. alleg. 3,229; cf. 3,228.

[69] τῶν σωματικῶν μὲν καὶ τῶν ἐκτός.

[70] ἀπιστεῖ θεῷ.

[71] De Abr. 269. Again This understanding of faith is foreign to Hebrew thinking (cf. Heb. 11; Hab. 2,4). Rather it is rooted in the dualism of Philo's Hellenistic heritage.

[72] De Abr. 263: "For in what else should one trust? In high offices or fame and honours or abundance of wealth and noble birth or health and efficacy of the senses or strength and beauty of body?" Cf. Josephus, Ant. 8,279. N.B: The idea of τίνι πιστευτέον is completely foreign to NT use of πιστεύειν.

[73] Cf. Lk. 14,26; Jn. 12,43. Also closely related is the teaching of Jesus that the one who finds/seeks/loves (εὑρίσκειν/ζητεῖν/φιλεῖν) his own soul will lose it, but whoever loses it for Jesus' sake will find it (Mt. 10,39; Lk. 17,33; Jn. 12,25; cf. Mt. 16,25 par.). Here again there is a direct moral contrast as in Philo, but the NT terminology in this context is not faith terminology.

Just as it is the case with ἡ πρὸς θεὸν πίστις, so in the formula πιστεύειν τῷ θεῷ faith is more a goal than a given.

> To trust in God alone and join no other with Him is no easy matter,[74] by reason of our kinship with our yoke fellow, mortality, which works upon us to keep our trust placed in riches and repute and office and friends and health and many other things.

> ...to trust in God, and in Him alone, even as He alone is worthy of trust — this is a task for a great and celestial understanding.... [75]

Πιστεύειν θεῷ also appears in connection with Philo's narrative about the life of Moses. In *de vit. Mos.* 1,225, for example, Moses assures the Israelites: "Our weapons and devices and all of our power lie alone in faith in God".[76] Also in *de vit. Mos.* 2,259 Moses exhorts the Israelites: "We must trust in God,[77] having experienced his kindness in deeds greater than we could have hoped for".[78] In *de vit. Mos.* 1,83 πιστεύειν is used absolutely in the context of God's self-revelation to Moses in the burning bush and the mission to return to Egypt. Philo reports that Moses 'believed' (πιστεύων). It is clear from the context that this faith was also directed toward God.[79]

Philo employs various epithets for God within the context of faith. In *de vit. Mos.* 1,284 Philo refers to faith in "the one ruler of the universe".[80] In *quis rer. div. heres* 99 Abraham's faith is said to be placed in God, the one who rides on the heaven and the one who guides the chariot of the whole cosmos.[81] In *de virt.* 218 Abraham's faith is directed toward none other than the 'Uncreated one' and 'Father of all'.[82] The one in whom it is necessary to believe[83] in *de mut. nom.* 166 is 'the one who promises, the Lord, the elder one'. And in *de sacr. Abel et Caini* 70, it is 'the savior God'[84] who is (not) the object of faith.[85]

---

[74] μόνῳ θεῷ οὐ ῥᾴδιον πιστεῦσαι.

[75] μεγάλης καὶ ὀλυμπίου ἔργον διανοίας ἐστί. *quis rer. div. heres* 92-93.

[76] ἐν μόνῳ τῷ πιστεύειν θεῷ.

[77] πιστεύειν δεῖ τῷ θεῷ.

[78] As already noted in Chapter Two, this is exactly the opposite of Abraham's faith in Gen. 15,6. Recalling the words of Otto Betz: "Gar nichts lag für Abraham am Tage, alles sprach gegen die Verheißung". For further references of πιστεύειν θεῷ, cf. *de opificio mundi* 45; *de migr. Abr.* 43; *de mut. nom.* 218; *de praem. et poen.* 28.

[79] Cf. *quis rer. div. heres* 101; *de mut. nom.* 178.

[80] ἑνὶ τῷ τοῦ κόσμου ἡγεμόνι πιστεύοντες.

[81] πεπιστευκέναι ... τῷ ἐπόχῳ τοῦ οὐρανοῦ καὶ ἡνιόχῳ τοῦ παντὸς κόσμου, θεῷ. This imagery also has its parallel in Hebrew tradition; cf. e.g., Ps. 18,7ff; 19,1-6.

[82] πιστεύσαντα δὲ μηδενὶ ... πρὸ τοῦ ἀγενήτου καὶ πάντων πατρός.

[83] ᾧ πιστεύειν ἀναγκαῖον.

[84] τῷ σωτῆρι θεῷ.

[85] In the OT the proper response to God's attributes as 'father' and 'Lord' is love rather than faith (cf. esp. Dt. 6,4f.).

There is a subtle shift here in Philo's use of the πιστ‑ word group. By employing divine epithets as objects of faith Philo creates creedal statements from normal OT terminology. The emphasis of faith is no longer simply a relationship of trust and faithfulness to God, but now in‑cludes further the acceptance of a dogma; i.e., that God *is* the one ruler of the universe, that God *is* the Uncreated one and Father of all, etc. In this shift of emphasis Philo reveals once again his Hellenistic heritage.

There are other persons or things which, by virtue of their close connection to God, can also be the objects of faith in Philo; e.g., "the godly love of wisdom"[86] in *quis rer. div. heres* 14. The leaving of fatherland without possibility to return and live there again is a grievous inner battle for the one who does not trust in the divine messages or promises.[87] In *de agricultura* 50 Philo refers to the author of Psalm 23,1 as "a prophet, whom we do well to believe".[88] Moses was also the object of the faith of the Israelites when he spoke the word of God,[89] or simply because of his record of accuracy and reliability.[90] The fact that faith in Moses is dependent upon Moses' close relationship with God is clearly displayed in *leg. alleg.* 2,89 where Philo quotes from Ex. 4,1: ἵνα πιστεύσωσί σοι [Μωυσεῖ], and makes this statement directly parallel to πιστεύειν θεῷ in the following lines:

πῶς ἄν τις πιστεύσαι θεῷ; ἐὰν μάθῃ ὅτι[91] πάντα τὰ ἄλλα τρέπεται, μόνος δὲ αὐτὸς ἄτρεπτός ἐστι.

This passage again points to the dualism in Philo's concept of faith, indicating the ethical nature of his understanding of faith.

The formula πιστεύειν θεῷ of course does not exhaust the use of the verb πιστεύειν in Philo. Philo employs the verb in a non-religious sense as well.[92] But Philo's religious use of the verb is predominant and almost exclusively refers to faith or trust placed in God.

---

[86] τοὺς ἔρωτι σοφίας θείῳ πεπιστευκότας.
[87] τῷ μὴ θεοπροπίοις καί τισι θεσφάτοις πεπιστευκότι. *quis rer. div. heres* 287; cf. *de Abr.* 275: περὶ ὧν ὁ θεὸς ὁμολογεῖ, προσῆκεν πιστεύειν.
[88] προφήτης ἐστίν, ᾧ καλὸν πιστεύειν.
[89] καὶ Μωυσεῖ λέγοντι πιστεύειν; *de somniis* 2,24; cf Dt. 1,17.
[90] *De vit. Mos.* 1,196.
[91] Cf. Philo's similar use of the formula πίστιν μαθεῖν in *de ebrietate* 40.
[92] E.g., πιστεύειν as 'trust, believe' in purely human relationships; cf. *in Flaccum* 86; *de planta-tione* 92; *de migr. Abr.* 138. Schlatter cites more references of πιστεύειν 'im menschlichen Verkehr', *Glaube im NT*, p. 579. Πιστεύειν in the profane sense of 'to entrust' also occurs in Philo; cf. *de cherubim* 24; *quis rer. div. heres* 129; *de Iosepho* 149.

3 A THEOLOGICAL ASSESSMENT

3.1 Philo as 'The First Great Psychologist of Faith'

3.11 Greek and Hebrew Influences upon Philonic Use

This investigation indicates that πίστις and πιστεύειν in Philo undergo a
further major development as faith terminology. This is a development
beyond other uses of the word group examined thus far. It is a
development rooted both in Old Testament literary tradition and in
Hellenistic Greek philosophical tradition. Thus, Philo's use of the πιστ-
words is truly a new development. Bousset writes:

> Zum ersten Mal in der Religionsgeschichte begegnet uns bei Philo im
> Centrum der Religion der Gedanke des Glaubens, Philo ist der erste große
> Psychologe des Glaubens.[93] Im Spätjudentum begann man abgesehen von
> Philo die Bedeutung des Glaubens für die Frömmigkeit bereits hier und da
> zu vergegenwärtigen. Aber daß dies mit Bewußtsein geschah, war doch nur
> selten und vorübergehend.[94]

The Hellenistic understanding of πίστις as a 'creed' and of πιστεύειν ὅτι
or πιστεύειν with the indirect discourse as an intellectual creedal formula
does indeed appear in Philo. The new development, however, is his use
of the formulas πιστεύειν θεῷ and ἡ πρὸς θεὸν πίστις, where faith is
always directed toward the person of God. Indeed, God alone is the proper
object of human faith and only ὁ πεπιστευκὼς θεῷ practices the right
kind of faith.   In this respect, writes Schlatter, "bleibt Philos
Sprachgebrauch mit dem der Palästiner parallel".[95] With his frequent use
of Gen. 15,6 and Abraham as the supreme example of faith in God, Philo
remains true to his Jewish background. Yet, as noted above, there is a
subtle difference. Philo presents a concept of faith emphasizing an intellectual acknowledgement of God. Consequently, the element of personal
commitment is virtually de-emphasized. This tendency in Philo is not
reconcilable with the Hebrew concept of faith.[96]
     Bousset defines Philo's concept of faith in God in terms of "Gott
finden". He explains:

---

93   David M. Hay takes up this thesis from Bousset and develops it further in an article entitled:
     "The Psychology of Faith in Hellenistic Judaism", *Aufstieg und Niedergang der Römischen
     Welt*, Teil II: Principat, Vol. 20.2, ed. by Wolfgang Haase (Berlin: Walter de Gruyter, 1987),
     pp. 881-925.
94   Bousset, *Religion des Judentums,* p. 421; cf. pp. 175ff.
95   Schlatter, *Glaube im NT,* p. 61; cf. also Bultmann, *TDNT* 6, p. 201.
96   It is interesting to note that any hint of the Hebrew construction of אמן with the preposition ־ב
     (e.g., πιστεύειν ἐν) is absent in Philo's use of πιστεύειν.

Gott finden ist ein Willensakt. Gott finden heißt erkennen, daß diese
sichtbare Welt nicht auf sich selbst ruht; Gott finden heißt alles Sichtbare
und Greifbare für unsicher und ungewiß halten und für gewiß das
Unsichtbare und Ungreifbare; Gott finden heißt sich selbst aufgeben, das
eigene Ich aus dem Centrum der Welt herausrücken und ein höheres
allmächtiges Wesen an seine Stelle treten lassen. Gott finden heißt
Glauben.[97]

With similar language H. Windisch defines Philo's faith as "das Erleben
Gottes".[98] A basic component of this 'finding' God or this 'experience' of
God (i.e., 'faith') is, according to Grässer, *steadfastness*.

> [Die Festigkeit] fanden wir als Strukturelement auch des alttestamentlichen
> Glaubensbegriffes. Aber niemand hat sie mit solcher Intensität zum
> eigentlichen Wesenmerkmal der Pistis erklärt wie Philo: Πίστις und
> βεβαιότης sind Synonyme.[99]

It is not surprising, then, that Schlatter identifies the opposite of faith for
Philo as 'wavering' or 'doubt'.[100]   For this reason also 'faith' and
'faithfulness' are very closely related in Philo. According to Schlatter, the
two terms imply precisely one and the same human conduct toward
God.[101]

3.12 Philonic Departure from Greek and Hebrew Use

As much as these concepts of faith in Philo may appear to reproduce the
use of πιστ- in the OT (i.e., πιστ- = אמן), a closer examination reveals
that Philo has something much different in mind when he employs
πίστις and πιστεύειν as faith terminology. Gen. 15,6 is merely a
starting point for him. Granted, it is a starting point firmly rooted in
Jewish tradition; but with his Greek philosophical tools he proceeds to
shape a concept of πίστις as 'faith' which extends beyond that of the
LXX.

---

97   Bousset, *Religion des Judentums,* p. 421; cf. *de migr. Abr.* 132. Bousset indicates that this
     Philonic concept of faith is in contrast to the Greek philosophical understanding of faith. There
     are serious problems with this viewpoint. Far to the contrary, this is precisely the form which
     the Greek understanding of faith takes. All of these aspects of "Gott finden" which, according to
     Bousset represent Philonic faith, are clearly shot through and through with Platonic philosophy.
98   Windisch, *Die Frömmigkeit Philos,* pp. 28-29.
99   Grässer, *Glaube im Hebr. Brief,* p. 144.
100 Schlatter, *Glaube im NT,* p. 62.
101 Ibid., p. 65.

3.2 Philonic Faith as Superstition

3.21 Conceptual Differences Between Philonic and Biblical Faith

Although there may be some structural similarities between Philo's use of πιστ- and the use of the word group in the LXX and NT, there are nonetheless "fundamental differences" between the concepts of faith represented by πίστις in Philo and in the biblical material.[102] Πίστις in Philo is, in some respects, not so much faith as it is superstition—*kein Glaube, sondern Aberglaube*.[103] This is particularly true in passages where Philo views faith as a means to happiness in the present life.

3.22 Faith in Philo and the Hebrews Epistle

This difference is particularly clear when Philo is seen in contrast to the NT epistle to the Hebrews, especially Heb. 11.[104] Ronald Williamson notes quite correctly:

> There is virtually no eschatology in Philo and therefore no eschatological faith. Faith for the Writer of Hebrews involves a response to the 'last things' that have invaded the present; for Philo there are no 'last things' and for him, therefore, faith cannot consist in a response to them.[105]

The fact that this eschatological hope is lacking points to a shift in Philo's understanding of faith. Faith must prove its worth in the present life—in the here and now. This is in direct contrast to the 'heroic faith' of the faithful ones in Heb. 11 who displayed their faith *in spite of* the hardships of the present life.

In Hebrews 11 (e.g., vss.1. 3) faith is the starting point for the proper relationship to God, not the goal as in Philo. Indeed, faith is the prerequisite for this proper relationship (vs. 6). The occasion of faith does not lie so much in present realities but in future possibilities (vs. 8), and even in human impossibilities (vs. 11). Faith is no guarantee for a happy, bountiful earthly life, as the catalog of martyrs in Heb. 11,32-38 clearly shows. Far from being a goal in this life, the faith of these martyrs is displayed in that they died before they attained their goal, the promise of God.

---

[102] Williamson, *Philo and Hebrews*, p. 372.
[103] The term 'superstition' may be a bit exaggerated. Perhaps a better term is 'utilitarianism'. At any rate, the idea is that Philo sees in πιστιw a direct link with 'the good life' and the good things in life. I owe this observation to Prof. Dr. Otto Betz.
[104] Cf. esp., Ronald Williamson, *Philo and Hebrews* (esp. pp. 309-85); E. Grässer, *Glaube im Hebr. Brief* (esp. pp. 79-146); C. Spiq, *L' Épître aux Hebreaux*.
[105] Williamson, *Philo and Hebrews*, p. 371.

This concept of faith is foreign to Philo. For him,

> Faith in God, then is the one sure and infallible good, consolation of life,
> fulfillment of bright hopes, dearth of ills, harvest of goods, inacquaintance
> with misery, acquaintance with piety, heritage of happiness, all-round
> betterment of the soul.[106]

Philonic faith is a direct link to the good things in life—to a happy and
richly blessed life: "He lacks faith, if he has no belief that both in the
present and always the good gifts of God are lavishly bestowed on those
worthy of them".[107] The faith in God which produces these happy results
is a faith based in experience of God. This is seen in Moses' exhortation:
"We must trust in God, having experienced his kindness in deeds greater
than we could have hoped for".[108] As noted above, this is exactly the
opposite of the faith of Abraham in Gen. 15,6. But Philo even bases
Abraham's faith in his experience of God in *de migr. Abr.* 122:
"...Abraham, the wise, when he had made trial of God's unvarying loving-
kindness, believed...".[109]

The 'other things' which Philo sees as rivals for faith in God—high
offices, fame, honors, wealth, health, noble birth, friends, bodily
strength, "and many other things"[110]—show clearly that Philo's concept
of faith is quite different from that of the OT and NT. Nowhere in the
LXX or in the NT do any of these 'other things' appear as the object of
πιστεύειν. That Philo chooses to employ faith terminology at this
juncture says a great deal about his understanding of faith. God is indeed
the only proper object of human faith. The reason for this, however, is a
Greek notion, not Hebrew. This exclusive faith in God is only possible
when one learns that all other things are subject to change (τρέπεται),
but God alone is unchanging (ἄτρεπτός).[111] In other words, God alone
is the most reliable 'talisman' which guarantees the good, blessed life, not
all the other things upon which people are tempted to rely.[112]

---

[106] *De Abr.* 268.

[107] *Leg. alleg.* 3,164.

[108] *De. vit. Mos.* 2,259.

[109] Philo is not consistent at this point. In *de migr. Abr.* 43-44, for example, it is not
'accomplished facts', but rather 'the expectation of what was to be' which was the hallmark of
Abraham's faith. But even here, faith is a goal, a prize for the soul which clings "in utter
dependence on a good hope and deeming that things not present are beyond question already
present by reason of the sure steadfastness of Him that promised them". The good things in life
comprise the substance of the hope and of the promise. Faith is the 'power of positive thinking',
so to speak, which helps to experience these future goals as present realities.

[110] *Quis rer. div. heres* 92-93; *de Abr.* 263.

[111] *Leg. alleg.* 2,89.

[112] This was the problem with Jethro in *de ebretate* 40, that he had not learned *the true faith*, so dear
to real men.

But this rather sophisticated superstition is by no means an easy superstition to follow. The temptation to 'trust' other things is great because of our kinship to our yoke fellow, mortality. In order for some-one to trust exclusively in God, it is necessary to put forth much effort, or, in the words of Philo, "this is a task for a great and celestial under-standing".[113] This 'faith' for Philo is an 'intellectual superstition'.[114] It is the "crown of intellectual achievement".[115] And, as Grässer points out, this intellectual element is "genuin griechisches Erbe".[116]

3.23 Philonic Faith is Not the Same as Biblical Faith

Bousset is correct when he calls Philo the first great psychologist of faith.[117] But he sets the Philonic concept of faith too much in contrast to the Hellenistic when he maintains: "Für die griechische Philosophie ist die Gottheit in zu geringem Maße eine konkrete Realität, als daß der Begriff 'Glaube' entstehen könnte. Bei Philo kommt der Begriff des Glaubens zu klarer und bewußter Erfassung".[118]

Bousset's first assertion is certainly true, as we have pointed out earlier.[119] But that Philo sharpened a (Jewish) concept of faith in contrast to Hellenistic philosophy is dubious. When in the same context Bousset defines Philonic faith as "Gott finden", he is trying to interpret Philonic faith in light of Hebrews 11.[120] When he maintains that this "Gott finden heißt ... das eigene Ich aus dem Centrum der Welt heraus-rücken...", it is absolutely not consistent with Philonic faith. For in Philo it is the "eigenes Ich" that receives all of the good things in life as the reward from God for faith.

Grässer is probably correct in his assertion that βεβαιότης is a link between Philo's πίστις and the root אמן of the OT.[121] Schlatter's equation of faith and faithfulness in Philo, in the OT sense of אמן, is also quite correct.[122] Nevertheless, πίστις and πιστεύειν in Philo are, as we have shown, radically different from πίστις and πιστεύειν in the LXX and NT.

---

113 *Quis rer. div. heres* 92-93.
114 I.e., πιστεύειν = νομίζειν!
115 Williamson, *Philo and Hebrews*, p. 350.
116 Grässer, *Glaube im Hebr. Brief*, p. 145.
117 Bousset, *Religion des Judentums*, p. 421.
118 Ibid.; cf. pp. 175ff.
119 Cf. above, Chapter One.
120 "Gott finden heißt alles Sichtbare und Greifbare für unsicher und ungewiß halten und für gewiß das Unsichtbare und Ungreifbare"; Bousset, *Reiigion des Judentums*, p. 421.
121 Grässer, *Glaube im Hebr. Brief*, p. 144.
122 Schlatter, *Glaube im NT*, p. 65.

It is therefore misleading when Schlatter writes:

> Philos Worte über das Glauben machen deutlich, daß die Boten Jesu nicht
> nur in Jerusalem, sondern auch in einer griechischen Synagoge unbesorgt
> ihre Weisung so formulieren konnten: Glaubt an Christus. Sie wurden
> verstanden; man wußte, was es heiße, an Gott gläubig sein.[123]

On the contrary, if a *Philonic* concept of faith was the only reference
point which someone had, there would have been no guarantee at all that
this person would have correctly understood the Christian proclamation:
"Believe in Christ". Faith in Christ for the Christian mission was *faith
in the cross*. Precisely this kind of faith was a scandal to the Jews and
folly to the gentiles,[124] and precisely this kind of faith would not have fit
well into Philo's concept of faith.[125]

3.3 Philonic Faith as a Virtue

On the other hand, Schlatter is correct when he writes:

> [Philo] denkt sich das Glauben nicht konkret, wie es die einzelnen
> Bewegungen der Persönlichkeit leitet, sondern er denkt an die abstrakte
> 'Tugend' Glaube, die als bleibende Eigenschaft in der Seele sitzt. ...Er
> denkt es nicht als Wurzel, sondern als Frucht der Erkenntnis Gottes und
> darum so unverlierbar wie diese.[126]

Indeed, as we have seen above, faith for Philo is not merely a virtue—it
is the queen of virtues;[127] it is the most perfect of virtues;[128] it is the
most certain of virtues; it is a perfect good.[129] Grässer maintains that the
placing of πίστις within the ranks of the ἀρεταί was but a small step for
Philo in light of his understanding of πίστις as steadfastness, as
Festigkeit.[130] It is nevertheless significant that Philo took this step.
Wolfson comments: "In Greek Philosophy prior to Philo neither faith in
general nor faith in God in particular is spoken of as a virtue on par with
piety, the fear of God and holiness".[131] It is because of the close

---

[123] Ibid., p. 74.

[124] 1 Cor. 1,21ff.

[125] Perhaps this is a point where the Epistle to the Hebrews was influenced by Philo's concept of
faith; a point where a redefinition and a clear contrast to Philonic faith had to be made for the sake
of the Christian mission!

[126] Schlatter, *Glaube im NT*, pp. 72f; cf. p. 61.

[127] τὴν βασιλίδα τῶν ἀρετῶν, *de Abr.* 270.

[128] τὴν τελειοτάτην ἀρετῶν, *quis rer. div. heres* 91.

[129] Cf. *de migr. Abr.* 44.

[130] Grässer, *Glaube im Hebr. Brief,* pp. 144-45.

[131] Henry A. Wolfson, *Philo: Foundations of Religious Philosophy in Judaism, Christianity and
Islam* Vol. 2 (Cambridge, MA: Harvard University Press, 1948), p. 216.

relationship between faith and righteousness in Gen. 15,6 that Philo is able to elevate πίστις also among the ranks of the virtues.[132]

4 SUMMARY

Philo's employment of πίστις and πιστεύειν as faith terminology is an excellent example of his attempt to synthesize the best of his Jewish heritage with the best of his Greek education. His concept of faith grows out of his understanding of the OT scriptures and is embellished by Greek philosophy. Yet at the same time it is neither a truly Jewish concept nor truly Greek. It is indeed a synthesis, but it is more than a synthesis, so that it is appropriate to speak of a Philonic concept of faith. For this reason, one must be careful in drawing strict parallels between faith in Philo and in the LXX or between faith in Philo and in Hellenistic Greek literature.[133] Likewise caution is to be urged in calculating the influence of the Philonic concept of faith upon the concept of faith in the NT solely upon the basis of similar terminology.[134] The stronger influence of Philo upon the use of the πιστ- word group in Christian writings is probably not to be found until the time of the Church Fathers who were mainly responsible for preserving his writings.[135]

But we must also be careful not to underestimate the importance of Philo's understanding and use of πίστις and πιστεύειν as faith terminology also for the Christian mission of the first century C.E. With Philo there is room for a new understanding of the word group in a Hellenistic setting—an understanding of πίστις and πιστεύειν with at least some roots in the OT concept of faith in God or faithfulness towards God—and an understanding of πίστις and πιστεύειν apart from the normal religious use of the word group in secular Greek with πίστις as 'content of faith' and πιστεύειν ὅτι as a creedal formula. Philo has expanded the use of πίστις and πιστεύειν as faith terminology, and, in so doing, he has opened the possibility for further expansion and further development in other directions.

---

[132] Ibid.

[133] Except, of course, when Philo uses the purely Greek creedal formulas.

[134] We have disucssed above the dissimilarities between Philo and the Hebrews epistle. Concerning differences between Philo and Paul in the use of πίστις, see Schlatter, *Glaube im NT*, pp. 75ff.

[135] E.g., Clement of Alexandria, Origen, Ambrosius; cf. L. Baur, "Philo", *Lexikon für Theologie u. Kirche*, vol. 8, col. 244.

PART II:

THE ΠΙΣΤ- WORDS AS FAITH TERMINOLOGY IN
THE WRITINGS OF FLAVIUS JOSEPHUS AND IN
THE NEW TESTAMENT

CHAPTER FIVE

ΠΙΣΤΙΣ IN THE WRITINGS OF FLAVIUS JOSEPHUS AND THE NT

1 GENERAL USE OF ΠΙΣΤΙΣ IN JOSEPHUS

1.1 Introduction

The substantive πίστις appears precisely two hundred times in the writings of Josephus.[1] In as many as fifty instances it is possible to identify
religious elements within the immediate context, though in most cases
the word πίστις itself has no religious significance. Actually, only ten
percent of the total occurrences or fewer represent a religious or
theological use of the substantive. These religious uses of πίστις will be
discussed at a later point. But first it will be helpful to present an
overview of Josephus' general use of πίστις. This overview will then
serve as the backdrop against which Josephus' religious use of the
substantive must be understood and interpreted.

A. Schlatter makes this observation concerning the general use of
πίστις and πιστεύειν in the writings of Josephus: "Bei Josephus umfaßt
die Wortgruppe ähnlich wie bei [Polybius] die ganze Mannigfaltigkeit des
menschlichen Verkehrs, doch so, daß sie spürbar matter, leerer geworden
ist".[2]

Liddel and Scott identify six basic meanings of πίστις in Greek literature at large:

> 1) trust, faith, confidence, in a subjective sense as well as an objective
> sense
> 2) that which causes or gives confidence, faith, trust
> 3) that which is entrusted
> 4) political protection
> 5) a name for the number 'ten' (in Pythagoras)
> 6) 'Pistis', as a personification[3]

The latter two definitions are completely lacking in the writings of
Josephus, as well as in the NT, and may be dismissed in this discussion.

---

[1] Including the textual variants.
[2] Schlatter, *Glaube im NT*, p. 582.
[3] H. Liddell and R. Scott, *A Greek-English Lexicon*, 9th ed. (Oxford: Clarendon Press, 1940, reprint 1958), p. 1408.

The first four definitions, however, provide a good outline of the general use of πίστις in Josephus.

1.2 Πίστις as Trust or Faith

Liddell and Scott further qualify this first meaning of πίστις with reference to its focus upon an object (faith or trust *in* someone or something) and its focus upon a subject (faithfulness or trustworthiness *of* someone). Josephus employs the term with both emphases.

1.21 Focus upon the Object of Faith

Josephus uses the simple dative to speak about putting trust in a person: "They kept watch over their enemies from a distance, nor was there even trust in friends who approached."[4] Πίστις can also represent faith that is placed in some *thing*, as in *Ant.* 15,201: "This caused Caesar to have even greater faith in [Herod's] loyalty and devotion."[5]   Similarly, Josephus employs πίστις to mean 'trust' or 'confidence' in an absolute sense with no explicitly stated object: "For two days the Scythopolitans made no move, enticing the confidence of the Jews."[6]

A somewhat different focus with this objective use is πίστις as 'belief' in the sense of a persuasion that something is true—i.e., that something is or is not the case. In *Bel.* 1,485, "Herod was led to belief (= persuasion) in the things being reported."[7] Likewise in *Ant.* 16,117: "But if you have no cause for complaint and can discover no plot against you, what is it that has the power in itself to lead you to the belief [πίστιν] of so great an impiety?"[8]

1.22 Focus upon the Subject of Faith

In comparison with the other uses of πίστις in Josephus, the objective sense of faith or trust in someone or something occurs relatively seldom. More common is the subjective emphasis in the sense of the 'loyalty, fidelity, faithfulness' of someone (or something). This sense of πίστις accounts for over one fourth of the total number of occurrences of the substantive in Josephus. In particular, political and military situations play

---

4   οὐδὲ τοῖς φίλοις πίστις ἦν, *Bel.* 2,257.
5   πίστιν εὐνοίας καὶ προθυμίας; (objective genitives) cf. *Ant.* 17,246; 15,87; 19,58.
6   τὴν πίστιν αὐτῶν δελεάζοντες, *Bel.* 2,468; cf. *Ant.* 17,327.
7   εἰς πίστιν ὑπαχθῆναι τῶν λεγομένων (objective genitive).
8   εἰ δὲ μήτ᾽ αἰτίας ἔχεις μήτ᾽ ἐπιβουλὰς εὑρίσκεις, τί σοι πρὸς πίστιν αὔταρκες τοιαύτης δυσσεβείας;

a significant role in Josephus' understanding and implementation of πίστις in this subjective sense. In many instances Josephus speaks of loyalty to political leaders and institutions. He refers, for example, to the loyalty of the Greeks to Alexander,[9] the loyalty of the Jews to Demetrius,[10] Joab's loyalty to King David,[11] etc. Josephus speaks of the loyalty of the Jews to the nation of Rome,[12] loyalty between allies and members of a particular group or party,[13] loyalty toward foreigners[14] and even loyalty between fellow conspirators.[15] It is worth noting that this sense of the word πίστις dominates the use of the term in the *Vita*. In seventeen of the twenty-one times that πίστις occurs in the *Vita*, it is employed in the sense of loyalty within a political context. Quite often it refers to loyalty displayed towards Josephus himself.[16]

Πίστις in Josephus can also describe a more personal level of fidelity. In *Ant.* 6,276 Jonathan renews his oaths of life-long mutual affection and fidelity[17] to David. Πίστις appears in reference to the marital fidelity of wives to husbands. In *Bel.* 2,121 Josephus discusses the views of the Essenes on marriage: "[The Essenes] wish to protect themselves against women's wantonness, being persuaded that none of the sex keeps her plighted troth to one man."[18] On a less personal level Josephus refers to "the undauntedness of the loyalty of the Jewish people toward their laws."[19]

Another subjective sense of πίστις appears in passages where the substantive is used in the sense of 'good faith'. In *Ant.* 7,43 Josephus reports that David was loved by the people because he had kept πίστιν with the murdered Abner by mourning his death. *Ant.* 15,134 reads: "If indeed good faith has some place toward the greatest of enemies, it must most necessarily be kept also toward friends." This good faith may also carry the idea of 'reliability', as in *Ant.* 2,61 where Josephus reports that the Egyptian jailer noticed Joseph's "reliability in the tasks assigned to him."[20] Likewise, Antiochus III praised the Jewish people for having

---

[9]   *Bel.* 1,94.
[10] *Ant.* 13,48.
[11] *Ant.* 7,160.
[12] *Bel.* 2,341; *Ant.* 14,192; 16,48; 19,289; *Ap.* 2,134.
[13] *Bel.* 5,121; 6,330; 7,365; *Ant.* 20,77.
[14] *Bel.* 2,476; *Ant.* 14,186.
[15] *Ant.* 19,273.
[16] E.g., *Vi.* 84; 87; 123; 160; 167; 333.
[17] ὅρκους … εὐνοίας καὶ πίστεως.
[18] τὴν πρὸς ἕνα πίστιν.
[19] τὸ τῆς ὑπὲρ τῶν νόμων πίστεως ἀκατάπληκτον; *Ant.* 15,291.
[20] τὴν πίστιν … ἐν οἷς τάξειεν αὐτόν.

shown "reliability in whatever they were called upon to do."[21] There are a few other instances where πίστις appears in the sense of good faith with reference to political protection or amnesty. We shall return to these at a later point.

Before leaving the discussion of πίστις as fidelity, one last reference must be noted where the substantive is used in this absolute sense. In his discussion of the Essene sect in *Bel.* 2,135 Josephus describes the group as a whole as "righteous tamers of wrath, masters of temper, champions of fidelity,[22] servants of peace." In this passage Josephus is testifying to the morally upright lifestyle of the Essenes, so that πίστις in this context is referring to faith in the sense of 'personal fidelity'. As in Philo, so also here, πίστις represents a moral category, an ἀρετή.

1.3 Πίστις as the Ground for Trust or Faith

David M. Hay[23] identifies as many as 78 instances, approximately forty percent of all occurrences of πίστις in Josephus, where πίστις as 'pledge' or 'evidence' refers to that which inspires faith or trust; or, in Hay's terminology, πίστις is the 'ground for faith'. This understanding of πίστις is thus quite common in Josephus and occurs in several different contexts and with various nuances.[24]

1.31 Military and Political Use

Josephus employs πίστις quite often in the sense of 'pledge, guarantee, proof'. Here again, as in the case with πίστις as 'loyalty', military and political situations play a dominant role. In a number of instances πίστις refers to a pledge of safety, as in *Bel.* 3,334: "One of the many fugitives who had taken refuge in the caverns besought Antonius to extend his hand to him, as a pledge of protection."[25]

---

21 πίστιν ... εἰς ἃ παρακαλοῦντα; *Ant.* 12,150; cf. 12,147.
22 [πίστεως].
23 Hay, "*Pistis* as 'Ground for Faith'", pp. 468-470.
24 Hay is accurate in his assessment of Josephus' use of πίστις as ground for faith. But the 'leap' which he makes from this basis to identify similar usage of πίστις in Paul is misguided. This understanding of πίστις as ground for faith is purely Hellenistic and almost exclusively secular in its application, as even Hay notes of Josephus' usage: "[Josephus] does not often link the term specifically with religion, however, and only rarely uses it to mean 'evidence on which faith in God may be secured'" (ibid., p. 470).
25 Literally, a pledge of *salvation*: πίστιν σωτηρίας. Cf. *Ant.* 12,396 and 20,62 where πίστις is linked with the term 'amnesty' (ἀμνηστία).

Similarly, Josephus employs πίστις in a few instances to refer to 'a word of honor' which is given or kept. In *Ant.* 16,390 Herod gives his word of honor to grant safety to an informant in exchange for information concerning a conspiracy against himself.[26] Πίστις occurs here in a political context. But Josephus also uses the substantive to refer to a word of honor in a more general sense, as in *Ant.* 1,321 where he reports that Laban did not keep his word to Jacob[27] to give to Jacob the livestock he had promised. In some instances πίστις has the technical meaning: 'treaty'.[28] And again, in a more general sense, πίστις can refer to an 'assurance' or 'pledge'.[29] Πίστις as 'pledge' may also carry the force of an oath.[30]

1.32 Πίστις in the Plural

Particularly striking in this context is Josephus' use of πίστις in the plural: πίστεις. Of the two hundred times that πίστις occurs in Josephus' writings, it appears 34 times in the plural. The plural noun πίστεις is completely foreign to the NT, but it is not at all uncommon in other Greek literature. We have already seen that Philo makes use of the substantive in the plural.[31] Liddell and Scott cite occurrences of πίστεις in Thucydides, Plato, and Democritus.[32] In Josephus the plural is used very much the same as the singular πίστις. That is, πίστεις can be pledges of political safety,[33] pledges having the force of oaths,[34] assurances,[35] the pledges of Jonathan to David,[36] political treaties[37] and words of honor.[38]

---

[26] Cf. *Bel.* 2,639.

[27] οὐκ ἐφύλαττε πίστιν.

[28] *Bel.* 5,453; *Ant.* 7,107.

[29] E.g., *Ant.* 9,153, where Jehoiada compels the king to give him a pledge (πίστιν δοῦναι) that he will honor God and not transgress the laws of Moses. Cf. *Ant.* 4,136.

[30] E.g., *Ant.* 9,145: ὁ δὲ πίστιν ἤτησεν ἔνορκον. Cf. *Bel.* 3,391.

[31] Cf. Schlatter, *Der Glaube im NT*, p. 576.

[32] Liddell & Scott, *Greek-English Lexicon*, p. 1408.

[33] *Bel.* 3,345; 4,61; 6,345; *Ant.* 5,131.

[34] *Ant.* 1,242; in this passage Abraham binds his servant with μεγάλαις πίστεσι concerning the choice of a wife for Isaac. Cf. *Ant.* 2,253; 7,24; 10,63.

[35] *Ant.* 4,86.

[36] *Ant.* 6,234; cf. 6,291.

[37] *Ant.* 10,108; 14,27.

[38] *Ant.* 12,8.

1.33 Πίστις as Proof, Evidence

With a slightly different emphasis, Josephus often uses πίστις to mean
'proof, evidence'. In *Bel.* 4,337 we read: "There was neither proof nor
evidence of the accusations, but they said that they themselves were
completely convinced [of the truth of the accusations] and they considered
this to be *proof* of the truth."[39] Josephus reports in *Bel.* 4,418 that the
people of Gadara tore down their city walls as a *sign* to the Romans that
they were lovers of peace and did not intend to resist the Roman invasion.
A reason for Josephus' recounting of the death of Gaius in *Ant.* 19,16 is
that it provides great 'evidence'[40] of God's power. In a technical legal
sense in *Ant.* 18,156 πίστις represents a 'security' or 'guarantee' for the
lending of money.

1.34 Πίστις as Reputation

In some instances Josephus employs πίστις with the meaning
'reputation'. He introduces the Egyptian false prophet in *Bel.* 2,261 as
one who had gained for himself the reputation of a prophet[41] among the
Jews. According to *Ant.* 5,52 the Gibeonites, in their deception of
Joshua, reported that they had come to him because of the great reputation
of his virtue.[42] Because the prophecies of Daniel always came to pass, he
gained a reputation for truthfulness.[43]

1.4 Πίστις as That Which is Entrusted

Josephus is familiar with the use of πίστις in the sense of 'a trust', or
'that which is entrusted', but he employs the term in this sense only three
times. In *Ant.* 2,57 πίστις is the 'charge' or 'stewardship' which Joseph
exercised over the estate of Potiphar.[44] The assassins of Ishbosheth in
Ant. 7,47 considered that they would receive in return for this act some
gift from David: either a military command or some other trust (=
'office').[45] In *Ant.* 12,47 πίστις refers to a position of trust in the royal
court of Ptolemy. Although in Josephus the substantive πίστις very

---

39 ἦν δὲ οὔτ' ἔλεγχός τις τῶν κατηγορουμένων οὔτε τεκμήριον, ἀλλ' αὐτοὶ πεπεῖσθαι καλῶς
    ἔφασαν καὶ τοῦτ' εἶναι πίστιν τῆς ἀληθείας ἠξίουν.
40 πολλὴν ἔχει πίστιν. See also *Ap.* 1,72; 2,18.
41 προφήτου πίστιν ἐπιθεὶς ἑαυτῷ.
42 κατὰ πίστιν [variant of πύστιν] τῆς ἀρετῆς αὐτοῦ πολλήν.
43 ἀληθείας πίστιν, *Ant.* 10,268; cf. *Vi.* 22.
44 Cf. Philo, *de Iosepho* 258.
45 ἤ τινος ἄλλης πίστεως.

seldom relates the idea of 'that which is entrusted', it should be noted that the verb πιστεύειν commonly expresses the meaning: to entrust.[46]

1.5 Πίστις as Political Protection

We have already dealt in part with the understanding of πίστις as political protection under the consideration of πίστις as that which causes trust. There is a fine line of distinction between the use of πίστις in the passages treated above and the ones we shall examine presently. In the former passages πίστις in the sense of a 'pledge of protection' was generally linked with another noun.[47] We shall presently encounter instances where πίστις appears in an absolute sense not simply referring to a pledge of protection or security, but to the protection or security itself. A few examples should serve to clarify this distinction.

The construction δεξιαὶ πίστεως occurs in *Bel.* 4,96. 417 in the sense of 'pledges of protection'. Important here, however, is that the δε-ξιαί are the pledges and πίστις itself is the protection. In *Ant.* 18,328 Josephus writes: "[Artabanus] swore by his ancestral gods that he would do no harm to [his opponents] if they drew near to him *under his protection*."[48] In *Ant.* 17,246. 247 Josephus refers to the 'good faith' of Caesar.[49] The implication of this good faith is political security and protection.[50] Finally, Josephus writes in his *Vi.* 370 that he himself offered 'protection and security'[51] to any of the followers of John of Gischala who were prepared to change their political loyalty.

1.6 Additional uses of Πίστις in Josephus

In addition to the four definitions of πίστις from Liddell and Scott, there are two more senses in which Josephus employs the substantive πίστις. The first is his use of the substantive as belief, focusing upon the content of what is believed. This is primarily a religious usage and will be considered in more detail below. The second is Josephus' reference to belief in the sense of 'credibility'. Josephus relates in *Bel.* 5,509 that the wall around Jerusalem built by Titus in his siege of the city took only three days to construct, so that the speed of this construction surpassed

---

46   E.g., *Bel.* 4,140. 274; *Ant.* 2,104; 8,41. See below, Chapter Six, section 1.3.
47   E.g., πίστις σωτηρίας; πίστις εὐνοίας.
48   πίστει τῇ αὐτοῦ προσκεχωρηκότας. Cf. *Ant.* 14,346.
49   πίστιν Καίσαρος.
50   Cf. *Bel.* 6,231: "his good faith overcame his anger."
51   πίστιν καὶ δεξιάν.

belief.[52]   Concerning rumors that Alexander was plotting to murder his father, Josephus indicates in *Bel.* 1,472 that nothing lent more 'credit'[53] to these slanders than the pleading of Antipater on his brother's behalf. Finally, Josephus claims in *Ap.* 1,41 that Jewish histories written since the time of Artaxerxes have not been deemed worthy of equal 'credit'[54] with earlier records.

1.7 Summary

This examination of Josephus' use of πίστις under the definitions of Liddell and Scott confirms the observation of Schlatter that the substantive "umfaßt ... die ganze Mannigfaltigkeit des menschlichen Verkehrs."[55]   Josephus uses πίστις as faith or trust in someone or something, as well as loyalty or faithfulness to someone or something. Πίστις can be a pledge, oath, assurance, security, proof, reputation, guarantee or even a personal virtue. Πίστις represents an entrusted office of leadership or stewardship and also political safety and security. It signifies in some instances the content of what is believed as well as credibility itself. And in many of these senses Josephus employs the substantive πίστις within the context of political and military situations.

Dieter Lührmann summarizes Josephus' use of πίστις as follows: "Dominierend ist bei ihm die Verwendung von πίστις als Tugend der Treue, von πίστις bzw. πίστεις als Zusicherung(en) und von πίστις als 'Beweis'...."[56] With this general background in mind, we now turn our attention to Josephus' use of πίστις in a religious sense.

2 RELIGIOUS USE OF ΠΙΣΤΙΣ IN JOSEPHUS

As indicated above, the substantive πίστις occurs relatively seldom in the writings of Josephus within a directly religious context. For our purposes it will help to group these religious passages into two categories: 1) passages with a religious context, but with a profane use of πίστις; and 2) passages where πίστις itself carries some religious significance.

---

[52]   τὸ τάχος δ' ἡττᾶσθαι πίστεως. Cf. *Ant.* 1,14; 5,66.
[53]   πίστιν ἐχορήγει. Cf. *Bel.* 1,493; 2,586; *Ant.* 17,142.
[54]   πίστεως δ' οὐχ ὁμοίας ἠξίωται.
[55]   Schlatter, *Glaube im NT*, p. 582.
[56]   Lührmann, "*Pistis* in Judentum", pp. 26-27.

2.1 Religious Context; Profane Use of Πίστις

2.11 Πίστις and the National Gods

In *Ant*. 18,328 King Artabanus of Parthia assures safety and protection to the brothers Anilaeus and Asinaeus: "He swore by his national gods not to harm them when they approached him at his pledge of security."[57] Δεξιά also appears in this passage with the result that, although there is indeed religious terminology,[58] πίστις should be understood in the profane sense of a 'pledge of protection'.[59]

In *Ant*. 14,27 Josephus relates how Aristobulus and the priests of Jerusalem were double-crossed by their countrymen when attempting to buy sacrificial animals from them. The priests paid the price agreed upon, but when their countrymen had received the money, they broke the 'agreements' and acted impiously toward God by not delivering the sacrificial victims.[60] Here the plural πίστεις refers simply to the purchase contract(s) between the priests and their countrymen.

2.12 Πίστις and the Mosaic Law

In two instances πίστις occurs in connection with worshiping God and keeping the law of Moses, but the substantive itself simply means 'pledge, oath'. In *Ant*. 9,153, e.g., Jehoida the high priest compels the king to give a pledge[61] that he will honor God and not transgress the laws of Moses. Similarly in *Ant*. 10,63 King Josiah compelled the assembly in Jerusalem to make an oath and a pledge to worship God and to keep the laws of Moses.[62]

2.13 Μεῖζον Πίστεως

There are also three interesting passages where πίστις appears in the sense of 'beyond credibility' or 'surpassing belief'. The context of *Bel*. 1,14; 6,297 and *Ant*. 5,350 is undoubtedly religious. In *Bel*. 1,14 Josephus spells out the lesson to be learned from the history of Israel that those

---

[57] πίστει τῇ αὐτοῦ.

[58] I.e., 'swearing by the national gods'.

[59] Cf. *Ant*. 6,276.

[60] κἀκεῖνοι λαβόντες οὐκ ἀπέδωκαν τὰ θύματα, ἀλλ' εἰς τοῦτο πονηρίας ἦλθον ὥστε παραβῆναι τὰς πίστεις καὶ ἀσεβῆσαι εἰς τὸν θεόν, τὰ πρὸς τὴν θυσίαν μὴ παρασχόντες τοῖς δεομένοις.

[61] πίστιν δοῦναι = 'to take an oath'.

[62] ὅρκους ποιήσασθαι καὶ πίστεις ἠνάγκασεν ἦ μὴν θρησκεύσειν τὸν θεόν καὶ φυλάξειν τοὺς Μωυσέος νόμους.

who conform to God's will and do not transgress God's laws prosper in all things beyond belief.[63] *Bel.* 6,297 relates one particular divine phenomenon which appeared in Jerusalem shortly before the fall of the city and which was beyond belief.[64] *Ant.* 5,350 deals with God's revelation to the boy Samuel concerning what was to happen to Israel and to Eli and his sons. God revealed to Samuel that a calamity would come upon the Israelites which would be beyond reason or belief[65] to those who experienced it.

In spite of the religious subject matter of these passages, the word πίστις in these references is a non-religious term, simply meaning credibility (or incredibility). In fact, in most of the occurrences of πίστις in the writings of Josephus where religious subject matter constitutes the immediate context, πίστις itself carries little or no religious significance.

2.14 Πίστις as a Semi-Religious Term

There are three passages in *Ant.* where πίστις, although employed in a profane sense, assumes a religious 'flavor'. Josephus mentions in *Ant.* 12,147 a letter from Antiochus III to Zeuxis, the governor of Lydia, in which Antiochus testifies to the εὐσέβειάν τε καὶ πίστιν of the Jewish people. Πίστις here is probably best understood as 'loyalty' or 'faithfulness', but its connection with εὐσέβεια (= 'piety') is striking. Likewise in *Ant.* 15,291 Josephus refers to the undauntedness of the πίστις of the Jewish people with respect to their laws. Again, πίστις in this context simply means 'loyalty', but it is significant that this loyalty is directed toward the Jewish νόμοι.

In *Ant.* 19,16 Josephus recounts the death of Gaius because, he says, it provides 'convincing proof'[66] of God's power. The definition of πίστις in this text as a proof of God's power brings us another step closer to a religious understanding of πίστις in Josephus' writings. The next step then is to view the passages in Josephus where πίστις appears as a religious term meaning 'faith' or 'faithfulness'.

---

[63] πέρα πίστεως.
[64] φάσμα τι δαιμόνιον ὤφθη μεῖζον πίστεως.
[65] λόγου μείζονα καὶ πίστεως.
[66] πολλὴν πίστιν.

2.2 Religious Context; Religious Use of Πίστις

2.21 Πίστις τοῦ Θείου

The formula πίστις τοῦ θείου appears in *Ant.* 17,284. At first glance one would take the genitive τοῦ θείου as an objective genitive and translate: 'faith in God'. The context, however, does not point clearly in this direction. Josephus refers in this passage to a certain Athronges who made himself king and, with the help of his four brothers, attempted to lead a revolt against Rome. When the last of his brothers was captured, Athronges himself capitulated to Archelaus ἐπὶ δεξιαῖς καὶ πίστει τοῦ θείου. Πίστις is again employed in the sense of a pledge of protection alongside δεξιαί, but what is meant by the τοῦ θείου is at first puzzling. R. Marcus translates here: "...he surrendered to Archelaus having received a pledge sworn by his faith in God (that he would not be harmed)."[67] D. Lührmann takes note of Marcus' translation, but maintains the following:

> Wenn das Substantiv πίστις bei Josephus sonst nicht 'Glaube' als das Gottesverhältnis ganz nennender Begriff meint, dann wird diese Bedeutung wohl auch für die schwierige Stelle *Ant.* 17,284 auszuschließen sein. ...In der auch bei Josephus nicht selten belegten Zusammenstellung mit δεξιαί heißt πίστις wie dieses 'Zusicherung', beides zusammen etwa 'verläßliche Zusicherung'; der Genitiv τοῦ θείου bleibt rätselhaft.[68]

But I would contend, contrary to Lührmann, that the genitive τοῦ θείου is not puzzling at all. The faithfulness of God[69] is an important component of a binding oath of security. The securities[70] of a human party are not sufficient to warrant the risking of one's life through capitulation in war. The further security of God's faithfulness, however, serves to make the human oaths binding and trustworthy.

Πίστις τοῦ θείου occurs also in *Ant.* 17,179, where Josephus recounts how Herod, shortly before his own death, gave instructions to his soldiers to assure that he would be properly mourned and honored after his death. He pleaded with them and appealed to the "good will of kinship and to the faithfulness of God"[71] that he would not be dishonored. As in *Ant.* 17,284, πίστις τοῦ θείου in this passage is a sort of security or oath by which Herod binds his troops to honor him after his death. And

---

[67] *Loeb Classical Library.*
[68] Lührmann, "*Pistis* in Judentum", p. 28.
[69] Subjective Genitive!
[70] δεξιαί.
[71] καὶ τοῦ συγγενοῦς τὴν εὔνοιαν καὶ πίστιν τοῦ θείου.

it is an oath which they agree not to break. But it must also be seen as an oath in a particular religious sense, in which πίστις marks the trustworthiness of God in the same way that τοῦ συγγενοῦς τὴν εὔνοιαν marks the trustworthiness of kinship.

Here Josephus displays traces of a Hebrew heritage with this understanding of πίστις as God's faithfulness.[72] It should be noted, however, that Josephus employs the neuter substantive: τὸ θεῖον instead of the more direct and more personal: ὁ θεός. Josephus distances himself from the terminology of Jewish religion and accommodates himself to a secular, Greek-speaking audience.

2.22 God as the Giver of Πίστις

There is a stronger theological implication for πίστις in *Bel.* 3,404 and *Ap.* 2,218, where God is the one who rouses or provides faith. In the former passage this relationship is seen indirectly. After Josephus' speech to Vespasian in which he indicated that God was going to give him (Vespasian) the emperorship, Vespasian's initial response was disbelief,[73] for he thought that Josephus was simply trying to save his own life with such favorable words. Little by little, however, he was led to belief (i.e., belief in the words of Josephus), for God was rousing him to the position of sovereignty and was already indicating through other signs the scepter of leadership.[74]

In *Ap.* 2,218 the connection is more direct. Josephus speaks in this passage of the Jewish 'belief' in the reward of a future life:

> For those who live their lives according to the laws the reward is not one of silver nor of gold, neither a victor's wreath of olive boughs nor of parsley nor of any such fame. Rather, each individual having a conscience testifying in himself, *has believed*, upon the basis of the lawgiver's prophecy, and on the basis of *God's having provided the strong faith*, that to those who have kept the laws ... God has given a new existence and a better life in the turning about of things.[75]

---

[72] The idea here is particularly akin to the formula πιστὸς ὁ θεός, e.g., in Dt. 7,9; 32,4; 1 Cor. 1,9; Heb. 10,23; et al.

[73] ἀπιστεῖν.

[74] κατὰ μικρὸν δὲ εἰς πίστιν ὑπήγετο, τοῦ θεοῦ διεγείροντος αὐτὸν εἰς τὴν ἡγεμονίαν ἤδη καὶ τὰ σκῆπτρα δι' ἑτέρων σημείων προδεικνύντος.

[75] Τοῖς μέντοι γε νομίμως βιοῦσι γέρας ἐστὶν οὐκ ἄργυρος οὐδὲ χρυσός, οὐ κοτίνου στέφανος ἢ σελίνου καὶ τοιαύτη τις ἀνακήρυξις, ἀλλ' αὐτὸς ἕκαστος αὑτῷ τὸ συνειδὸς ἔχων μαρτυροῦν πεπίστευκεν, τοῦ μὲν νομοθέτου προφητεύσαντος, τοῦ δὲ θεοῦ τὴν πίστιν ἰσχυρὰν παρεσχηκότος, ὅτι τοῖς τοὺς νόμους διαφυλάξασι κἂν εἰ δέοι θνήσκειν ὑπὲρ αὐτῶν προθύμως ἀποθανοῦσι δέδωκεν ὁ θεὸς γενέσθαι τε πάλιν καὶ βίον ἀμείνω λαβεῖν ἐκ περιτροπῆς [cf. *Bel.* 3,374]. Cf. also the Pharisaic belief expressed in *Ant.* 18,14.

This passage is extremely important because, 1) πίστις occurs in the context of a theological discussion focusing upon the *content of faith* (πιστεύειν ὅτι); 2) God is the very one who supplies this πίστις to those who keep God's laws; and 3) Moses is represented as the prophet and lawgiver whose prophecies and laws make up the content of this faith.

2.23 Πίστις as Content of Faith

In *Ant.* 18,14 πίστις represents the content of what is believed by the sect of the Pharisees: "They believe that souls have the power to survive death and that there are rewards and punishments under the earth for those who have led lives of virtue or vice, etc."[76] The idea that faith involves rewards is comparable to a similar tendency we have noted in Philo's use of πίστις. Josephus, however, includes an eschatological element (i.e., in the teachings of Pharisaism) which is missing in Philo. The formula ἡ περὶ θεοῦ πίστις, which occurs twice within a limited context in *Ap.*, also stresses the *content* of the Jewish faith.[77]

Moses in his role as lawgiver is presented as the source of the content of faith. Josephus argues in *Ap.* 2,163: "...the question of who was the most successful at setting up laws and discovering the most correct faith about God[78] is to be seen from the laws themselves." The important point here is that the Mosaic law serves Josephus not only as the content of, but also the justification for faith in God. A few lines further in *Ap.* 2,169 Josephus writes: "Our lawgiver, however, providing actions which were harmonious to his words, not only persuaded those who were about him, but also implanted into their offspring forever the immovable faith about God."[79] Again this displays a similarity to Philo's understanding of faith in God as the 'true doctrine'.[80]

---

[76] ἀθάνατόν τε ἰσχὺν ταῖς ψυχαῖς πίστις αὐτοῖς εἶναι καὶ ὑπὸ χθονὸς δικαιώσεις τε καὶ τιμὰς οἷς ἀρετῆς ἢ κακίας ἐπιτήδευσις ἐν τῷ βίῳ γέγονεν, καὶ ταῖς μὲν εἱργμὸν ἀΐδιον προτίθεσθαι, ταῖς δὲ ῥᾳστώνην τοῦ ἀναβιοῦν. It is not clear from this passage nor from *Ap.* 2,218 whether Josephus believed in a bodily resurrection, as was the normal belief of the Pharisees.

[77] I.e., 'faith *about* God'. The similar formula: ἡ πρὸς θεὸν πίστις appears in Philo.

[78] τῆς δικαιοτάτης περὶ θεοῦ πίστεως ἐπιτυχών.

[79] οὐ μόνον τοὺς καθ᾽ αὑτὸν ἔπεισεν, ἀλλὰ καὶ τοῖς ἐξ ἐκείνων ἀεὶ γενησομένοις τὴν περὶ θεοῦ πίστιν ἐνέφυσεν ἀμετακίνητον. Cf. Ex. 19,9.

[80] ἀληθὲς δόγμα; *leg. alleg.* 3,229.

2.24 Πίστις and Moses

The person and the work of Moses are central in Josephus' religious use
of πίστις. According to *Ant.* 2,218 the birth of Moses provided faith[81] in
the things that were foretold by God. But it is in connection with Moses'
role as prophet and lawgiver that Josephus attributes to πίστις its main
religious significance.[82] In *Ant.* 2,272 Josephus records God's reassuring
words to Moses that God would be with him and provide for him in the
task of deliverance to which God was calling him. God commanded
Moses to throw his staff on the ground and to receive a sign (πίστιν) of
or in the things which had been promised. Although the word 'sign'[83]
does not explicitly appear in the text at this point, the inference is that
Moses was indeed receiving a sign and that this sign was meant to create
faith in God's promises.[84] In *Ant.* 2,283 the relationship between signs
and faith is more clearly spelled out. Here Moses recounts before Pharaoh
his call from God which he received on Mt. Sinai.

> He related in detail the things which he experienced on Mt. Sinai and the
> utterances of God and the signs[85] displayed by him (i.e., Moses) for the
> purpose of establishing faith in whatever God would instruct him.[86]
> Furthermore, he urged Pharaoh not to disbelieve these things[87] and by so
> doing set an obstacle in the way of God's will.

2.25 Πίστις and the Prophets

Generally speaking, Josephus employs the verb πιστεύειν more
frequently than he does the substantive πίστις in connection with the OT
prophets.[88] Nevertheless, there are a few significant occurrences of the
substantive in this context. In *Ant.* 10,268 πίστις appears in connection
with the OT office of a prophet. In this passage Josephus relates concerning the prophet Daniel:

> And whereas the other prophets foretold disasters and were for that reason
> in disfavor with kings and people, Daniel was a prophet of good tidings to

---

81 πίστιν παρεῖχε.

82 Moses as a 'point of departure' for a religious use of πίστις is at least a stuctural point which
Josephus shares in common with Philo of Alexandria, although the concepts of faith developed
by the respective authors often differ greatly from one another.

83 σημεῖον.

84 This corresponds to the context of Ex. 4 where in the LXX σημεῖα and πιστεύειν belong very
much together. Concerning this third sign to Moses, cf. also Philo, *de vit. Mos.* 1,82.

85 σημεῖα.

86 πρὸς πίστιν ὧν [ὁ θεὸς] αὐτῷ προστάξειεν.

87 μὴ ἀπιστοῦντα τούτοις.

88 See below, Chapter Six.

> them so that through the auspiciousness of his predictions he attracted the
> goodwill of all, while from the realization [of the prophecies] he gained
> 'credit' among the multitude for his truthfulness and at the same time he
> won their esteem for his divine power.[89]

It is important to note the close relationship in this passage between faith
and truth, πίστις and ἀλήθεια. Both concepts are, as we have shown
above in Chapter Two, integral elements of the Hebrew root אמן. It is
quite possible, however, that Josephus here employs πίστις simply in the
(non-religious) sense of 'reputation'. It is further interesting that πίστις
is directly parallel in syntax and (very likely) in meaning to δόξα, which
itself represents no theological concept in this setting. Both substantives
refer to the simple idea of reputation.

Similarly, *Bel.* 2,261 reports that the Egyptian false prophet gained
for himself the reputation of a prophet[90] among a number of Palestinian
Jews. While πίστις can indeed represent 'that which causes belief', and
while the definition 'reputation' readily fits into this category, πίστις in
this sense is not necessarily a religious term.

If John of Gischala in *Bel.* 2,586 may be placed in this category of
(false) prophets, then it becomes all the more clear that πίστις does not
necessarily have a religious significance within this context. Josephus
writes in this passage concerning John: "He was a conniving man ...
most base and most deceptive.... On the one hand ready and eager to lie,
and on the other hand skillful at gaining *credit* for his lies."[91] In all of
these instances πίστις should simply be interpreted in light of the
normal, profane use of the term in Josephus.

2.3 Summary

The above passages clearly show that Josephus knew the term πίστις as a
religious *terminus technicus* within the context of Jewish religion. It is
striking, however, that he does not employ πίστις in this sense to any
great extent. This is particularly evident in light of the religious use of
πίστις as compared with the bulk and variety of the non-religious use of
the substantive by Josephus. D. Lührmann tries to rule out as much as
possible the influence of the OT (LXX and MT) and the Hellenistic-
Jewish use of πίστις upon Josephus. But he is willing to concede the
following:

---

[89] ἀληθείας πίστιν καὶ δόξαν ὁμοῦ θεότητος παρὰ τοῖς ὄχλοις ἀποφέρεσθαι.
[90] προφήτου πίστιν ἐπιθεὶς αὐτῷ.
[91] δεινὸς δ' ἐπιθεῖναι πίστιν τοῖς ἐψευσμένοις. Cf. *Ap.* 1,41.

Deutlich wird der Einfluß der [alttestamentlichen] Vorlage freilich [nur] in zwei Zusammenhängen. Einmal verwendet Josephus πίστις und πιστεύειν in der Wiedergabe von Ex. 4, wo Gott dem Mose verheißt, daß die Israeliten ihm 'glauben' werden, und ihn zu Wundern befähigt.[92] Zum anderen begegnen sie in der ja schon alttestamentlichen Formulierung, daß jemand den Propheten (nicht) Glauben schenkt. Daß Josephus nicht zufällig gerade diesen auch für griechische Ohren verständlichen Sprachgebrauch aufnimmt und nicht sklavisch seiner Vorlage folgt zeigt sich daran, daß der Stamm πιστ- fehlt im Umkreis der Abrahamsüberlieferung, also des klassischen Zusammenhangs für 'Glaube'.[93]

3 ΠΙΣΤΙΣ IN JOSEPHUS AND THE NEW TESTAMENT

3.1 Similarities in Use

3.11 Profane Use

In sharp contrast to Josephus the NT makes almost no use of πίστις in a profane sense. There are only two instances where a profane sense of the word occurs. Tit. 2,9-10 gives this admonition to slaves: "Bid slaves to be submissive to their masters and to give satisfaction in every respect; they are not to be refractory, nor to pilfer, but to show entire and true *fidelity*, so that in everything they may adorn the doctrine of God our Savior".[94] Πίστις in this passage is clearly a virtue of faithfulness or trustworthiness in relationship to another person and not (necessarily) in relationship to God.

This 'faithfulness' or this 'acting in good faith' is precisely the same profane use of the substantive which appears with much greater frequency in Josephus. In more than fifty of the two hundred occurrences of πίστις in Josephus' writings, the substantive means 'fidelity, trustworthiness, good faith'. In most of these instances Josephus speaks of faithfulness to political or military leaders.[95] In the sense of fidelity or acting in good faith, as in Tit. 2,10, Josephus writes in *Ant.* 2,61 about Joseph in the

---

[92] It is misleading when Lührmann limits the sphere of influence upon Josephus' use of πιστ- in connection with Moses to Ex. 4. Ex. 14,31 and 19,(9) undoubtedly play an equally important role.

[93] Lührmann, "*Pistis* in Judentum", pp. 27-28.

[94] Δούλους ἰδίοις δεσπόταις ὑποτάσσεσθαι ἐν πᾶσιν, εὐαρέστους εἶναι, μὴ ἀντιλέγοντας, μὴ νοσφιζομένους, ἀλλὰ πᾶσαν πίστιν ἐνδεικνυμένους ἀγαθήν, ἵνα τὴν διδασκαλίαν τὴν τοῦ σωτῆρος ἡμῶν θεοῦ κοσμῶσιν ἐν πᾶσιν.

[95] E.g., *Bel.* 1,94; *Ant.* 7,160; 13,48.

Egyptian jail: "...the keeper of the prison took note of Joseph's *fidelity* in the tasks committed to him."[96]

Πίστις in Tit. 2,10 is not a religious *terminus technicus.* Nevertheless the πίστις of a slave to his master has a clearly 'religious' implication: one's fidelity to his fellow human being serves to "adorn the doctrine of God our Savior." Therefore even this profane πίστις must be understood with religious overtones.

The other profane use of πίστις in the NT appears in 1 Tim. 5,11-12. In a series of admonitions concerning widows in the church there is a word of caution against enrolling younger widows (to receive church aid). The reason for this caution is: "...for when they grow wanton against Christ they desire to marry, and so they incur condemnation for having violated their *first pledge*."[97] Josephus also employs πίστις on one occasion referring to the marital pledge. In *Bel.* 2,121 the Essene practice of celibacy is grounded upon their (the Essenes') persuasion that there is no woman who keeps her *plighted troth* to one man.[98]

But again in 1 Tim. 5,12 it is difficult to say with complete certainty that the first pledge refers only to the marital pledge of a widow to her first husband. The violation of this first pledge is directly parallel to "growing wanton against Christ", so that the first pledge could also conceivably refer to faithfulness to Christ himself. The latter nuance is clearly present in the charge against the Church in Ephesus (Rev. 2,4), that she had abandoned her *first love*.[99]

3.12 Syntactical Similarities

There are a number of syntactical similarities in the use of πίστις in the NT and in Josephus. A. Schlatter provides a register of what he identifies as parallel uses of πίστις in Josephus and the NT.[100] He lists the following:

μεγάλη σου ἡ πίστις Mt. 15,28. Der Wächter der Mariame [sic] οὐκ ἂν ἐξειπεῖν ἃ κατ᾽ ἰδίαν ἤκουσεν μὴ μεγάλης αὐτοῖς πίστεως ἐγγενομένης *Ant.* 15,87.

---

96 ὁ γὰρ δεσμοφύλαξ τήν τε ἐπιμέλειαν καὶ τὴν πίστιν αὐτοῦ κατανοήσας ἐν οἷς τάξειεν αὐτόν. Cf. also *Ant.* 12,147. 150.
97 νεωτέρας δὲ χήρας παραιτοῦ· ὅταν γὰρ καταστρηνιάσωσιν τοῦ Χριστοῦ, γαμεῖν θέλουσιν ἔχουσαι κρίμα ὅτι τὴν πρώτην πίστιν ἠθέτησαν.
98 καὶ μηδεμίαν τηρεῖν πεπεισμένοι τὴν πρὸς ἕνα πίστιν.
99 τὴν ἀγάπην τὴν πρώτην.
100 Schlatter, *Der Glaube im NT*, pp. 583-84.

παρ' οὐδενὶ τοσαύτην πίστιν ... εὗρον Mt. 8,10. τοῦ δικαίως
ἀνταίρειν ὅπλα πίστιν εὑρεῖν *Vi.* 22.

τὸ ἔλεος καὶ τὴν πίστιν Mt. 23,23. ἡ πρὸς ἐκείνους τὴν ἐκληπίαν
εὔνοια καὶ πίστις *Bel.* 7,365. Vgl. Polyb.

ἵνα μὴ ἐκλίπῃ ἡ πίστις σου Lk. 22,32. ἄδικον ἡγεῖτο τῆς πρὸς
τοὺς συνωμότας πίστεως *Ant.* 19,273.

ἐμμένειν τῇ πίστει Apg. 14,22. ἐμμένειν συνεβούλευον τῇ πρὸς
τοὺς Ῥωμαίους πίστει *Vi.* 34. κεκρικότες τῇ πρὸς Ῥωμαίους ἐμμεῖναι
πίστει *Vi.* 104.

Gott πίστιν παρασχὼν πᾶσιν Apg. 17,31. τοῦ θεοῦ τὴν πίστιν
ἰσχυρὰν   παρεσχηκότος, siehe bei πιστεύειν *Ap.* 2,218. τοῖς
προκατηγγελμένοις ὑπὸ τοῦ θεοῦ πίστιν ὁ τοκετὸς τῆς γυναικὸς
παρεῖχε *Ant.* 2,218.

βεβαιούμενοι τῇ πίστει Kol. 2,7. δύο τῶν περὶ ἐμὲ σωματο-
φυλάκων τοὺς κατ' ἀνδρείαν δοκιμωτάτους καὶ κατὰ πίστιν
βεβαίους *Vi.* 293.

ἀποστήσονταί τινες τῆς πίστεως 1 Tim. 4,1. ἀποστάντας τῆς
πρός με πίστεως προστίθεσθαι αὐτῷ *Vi.* 37.

τῆς ἐν σοί [sic] πίστεως 2 Tim. 1,5. τὸ βέβαιον τῆς ἐν σφίσι
πίστεως *Ant.* 13,411.

τὴν πίστιν τετήρηκα 2 Tim. 4,7. ἥ γε πίστις ἔχουσα καὶ πρὸς
τοὺς πολεμιωτάτους τόπον τοῖς γε φίλοις ἀναγκαιοτάτη τετηρῆσθαι
Ant. 15,134. τὴν μὲν εἰς τὸ παρὸν οὐκ ἐφύλαττε πίστιν mit dem
Gegensatz εἰς ἔτος *Ant.* 1,321. ὡς μηδὲ τὴν πρὸς ἐκεῖνον πίστιν
φυλαξάντων *Vi.* 93.

ἡ πίστις ὑμῶν ἡ πρὸς τὸν θεόν 1 Thes. 1,8. Für die zwischen den
Menschen bestehende Gemeinschaft verwendet Josefus regelmäßig πρός.

ἔχετε πίστιν θεοῦ Mk. 11,22. Josefus hat den Genetiv bei πίστις
vermieden. Mose τοῖς ἀεὶ γενησομένοις τὴν περὶ θεοῦ πίστιν
ἐνέφυσεν ἀμετακίνητον *Ap.* 2,169. Mose ὁ τῆς δικαιοτάτης περὶ θεοῦ
πίστεως ἐπιτυχών *Ap.* 2,[168]. τὸ τῆς ὑπὲρ τῶν νόμων πίστεως
ἀκατάπληκτον *Ant.* 15,291. Einen Genitiv des Objekts bei πίστις gibt
die Formel εἰς πίστιν ὑπαχθῆναι τῶν λεγομένων *Bel.* 1,485; vgl.
πίστιν εὑρεῖν *Vi.* 22.

At first glance Schlatter's register gives the impression that there is a significant amount of parallel use of πίστις in Josephus and the NT—particularly since the register is not purported to be exhaustive. Upon closer
examination, however, it becomes clear that this register records primarily
syntactical similarities. Josephus' concept of πίστις is, in the majority
of instances, much different from the concept of πίστις in the NT.
Schlatter's register does, however, indicate some parallel conceptual use of
πίστις in the NT and in Josephus and therefore provides a good starting
point for comparison.

3.13 Conceptual Similarities from Adolf Schlatter's Register

Πίστιν παρέχειν in Acts 17,31 [101] is not only syntactically identical to Josephus' use of the same formula in *Ap.* 2,218; *Ant.* 2,218 but also conceptually.[102] In each instance πίστις is a 'proof' or a 'sign' which provides grounds for [religious] belief, and God is the one who provides[103] this proof. Although these are parallel uses, it is important to note that πίστις as a proof for religious faith, or even as a proof in a profane sense, is not at all common in the NT.

Acts 17,31 is the only passage in the NT where πίστις appears in this sense. Moreover it is significant that πίστις occurs in this passage in the context of Paul's speech before a primarily non-Jewish, Greek-speaking audience in the Athenian Areopagus. Therefore a more typically Greek use of the substantive may be demanded by the context itself. At any rate, it is safe to say that this is not the normal use of πίστις in the NT. Josephus, on the other hand, frequently employs πίστις in the sense of 'proof, evidence, etc.', although generally in a non-religious sense.[104]

The formula πίστιν τηρεῖν in 2 Tim. 4,7 means 'to remain faithful or loyal'. This is parallel to Josephus' use of the same formula in *Ant.* 15,134, as indicated by Schlatter. Here the object of faithfulness or loyalty is marked either by the preposition πρός (with the accusative)[105] or by the simple dative.[106] In two instances this formula in Josephus signifies the keeping of pledges.[107] In this sense the formula is not parallel to the use in 2 Tim. 4,7.

More frequent in Josephus is the formula πίστιν φυλάττειν, for example in *Ant.* 1,321 or in *Vi.* 93. Πίστιν φυλάττειν is synonymous to πίστιν τηρεῖν. Sometimes the formula refers to the keeping of oaths or pledges;[108] and in other instances it refers to remaining faithful,[109] as

---

[101] καθότι ἔστησεν ἡμέραν ἐν ᾗ μέλλει κρίνειν τὴν οἰκουμένην ἐν δικαιοσύνῃ, ἐν ἀνδρὶ ᾧ ὥρισεν, πίστιν παρασχὼν ἀναστήσας αὐτὸν ἐκ νεκρῶν.

[102] This is in contrast to the opinion of David Hay, "*Pistis* as 'Ground for Faith'", pp. 471ff. It is clear that πίστις in Acts 17,31 is functioning quite differently than, e.g., in Gal. 3,23-25, where Hay argues for a similar understanding of πίστις as 'ground for faith'.

[103] ὁ παρασχών; in *Ant.* 2,218, however, God is only indirectly the provider of πίστις.

[104] Cf. further *Ant.* 2,37. 111. 272; 6,245; 15,69. 260; et al.

[105] πρὸς τοὺς πολεμιωτάτους. ἡ πίστις πρὸς ... occurs quite frequently in Josephus; cf. *Bel.* 2,121.

[106] τοῖς γε φίλοις.

[107] *Ant.* 13,207 (cf. 13,415); *Bel.* 6,345.

[108] E.g., *Ant.* 10,97. 101. 230; 12,396.

[109] Cf. *Ant.* 7,43; 12,8; *Vi.* 39; 43; 349.

does πίστιν τηρεῖν in 2 Tim. 4,7. The formula πίστιν φυλάσσειν, however, does not appear in the NT.[110]

Very similar in meaning to πίστιν τηρεῖν is the formula τῇ πίστει (ἐπι-, ἐμ-) μένειν, which occurs both in Josephus and in the NT.[111] This is simply another expression of the idea of remaining loyal or faithful [to someone]. Josephus always employs the formula in connection with the preposition πρός, indicating the *object* of the faithfulness or loyalty.[112] The formula occurs three times in the NT: Acts 14,22: ἐπιστηρίζοντες τὰς ψυχὰς τῶν μαθητῶν, παρακαλοῦντες ἐμμένειν τῇ πίστει; Col. 1,23: εἴ γε ἐπιμένετε τῇ πίστει; and 1 Tim. 2,15: ἐὰν μείνωσιν ἐν πίστει. Important to note in these latter instances, is that πίστις without an object signals, in contrast to Josephus, *Christian faith*.

While the concept of remaining loyal is common to Josephus and the NT in the appearance of the formulas πίστιν τηρεῖν (φυλάσσειν), τῇ πίστει μένειν,[113] there is one important distinction which must be made. Josephus employs the formula exclusively in a profane sense with refer-ence to human relationships. The formula in the NT occurs exclusively in a religious sense, referring to the relationship of individuals to God or to the Christian faith in general.

Schlatter rightly points out the parallel use of the formula: ἡ πίστις ἡ πρός [τινα] in the NT and in Josephus. In addition to 1 Thes. 1,8 cited by Schlatter, this formula also appears in Philem. 5: ἀκούων σου τὴν ἀγάπην καὶ τὴν πίστιν, ἣν ἔχεις πρὸς τὸν κύριον Ἰησοῦν καὶ εἰς πάντας τοὺς ἁγίους.[114] In the NT the formula refers either to faithfulness or simply to faith and occurs in both instances in a clearly re-ligious sense. Josephus, on the other hand, only employs the formula in a profane sense, referring to the faithfulness or loyalty of one person to another.[115]

---

[110] Πίστιν τηρεῖν appears also in Rev. 14,12: Ὧδε ἡ ὑπομονὴ τῶν ἁγίων ἐστίν, οἱ τηροῦντες τὰς ἐντολὰς τοῦ θεοῦ καὶ τὴν πίστιν Ἰησοῦ. The use of the formula here, however, is not parallel to the use in 2 Tim. 4,7 nor to the use in Josephus.

[111] Schlatter does not mention this parallel.

[112] E.g., *Ant.* 19,247: ὅρκους λαμβάνων ἢ μὴν ἐμμενεῖν πίστει τῇ πρὸς αὐτόν; also *Vi.* 46; 61; 104: τῇ πίστει τῇ πρὸς τοὺς Ῥωμαίους ἐμμένειν; cf. *Vi.* 346.

[113] The opposite of remaining faithful or loyal is expressed by the following formulas: πίστιν παραβῆναι, *Ant.* 14,27. 162; ἀποστεῖν τῆς πίστεως (cf. Schlatter), *Vi.* 87; 123; 1 Tim. 4,1 (cf. 6,10); ἐξίστασθαι τῆς πίστεως, *Vi.* 167; ἀρνεῖσθαι τὴν πίστιν, 1 Tim. 5,8; ἐκλειπία τῆς πίστεως, *Ant.* 19,273.

[114] This verse most likely represents a chiastic structure in which the object of faith is 'the Lord Jesus' and the object of love is 'all the saints'.

[115] Cf. *Ant.* 13,378; 15,134; 19,289; *Bel.* 1,207; and quite frequently in *Vi.*

3.14 Additional Similarities

In addition to the parallels indicated by Schlatter's register, there are other important similarities in the religious use of πίστις in Josephus and the NT. Generally it can be said that when Josephus employs πίστις in the sense of 'faith, trust, belief, faithfulness, etc.', this is comparable to the NT use in the majority of instances. The major difference is once again that Josephus normally uses the substantive in a profane sense while in the NT it occurs primarily in a religious sense. Outside of this general parallel usage there are a few special uses of πίστις which deserve more detailed attention.

In pointing out parallels in Josephus to the formula ἔχετε πίστιν θεοῦ in Mk. 11,22, Schlatter comments that Josephus generally avoided the genitive in connection with πίστις.[116] This observation is correct in this context. Josephus did indeed avoid the use of an *objective genitive* in connection with πίστις. Πίστις with a *subjective genitive*, however, occurs quite commonly.[117] Generally the accompanying genitive is a personal pronoun: *his* faithfulness;[118] *their* faith;[119] *your* faithfulness;[120] *our* faithfulness;[121] *my* faithfulness.[122] But the subjective genitive does not occur exclusively as a personal pronoun. *Ant.* 17,246 refers to the good faith of Caesar,[123] *Vi.* 84 to the loyalty of the Galileans towards Josephus[124] and *Bel.* 6,330 to the fidelity of allies.[125] Particularly interesting are two appearances of πίστις τοῦ θείου in *Ant.* 17,179. 284. In both instances the faithfulness of the Divinity[126] is introduced in the context of an oath or a pledge.

---

116 Schlatter, *Glaube im NT*, p. 584.
117 Of primary interest here are instances where πίστις refers either to 'faith, trust' or 'faithfulness, loyalty'.
118 [ἡ πίστις] αὐτοῦ, *Ant.* 2,61; 7,23; 17,246. 247; 18,156; *Bel.* 3,6.
119 [ἡ πίστις] αὐτῶν, *Bel.* 2,468.
120 [ἡ πίστις] σου, *Ant.* 13,45; ὑμῶν*Ant.* 13,48.
121 [ἡ πίστις] ἡμῶν, *Ant.* 14,186; ἡμέτερα, *Ant.* 16,48.
122 [ἡ πίστις] ἐμαυτοῦ, *Ant.* 18,337.
123 τὴν Καίσαρος ἀρετὴν καὶ πίστιν.
124 ἡ πρός με τοῦ πλήθους τῶν Γαλιλαίων εὔνοια καὶ πίστις.
125 πίστει ... συμμάχων.
126 I.e., the faithfulness of God. Ralph Marcus translates both of these instances (*Loeb Classical Library*) as objective genitives: i.e., faith in God. This sense does not logically fit into either passage. Moreover, the parallel construction τοῦ συγγενοῦς τὴν εὔνοιαν in *Ant.* 17,179 is itself obviously a subjective genitive. This is further evidence that [πίστις] τοῦ θείου should also be taken as a subjective genitive.

Parallels to this subjective genitive in Josephus appear throughout the NT. Πίστις with a genitive (possessive) personal pronoun is particularly frequent, occurring over forty times. Frequent in the synoptic narratives is the formula, "your faith has saved you."[127] But the use of the subjective genitive is not limited to this formula nor to the second person singular genitive pronoun σου.[128] In a few instances a noun may occur as a subjective genitive with πίστις. In Rom. 4,12. 16[129] Paul refers to the faith [of our father] Abraham; Rev. 13,10 speaks of the faith[fulness] of the saints;[130] the genitive with πίστις in Col. 2,12 is very likely a subjective genitive referring to the faithfulness of the power of God who raised [Christ] from the dead.[131]

Although syntactical and conceptual parallelism occurs in most of the instances in the NT and Josephus listed above where πίστις occurs with a subjective genitive, there is still an important distinction to be noted. The NT understands πίστις exclusively as religious faith[fulness], whereas Josephus employs the substantive in profane relationships. Πίστις with a possessive pronoun, which plays a significant role in the NT in the sense of "your faith has saved you",[132] is not to be found in Josephus. For this reason the most striking parallel between Josephus and the NT in the use of a subjective genitive with πίστις is Josephus' formula: πίστις τοῦ θείου in Ant. 17,179. 284 and the reference of Paul to the faithfulness of God in Rom. 3,3: τί γάρ; εἰ ἠπίστησάν τινες, μὴ ἡ ἀπιστία αὐτῶν τὴν πίστιν τοῦ θεοῦ καταργήσει; In Josephus and in Paul the clear idea of this formula is that God's faithfulness stands as a more certain basis for, or as a more certain basis than, human faithfulness.

Schlatter's observation that Josephus avoids the genitive with πίστις finds its proper context in the fact that Josephus does not employ the objective genitive of a personal noun in connection with πίστις.[133]

---

127 ἡ πίστις σου σέσωκέν σε, cf. Mt. 9,22; Mk. 5,34; 10,52; Lk. 7,50; 8,48; 17,19; 18,42.

128 Numerous examples can be found instantly with the help of a concordance.

129 τῆς ἐν ἀκροβυστίᾳ πίστεως τοῦ πατρὸς ἡμῶν Ἀβραάμ; ἐκ πίστεως Ἀβραάμ, ὅς ἐστιν πατὴρ πάντων ἡμῶν.

130 Ὧδέ ἐστιν ἡ ὑπομονὴ καὶ ἡ πίστις τῶν ἁγίων.

131 συνταφέντες αὐτῷ ἐν τῷ βαπτισμῷ, ἐν ᾧ καὶ συνηγέρθητε διὰ τῆς πίστεως τῆς ἐνεργείας τοῦ θεοῦ τοῦ ἐγείραντος αὐτὸν ἐκ νεκρῶν. (This is traditionally interpreted as an objective genitive: 'faith in the power of God'.) Ant. 19,16 reads similarly: πολλὴν ἔχει πίστιν τοῦ θεοῦ τῆς δυνάμεως. In this instance, however, πίστις carries the sense of 'proof' of God's power. This is not a close parallel.

132 E.g., Mt. 9,22; par.

133 I.e., in the sense of ἔχετε πίστιν θεοῦ in Mk. 11,22. The closest Josephus comes to this is his use of πίστις ὁμήρων in Bel. 6,357: καὶ τότε μὲν ἐν φρουρᾷ πάντας εἶχε, τοὺς δὲ τοῦ βασιλέως παῖδας καὶ συγγενεῖς δήσας ὕστερον εἰς Ῥώμην ἀνήγαγεν πίστιν ὁμήρων

Otherwise, there are only three instances where πίστις as 'faith, belief' occurs with an objective genitive: *Ant.* 2,283, "faith in the injunctions [of God]";[134] *Ant.* 15,201, "trust in the loyalty and devotion [of Herod]";[135] and *Bel.* 1,485, "Herod was led to belief in the things which were said."[136]

Josephus' rather sparse use of πίστις with an objective genitive does not correspond to the use of πίστις in the NT. Concepts such as πίστις θεοῦ (faith in God) in Mk. 11,22 or πίστις Ἰησοῦ Χριστοῦ (faith in Jesus Christ) in Rom. 3,22[137] are expressed differently by Josephus. Josephus uses, for example, the formula ἡ περὶ θεοῦ πίστις in *Ap.* 2,163. 169 or ἡ ὑπὲρ τῶν νόμων πίστις in *Ant.* 15,291. It is inter-esting, however, that the NT never implements either of these formulas to mark the object of faith or belief.

Perhaps the strongest point of contact between Josephus and the NT in the use of πίστις as a religious term is found in instances where πίστις refers to the content of what is believed. Πίστις appears quite often in the NT in this creedal sense. A classic example is μία πίστις in Eph. 4,5. But there are many other examples as well: Elymas the magician tried to turn away the proconsul from the faith;[138] the churches in Acts 16,5 were strengthened in the faith;[139] the word of faith which we preach;[140] stand in the faith;[141] the unity of faith;[142] the mystery of faith;[143] etc.

In Josephus πίστις in this sense occurs in only two contexts. The first is Josephus' reference to the 'belief' of the Pharisees in the immortal-

---

παρέξοντας. The sense of πίστις in this instance, however, is not 'faith, faithfulness' but rather 'pledge, deposit'. The genitive is neither objective nor subjective, but rather an *appositive genitive*, or perhaps even a *partitive genitive*; i.e., the pledge was the hostages, or the king's sons were a pledge or deposit of [the rest of the] hostages. The exact reverse of this formula, ὅμηρα τῆς πίστεως, appears in *Vi.* 79. In this passage it is clear that the hostages *are* the pledge of security/loyalty (i.e., an appositive genitive).

134 τά τε κατὰ τὸ Σιναῖον ὄρος αὐτῷ συντυχόντα καὶ τὰς τοῦ θεοῦ φωνὰς καὶ τὰ πρὸς πίστιν ὧν οὗτος αὐτῷ προστάξειεν ὑπ' αὐτοῦ δειχθέντα σημεῖα καθ' ἕκαστον ἐξετίθετο, παρεκάλει τε μὴ ἀπιστοῦντα τούτοις ἐμποδὼν ἵστασθαι τῇ τοῦ θεοῦ γνώμῃ.

135 εἰς πίστιν εὐνοίας καὶ προθυμίας.

136 τὸν Ἡρώδην εἰς πίστιν ὑπαχθῆναι τῶν λεγομένων. Cf. *Ant.* 16,117, πρὸς πίστιν ... τοιαύτης δυσσεβείας.

137 Cf. Rom. 3,26; Gal. 2,16. 20; 3,22; [Eph. 3,12]; Phil. 3,9. Note: There have been recent at-tempts to interpret πίστις Χριστοῦ in many of these passages as a subjective genitive. For a further discussion of this issue see further below.

138 Acts 13,8: ζητῶν διαστρέψαι τὸν ἀνθύπατον ἀπὸ τῆς πίστεως. Cf. 1 Tim. 4,1.

139 Αἱ μὲν οὖν ἐκκλησίαι ἐστερεοῦντο τῇ πίστει. Cf. Col. 2,7.

140 Rom. 10,8: τοῦτ' ἔστιν τὸ ῥῆμα τῆς πίστεως ὃ κηρύσσομεν. Cf. 1 Tim. 4,6.

141 1 Cor. 16,13: Γρηγορεῖτε, στήκετε ἐν τῇ πίστει, ἀνδρίζεσθε, κραταιοῦσθε. Cf. Col. 1,23.

142 Eph. 4,13: μέχρι καταντήσωμεν οἱ πάντες εἰς τὴν ἑνότητα τῆς πίστεως καὶ τῆς ἐπιγνώσεως τοῦ υἱοῦ τοῦ θεοῦ.

143 1 Tim. 3,9: ἔχοντας τὸ μυστήριον τῆς πίστεως ἐν καθαρᾷ συνειδήσει.

ity of the soul.[144] It is interesting that in passages where this 'Pharisaic creed' is mentioned in the NT, πίστις is not a part of the context. In Mt. 22,23ff. (par.) it is stated of the Sadducees that they *say* there is no resurrection.[145] In Acts 23,6ff. Paul, speaking as a Pharisee, claims that he is on trial concerning his hope in the resurrection of the dead.[146] There may be a stronger connection between Josephus' creedal use of πίστις and 1 Cor. 15,14. 16 where Paul writes that if there is no resurrection of the dead (and particularly, if Christ was not raised), then "your πίστις is empty (κενή); vain (ματαία)"—i.e., then πίστις is 'without content'.

However the parallelism between *Ant.* 18,14 and Mt. 23,23ff. shows that Josephus understands πίστις in the Hellenistic sense of an intellectual belief (πίστις αὐτοῖς = λέγοντες = νομίζοντες), without the aspect of personal commitment (*Verbindlichkeit*). Obviously the NT also views this Pharisaic 'belief' as something other than 'faith' in the Hebrew sense, for the πιστ- terminology is missing in this context. The other context where Josephus uses πίστις as the content of what is believed is in *Ap.* 2,163.169 where Moses the prophet and lawgiver is seen to be the founder[147] of the correct belief about God and the implanter[148] of the belief about God.[149]

There are a few instances in the NT and in Josephus where πίστις has the special sense of a *religious virtue* which is possessed or to be pursued. *Ant.* 12,147, for example, credits the Jewish folk with εὐσέβειάν τε καὶ πίστιν.[150] 1 Tim. 6,11 urges Timothy to pursue δικαιοσύνην εὐσέβειαν πίστιν, ἀγάπην ὑπομονὴν πραϋπαθίαν.[151] Πίστις is also

---

[144]   *Ant.* 18,14: ἀθάνατόν τε ἰσχὺν ταῖς ψυχαῖς πίστις αὐτοῖς εἶναι.

[145]   λέγοντες μὴ εἶναι ἀνάστασιν.

[146]   περὶ ἐλπίδος καὶ ἀναστάσεως νεκρῶν.

[147]   ἐπιτυχών.

[148]   ἐνέφυσεν.

[149]   In contrast to what Josephus says about Moses as the founder and implanter of πίστις, Heb. 12,2 affirms that Jesus is the founder and perfecter of faith: ἀφορῶντες εἰς τὸν τῆς πίστεως ἀρχηγὸν καὶ τελειωτὴν Ἰησοῦν.

[150]   Cf. *Ant.* 6,276; 7,212; 11,217; 15,368; 17,32. 194; *Bel.* 5,121; 7,365 *Vi.* 84;. Πίστις is also linked with such virtues as ἀρετή, *Ant.* 17,246; *Ap.* 2,42; τιμή, *Ant.* 6,326; 7,43; φιλία , *Ant.* 7,107; 19,289; προθυμία , *Ant.* 7,235; 12,150; ἀνδρεία, *Ant.* 13,45. 378; 14,186; σπουδή , *Ant.* 14,192; ἐγκράτεια, *Ant.* 16,246; ἐπιείκεια , *Ap.* 2,43; cf. further the list of 'virtues' for which the Essenes were known in *Bel.* 2,135: ὀργῆς ταμίαι δίκαιοι, θυμοῦ καθεκτικοί, πίστεως προστάται, εἰρήνης ὑπουργοί.

[151]   Cf. Tit. 1,1; 2 Tim. 2,22. Πίστις often appears in lists of 'Christian virtues' such as the fruit of the Spirit, Gal. 5,22-23; cf. also 1 Tim. 1,5. 19; 4,12; 2 Tim. 3,10; Tit. 2,2; Rev. 2,19. In these lists ἀγάπη is almost invariably included, and elsewhere πίστις and ἀγάπη are often listed together; cf. 1 Cor. 13,13, Rev. 2,19 and many other instances. In 2 Pet. 1,5 πίστις is mentioned in the same context with ἀρετή. Μακροθυμία is also a virtue with which πίστις is connected, Heb. 6,12; cf. ὑπομονή in Rev. 2,19; 13,10; 14,12.

employed by Josephus and the NT in connection with the birth of Moses[152] and in connection with the deeds harmonious with words.[153]

3.2 Differences in Use

3.21 Uses in Josephus Lacking in the NT

In spite of (and perhaps also in light of) the parallel uses of πίστις in the writings of Josephus and in the NT, there are also some very basic differences. The most fundamental difference lies in the fact that πίστις in Josephus occurs primarily in a profane sense, but in the NT almost exclusively in a religious sense. Simply upon the basis of this fundamental distinction, one would expect to find uses of πίστις in the NT which do not occur in Josephus and *vice versa*. Πίστις περί,[154] for example, is an expression not found in the NT. Josephus' use of the plural πίστεις has no parallel in the NT. Πίστις in the sense of a 'deposit, charge, trust'[155] is also lacking in the NT, and πίστις in the formula 'beyond belief'[156] is foreign to NT use.

Moses as prophet and lawgiver plays an important role in Josephus' religious understanding of πίστις, much more so than in the NT. But in the great majority of instances where Josephus' use of πίστις has no parallel in the NT, the meaning of the substantive is profane. The religious uses of πίστις in the NT which have no parallel in Josephus are of greater importance to the present study.

3.22 Religious Uses in the NT Lacking in Josephus

There are some obvious syntactical differences between the use of πίστις in the NT and in Josephus. Πίστις ἐν with a dative case form, for example, in the sense of 'faith in...' occurs seven times in the NT[157] but is completely lacking in Josephus. Likewise, the similar expression πίστις εἰς with an accusative case form also meaning 'faith in...'[158] has no

---

152 Heb. 11,23; *Ant.* 2,218.
153 Jas. 2; *Ap.* 2,169.
154 *Ap.* 2,163. 169. The verb πιστεύειν does occur with περί in Jn. 9,18 and Acts 8,12. In both instances, however, the prepositional phrase with περί plays a secondary role to the dative object of πιστεύειν.
155 E.g., *Ant.* 2,57; 6,326; 7,47.
156 παρὰ πίστεως; μεῖζον πίστεως; et al.; cf. *Ant.* 1,14; 5,350; *Bel.* 5,509; 6,297.
157 Rom. 3,25; Eph. 1,15; Col. 1,4; 1 Tim. (1,14); 3,13; 2 Tim. (1,13); 3,15.
158 Acts 20,21; 24,24; 26,18; Col. 2,5; 1 Pet. 1,21.

conceptual parallel in Josephus. [159] Πίστις ἐπί in Heb. 6,1 expresses the same idea, but this formula likewise does not appear in Josephus. These NT formulas are *Hebraisms*.[160] Josephus is obviously not influenced by the parallel Hebrew formulas. Instead he uses typical Greek formulas[161] to express the object of faith or belief. For this reason the purely syntactical differences between NT use of πίστις and the use in Josephus are of less importance

The apostle Paul uses the formula τὸ ῥῆμα τῆς πίστεως in Rom. 10,8, referring to the message which he preached. [162] Πίστις in this passage does signify the content of what is believed—a sense found in Josephus—but in this context it signifies something more. Πίστις *is* "the word which we preach."[163] 'The faith' is therefore not simply a creed—a doctrine or set of doctrines which a religious sect may hold to be true[164]—but it is also a word or words,[165] even a mystery,[166] which can be preached,[167] which can be taught[168] and which can be heard. [169]

In other words, πίστις as the content of what is believed takes on an added *missionary element* in Paul's understanding of τὸ ῥῆμα τῆς πίστεως—an element which calls not only for intellectual response on the part of the hearer, but also for a personal commitment. This missionary element is completely lacking in Josephus' understanding and use of πίστις, even when it refers to the content of religious faith. It is true that Josephus can refer to a spoken message as the object of belief or trust,[170] but he never uses the substantive πίστις as the equivalent of a *kerygma* or a *didache*.[171]

---

[159]   Josephus does indeed use the formula πίστις εἰς with an accusative case form (cf. *Ant.* 16,48; 17,194), but it is never in the same religious sense of 'faith in...' as in the NT. Rather the sense is 'faithfulness towards...', and then only in a profane (political) sense.

[160]   I.e., very literal translations of אמונה ב־ and האמין ב־.

[161]   E.g., πίστις περί in *Ap.* 2,163 or πίστις with a simple dative in *Bel.* 2,257.

[162]   ἀλλὰ τί λέγει; ἐγγύς σου τὸ ῥῆμά ἐστιν ἐν τῷ στόματί σου καὶ ἐν τῇ καρδίᾳ σου, τοῦτ' ἔστιν τὸ ῥῆμα τῆς πίστεως ὃ κηρύσσομεν.

[163]   I.e., the genitive is appositive.

[164]   E.g., the 'belief' of the Pharisees in the immortality of the soul; *Ant.* 18,14.

[165]   1 Tim. 4,6: Ταῦτα ὑποτιθέμενος τοῖς ἀδελφοῖς καλὸς ἔσῃ διάκονος Χριστοῦ Ἰησοῦ, ἐντρεφόμενος τοῖς λόγοις τῆς πίστεως καὶ τῆς καλῆς διδασκαλίας ᾗ παρηκολούθηκας.

[166]   1 Tim. 3,9: ἔχοντας τὸ μυστήριον τῆς πίστεως ἐν καθαρᾷ συνειδήσει.

[167]   Rom. 10,8; cf. Gal. 1,23.

[168]   Cf. Col. 2,7; 1 Tim. 4,6.

[169]   Cf. Rom. 10,17.

[170]   E.g., *Bel.* 1,485: τὸν Ἡρώδην εἰς πίστιν ὑπαχθῆναι τῶν λεγομένων.

[171]   Also in contrast to Josephus, πίστις in Philo sometimes has this missionary element. In *de ebrietate* 40, e.g., Philo uses the formula πίστιν μαθεῖν ('to learn the [true] faith'); cf. *leg. alleg.* 2,89.

Josephus does not use an objective genitive with πίστις in the same sense as ἔχετε πίστιν θεοῦ in Mk. 11,22. At best he only speaks of a πίστις περὶ θεοῦ;[172] i.e., a belief *about* God, but not a trust *in* God. Indeed, Josephus' use of the objective genitive with πίστις (in the sense of 'faith, faithfulness') is almost non-existent. Therefore the formula πίστις Χριστοῦ in its various forms[173] as faith *in* Christ represents a concept quite foreign to Josephus' use and understanding of πίστις.

Indeed the meaning of the πίστις Χριστοῦ formula in the NT itself is not undisputed. While the traditional view has been to treat the genitive with πίστις in these instances as an objective genitive, i.e., faith *in* Christ, there have been recent attempts by Morna D. Hooker,[174] by Sam K. Williams[175] and by Luke Timothy Johnson[176] to interpret the genitive as subjective, referring to 'Christ's faith' or 'Christ's faithfulness'. All three of these attempts seem to be spurred by an earlier article by Arland J. Hultgren[177] who defends the traditional interpretation of the formula as an objective genitive, primarily upon syntactical observations in the Pauline corpus,[178] but also upon exegetical grounds.

In my estimation none of the three attempts to interpret πίστις Χριστοῦ as a subjective genitive in the Pauline corpus has succeeded in dismantling the argument for the traditional interpretation posed by Hultgren. Johnson all but ignores Hultgren's syntactical observations and argues for a theological understanding of πίστις as obedience, whereby πίστις Ἰησοῦ in Rom. 3,26 *could* refer to Jesus' own obedience to God.[179] He interprets this passage, and other passages with this formula, accordingly.[180] Williams develops this argument further, contending

---

[172] *Ap.* 2,163. 169.

[173] The formula appears seven times in Paul: in Rom. 3,26 as πίστις Ἰησοῦ; in Gal. 2,16b and Phil. 3,9 as πίστις Χριστοῦ; in Rom. 3,22 and Gal. 3,22 as πίστις Ἰησοῦ Χριστοῦ; in Gal. 2,16a as πίστις Χριστοῦ Ἰησοῦ; and in Gal. 2,20 as πίστις τοῦ υἱοῦ τοῦ θεοῦ. Cf. also Eph. 3,12; Rev. 2,13; 14,12.

[174] Morna D. Hooker, "ΠΙΣΤΙΣ ΧΡΙΣΤΟΥ", *New Testament Studies* 35 (1989), pp. 321-42.

[175] Sam K. Williams, "Again *Pistis Christou*", *Catholic Biblical Quarterly* 49 (1987), pp. 431-47.

[176] L. Timothy Johnson, "Rom 3:21-26 and the Faith of Jesus", *Catholic Biblical Quarterly* 44 (1982), pp. 77-90.

[177] Arland J. Hultgren, "The *Pistis Christou* Formulation in Paul", *Novum Testamentum* 22,3 (July 1980), pp. 248-63.

[178] Cf. ibid., pp. 253-58.

[179] Cf. Johnson, "Faith of Jesus", pp. 85-90.

[180] It is interesting that Johnson earlier in his article (p. 80) places much emphasis upon the parallel formulation of the 'faith of Jesus' in Rom. 3,26 and the 'faith of Abraham' in 4,16. Because the latter is obviously a subjective genitive and because the two formulations are parallel, then the former must also represent a subjective genitive. If one follows Johnson's argument to its natural conclusion, then it would be necessary, because of the parallelism, to interpret the 'faith of

(from an argument of logic) that to be *in Christ*,[181] the Pauline description of 'the believer's relationship to Christ', means to share in every aspect of Christ's being:

> ...to 'believe in Christ' is the *means* by which one comes to be 'in Christ'. That means is adopting the life-stance, *pistis,* which marked Christ's own relationship to God, the life-stance of which he is the eschatological exemplar. To adopt this stance is to trust and obey Him who raised Jesus from the dead, to believe *like* Christ, and thereby to stand *with* Christ in that domain, that power field, created through his death and resurrection. To do so is to become the beneficiary of Christ-faith.[182]

Williams correctly rejects Hultgren's argument against a subjective genitive based on an anarthrous πίστις in the passages in question.[183] But this is only the first, and in my estimation the weakest, of Hultgren's syntactical observations.[184] With his translation "Christ-faith" Williams wants to integrate an objective genitive with the subjective in the formula πίστις Χριστοῦ:

> The *pistis* of believers, by its very nature, is always nothing else than that way which Christ created, just as *pistis Christou*, initially the faith of Jesus himself, is always that way which believers have taken as their own. In other words, Paul's phrase focuses attention on the pioneering faith of Christ, but *his* faith now marks the life of every person who lives in him. Thus, in its fundamental character, *pistis Christou* is identical with *pistis.*[185]

This theological observation may indeed be correct and the logical conclusions sound. But whether these conclusions can be drawn from the formula πίστις Χριστοῦ, or whether these conclusions, having been deduced from other sources, can be imposed upon the formula πίστις Χριστοῦ is quite another question.

Morna Hooker is sympathetic with Williams' argument for including both meanings, the subjective as well as the objective, in an

---

Abraham' in 4,16 also as obedience. It is probably safe to say that this is *not* what Paul had in mind in his understanding of Abrahamic faith!

[181] ἐν Χριστῷ; cf. Williams, *"Pistis Christou"*, pp. 438ff.

[182] Ibid., p. 443. 'Christ-faith' is Williams' proposed translation of πίστις Χριστοῦ; cf. p. 437.

[183] While it is indeed possible to speak of normal patterns for the use or non-use of the article with the noun, this does not rule out exceptions. Cf. ibid., pp. 431ff.

[184] Hultgren himself only develops this argument in one relatively short paragraph; cf. *"Pistis Christou* in Paul", p. 253.

[185] Williams, *"Pistis Christou"*, p. 447.

interpretation of πίστις Χριστοῦ.[186] She categorically rejects Hultgren's syntactical arguments for an objective genitive[187] and states: "This issue can be settled only by exegesis." Then proceeding to argue from 'logic' she affirms 1) "that Christ also had faith",[188] 2) "that in [Gal. 3,22] Paul is referring to the faith of Christ himself"[189] and, therefore, 3) "*that logic suggests that the subjective genitive is intended.*"[190] Nevertheless she concedes that logic alone is not enough to go on, and that, "though a case *can* be made out for the subjective genitive in all these passages, *the evidence is no more conclusive* than in those we have examined."[191]

A common concession in all of these attempts to interpret πίστις Χριστοῦ is that neither the designation subjective genitive nor objective genitive may be appropriate. Hultgren's final, and probably his strongest, syntactical observation is most convincing. Starting from Rom. 4,16b with the formula τῷ ἐκ πίστεως Ἀβραάμ, which is parallel to the formula τὸν ἐκ πίστεως Ἰησοῦ in 3,26, Hultgren points out that Paul is referring neither to faith *in* Abraham (objective genitive) nor strictly to the faith *of* "Abraham the individual person" (subjective genitive).[192] "Rather, Paul is here referring to what can be called the Abrahamic faith—or, more loosely, the faith of the people of God—i.e., Jewish and Gentile Christians who share in faith, as in the case of Abraham".[193] This, maintains Hultgren, is an instance of Semitic syntax underlying the Greek:

> While in Greek syntax the genitive is commonly determined by the governing noun, this is less the case in Hebrew and Aramaic. In Semitic usage it is more common that the governing noun (in construct state) is also determined by the genitive, whereby the latter takes on an adjectival function. The two words together form a unit, or compound idea, in which the interest is on the first word, but the second gives it particularity. Furthermore, the governing noun in construct state consistently lacks the definite article, and that is exactly what one finds in Paul's formulation. This Semitic usage, in which the genitive 'often provides an attribute which would normally be supplied by an adjective', has been called the 'genitive of quality', and it is fairly frequent in the New Testament.[194]

---

186 Cf. Hooker, "ΠΙΣΤΙΣ ΧΡΙΣΤΟΥ", p. 340.
187 "...the question is one which cannot be settled on the basis of appeals to grammatical construction alone"; ibid., p. 321.
188 Ibid., p. 328.
189 Ibid., p. 330.
190 Ibid., p. 333; italics mine.
191 Ibid., italics mine.
192 Hultgren sees this in contrast to the subjective genitive in reference to Abraham in Rom. 4,12.
193 Hultgren, "*Pistis Christou* in Paul", p. 256.
194 Ibid., pp. 256-57.

Hultgren concludes then that this 'genitive of quality' best explains the genitive Χριστοῦ in the formula πίστις Χριστοῦ.

> To emphasize the adjectival function of Χριστοῦ, one can speak (rather awkwardly) of 'Christic faith' or (more clearly) 'faith which is in and of Christ', i.e., the faith of the believer which comes forth as Christ is proclaimed in the gospel (cf. Rom. 10,8. 17; Gal. 3,2. 5).[195]

Such an understanding of the genitive in this formula provides an answer for one of the key arguments of Hooker, Williams and Johnson against the objective genitive and for the subjective genitive in these passages: i.e., that the objective genitive would be redundant in all of the passages where the formula appears, since the faith of the believer is also explicitly expressed. But if one views the genitive as a 'genitive of quality', then there is no redundancy at all. On the contrary, the genitive is very functional. In the words of Hultgren, "the addition of the word Χριστοῦ functions to qualify (or define) the [believer's] faith of which he speaks."[196]

Still the strongest argument for viewing πίστις Χριστοῦ as the faith which the believer has *in Christ* comes from the formulations in Gal. 2,16:

> εἰδότες [δὲ] ὅτι οὐ δικαιοῦται ἄνθρωπος ἐξ ἔργων νόμου ἐὰν μὴ διὰ πίστεως Ἰησοῦ Χριστοῦ, καὶ ἡμεῖς εἰς Χριστὸν Ἰησοῦν ἐπιστεύσαμεν, ἵνα δικαιωθῶμεν ἐκ πίστεως Χριστοῦ καὶ οὐκ ἐξ ἔργων νόμου, ὅτι ἐξ ἔργων νόμου οὐ δικαιωθήσεται πᾶσα σάρξ.

The first appearance of διὰ πίστεως Ἰησοῦ Χριστοῦ is parallel in meaning to καὶ ἡμεῖς εἰς Χριστὸν Ἰησοῦν ἐπιστεύσαμεν. In the first clause Paul states: "Now we know that a person is not justified by works of the law except through faith in Jesus Christ." In the second clause he states *emphatically* (not parenthetically, as Hultgren maintains): "and we *have* believed in Christ Jesus." In the second clause Paul personally and emphatically[197] affirms that which in the first clause he has only stated in terms of general knowledge.

The second occurrence of πίστις Χριστοῦ in vs. 16 provides further evidence that this is not to be taken as a subjective genitive. Ἐκ πίστεως Χριστοῦ is clearly parallel to ἐξ ἔργων νόμου. Νόμου in the

---

195 Ibid. It should be noted here that Hultgren does indeed retain the objective element here in so far as this faith is the faith *of the believer* and not the faith of Christ himself.
196 Ibid., p. 257.
197 I.e., with the use of καὶ ἡμεῖς.

formula 'works of the law' cannot be a subjective genitive. The law can-not perform works, it can only prescribe them. It is only a person[198] to whom these works can be ascribed. Πίστις Χριστοῦ must be understood in the same way: "...in order that we may be justified by [our] faith in Christ and not by [our] works of the law."

This use of πίστις with a genitive, be it an objective genitive or a genitive of quality, is missing in the writings of Josephus. At first the absence of an objective genitive of this sort in Josephus might appear to be a good argument for a subjective interpretation in the NT. But upon closer examination, it is clear that, even interpreted as a subjective genitive, πίστις Χριστοῦ has no parallel in Josephus. One factor which might account for the lack of a parallel in Josephus is that, as Hultgren maintains, πίστις Χριστοῦ represents a Semitic syntactical structure. Josephus, possessing a more Hellenistic understanding of faith and writing for a non-Jewish audience, tends to avoid Semitic formulas and concepts.

A more important factor, however, is that Josephus does not use πίστις in the sense of faith *in* God. He refers to the faith (belief) *about*[199] God or the faithfulness *of* God,[200] but not to faith in God. As we have seen above in the case with ῥῆμα τῆς πίστεως, Josephus does not think of πίστις in the sense of a *kerygma*. Πίστις Χριστοῦ is therefore very similar to ῥῆμα τῆς πίστεως, both having a missionary element. Indeed, ῥῆμα τῆς πίστεως in Rom. 10,8 is further determined by the 'sending word of Christ', the ῥήματος Χριστοῦ in Rom. 10,17. The message of faith is the message of Christ, and Christ is the *content* of Christian faith.

In its use of πίστις the NT takes up OT traditions which are missing in Josephus' writings. The most obvious of these is the faith of Abraham in Gen. 15,6.[201] This OT passage is quoted in Rom. 4,3. 9; Gal. 3,16 and Jas. 2,23—all passages where the nature of πίστις is being discussed. The faith of Abraham is an important theme in Hebrews (esp. Heb. 11,8-12). Gen. 15,6 and the faith of Abraham also play a very important role in Philo.[202] It is quite interesting that Josephus never mentions Abraham in connection with πίστις.[203] For him it is Moses

---

198 ἄνθρωπος, cf. Gal. 2,16a.
199 πίστις περί.
200 πίστις τοῦ θείου.
201 LXX: καὶ ἐπίστευσεν Ἀβραὰμ τῷ θεῷ, καὶ ἐλογίσθη αὐτῷ εἰς δικαιοσύνην.
202 See above, Chapter Four.
203 Or with any other member of the πιστ- word group!

who tends to be the 'father of faith'²⁰⁴ over against Abraham in the
Pauline epistles and in the Epistle to the Hebrews. Also missing in
Josephus' use of πίστις is any reference to Hab. 2,4,²⁰⁵ which plays an
important role in the discussions of πίστις in Rom. 1,17; Gal. 3,11 and
Heb. 10,38.

In the synoptic gospels πίστις is closely linked with miracles of
healing. This link is particularly evident in the formula: "Your faith has
saved you."²⁰⁶ The fact that healing was dependent upon πίστις is quite
clear from the passage Mk. 6,6, where Jesus was not able to perform any
miracles [of healing] in his home town of Nazareth because of ἀπιστία.
In Acts 14,9 πίστις is construed with an infinitive,²⁰⁷ referring again to
healing faith. Josephus never uses πίστις in the context of healing.

4 THE SUBSTANTIVE ΑΠΙΣΤΙΑ

4.1 Ἀπιστία in Josephus

4.11 Ἀπιστία as Disbelief, Incredulity

The substantive ἀπιστία appears 29 times in Josephus. In the majority
of instances the meaning is 'disbelief, incredulity' in a general profane
sense. A typical example is *Ant.* 19,127: "When the news of the death
of Gaius reached the theatre, there was consternation and incredulity."²⁰⁸
In one instance ἀπιστία occurs with a subjective genitive,²⁰⁹ twice with
an objective genitive²¹⁰ and once construed with the preposition περί.²¹¹

In three of these passages ἀπιστία carries a possible religious
significance. *Ant.* 2,327 reports how the Israelites during the exodus,
hemmed in between mountains and sea and the army of the Egyptians,
turned against Moses in the midst of their despair, responded to his
promises and encouragements with 'incredulity', and wanted to stone him

---

²⁰⁴ I.e., because of the important relationship of faith to the law.

²⁰⁵ LXX: ὁ δὲ δίκαιος ἐκ πίστεώς μου ζήσεται.

²⁰⁶ ἡ πίστις σου σέσωκέν σε; e.g., Mt. 9,22; par. This is also parallel to Hab. 2,4, especially in
the interpretation of the Habakuk commentary from Qumran, IQpHab 8,1f. Here the faith of the
house of Judah (וַאֲמָנָם) is the basis for the Lord's deliverance (יַצִּילֵם אֵל).

²⁰⁷ πίστιν τοῦ σωθῆναι.

²⁰⁸ Εἰς δὲ τὸ θέατρον ἐπεὶ ἀφίκετο ὁ λόγος περὶ τῆς Γαΐου τελευτῆς, ἔκπληξίς τε καὶ ἀπιστία
ἦν· Cf. also *Ant.* 2,47. 327; 8,171; 18,24; 19,109. 186. 204. 268; *Bel.* 1,628.

²⁰⁹ *Ant.* 10,142: τήν τε τῶν ἀνθρώπων ἄγνοιαν καὶ ἀπιστίαν.

²¹⁰ *Ant.* 18,197: ἀπιστία ... λόγων; *Bel.* 2,278: ἀπιστίαν τῆς ἀληθείας.

²¹¹ Denoting 'unbelief about...'; *Ant.* 18,239: οἱ δ' ἐν ἀπιστίᾳ περὶ τῶν γεγονότων ἦσαν.

and surrender to the Egyptians.[212] In *Ant.* 10,142 Josephus refers to the ignorance and disbelief of people who disregard divine prophecy.[213] In a less strictly religious sense, *Ant.* 18,197 refers to disbelief in a statement which interprets Divine Providence as the designer of deliverance from difficulties.[214]

4.12 Ἀπιστία as Mistrust

Closely related to the definition 'disbelief' is the idea of 'mistrust'. In five instances ἀπιστία carries this sense. A typical example is *Ant.* 13,132: "Now [Malchus] at first opposed this because of mistrust, but finally, after Tryphon had pleaded with him a long while, he was won over to the plan which Tryphon was urging him to accept."[215] In one instance ἀπιστία in the sense of mistrust appears with an objective genitive, referring to Samson's mistrust of [Delilah's] good will toward him.[216] In none of these instances does ἀπιστία appear in a religious sense.

4.13 Ἀπιστία as Disloyalty, Perfidy

Ἀπιστία as 'disloyalty, perfidy'[217] occurs eight times. In five instances the substantive appears with a subjective genitive referring to the disloyalty or untrustworthiness of the Parthians,[218] the barbarians,[219] the Tiberians[220] and perjurers.[221] In other instances ἀπιστία refers absolutely to 'disloyalty' or 'perfidy'.[222] Interesting are the opposites of ἀπιστία which appear in three passages. In *Bel.* 3,349 ἀπιστία is set over against

---

[212] καὶ τὸν Μωυσῆν ἠτιῶντο πάντων ἐπιλελησμένοι τῶν ἐκ θεοῦ πρὸς τὴν ἐλευθερίαν αὐτοῖς σημείων γεγονότων, ὡς καὶ τὸν προφήτην παρορμῶντα καὶ τὴν σωτηρίαν αὐτοῖς ἐπαγγελλόμενον ὑπὸ ἀπιστίας λίθοις ἐθελῆσαι βαλεῖν παραδιδόναι τε σφᾶς τοῖς Αἰγυπτίοις διεγνωκέναι.

[213] τήν τε τῶν ἀνθρώπων ἄγνοιαν καὶ ἀπιστίαν. The reference here is general, but the context has to do with Ezekiel's and Jeremiah's prophecies of the fall of Jerusalem and the unbelief and folly of Zedekiah (cf. 2 Ki. 25,6; Jer. 39,5).

[214] ἀπιστία δέ σοι λόγων, οἳ ἐπὶ διαφυγῇ κακοῦ τοῦ ἐφεστηκότος διαιροῖντο τοῦ θείου τὴν πρόνοιαν. The religious context is clearly pagan. Divine Providence here has to do with a prophecy arising from the appearance of an owl.

[215] ὁ δὲ τὸ μὲν πρῶτον ἀντεῖχεν ὑπ᾽ ἀπιστίας, ὕστερον δὲ πολλῷ χρόνῳ προσλιπαρήσαντος τοῦ Τρύφωνος ἐκνικᾶται τὴν προαίρεσιν εἰς ἃ Τρύφων παρεκάλει; see also *Ant.* 6,59; 16,384; 17,68.

[216] καὶ ἡ γυνὴ συνεχῶς ὁμιλοῦντος αὐτῇ τοῦ Σαμψῶνος δεινῶς ἔχειν ἔλεγεν, εἰ κατ᾽ ἀπιστίαν εὐνοίας τῆς πρὸς αὐτὸν μὴ λέγει ταῦθ᾽ ἅπερ δεῖται.

[217] Perhaps also, 'unfaithfulness, untrustworthiness'.

[218] *Ant.* 14,349.

[219] *Bel.* 1,268.

[220] *Vi.* 97.

[221] *Bel.* 3,382.

[222] E.g., *Ant.* 15,110.

φιλία; φιλία is the best thing there is, ἀπιστία the worst.[223] In *Bel.*
6,320 ἀπιστία occurs in contrast to the adjective πιστός ('trustworthy,
faithful').[224] And in *Ant.* 13,413 ἀπιστία is the opposite of πίστις (=
[political] loyalty).[225] Josephus never uses ἀπιστία in the religious
sense of 'unfaithfulness'.

4.2 *Ἀπιστία in the NT*

In contrast to Josephus, the NT employs ἀπιστία exclusively in a
religious sense. Whenever a genitive case form is construed with the
substantive it is always a subjective genitive. The sense of ἀπιστία as
'mistrust' is lacking in the NT. The substantive only occurs in the sense
of 'disbelief'[226] or 'unfaithfulness'.

4.21 Ἀπιστία as Unbelief

Ἀπιστία appears four times with the meaning: 'unbelief'—in each
instance with a subjective genitive. Mt. 13,58 reports that Jesus was not
able to perform many miracles in Nazareth because of the unbelief of the
people there.[227] In Mk. 9,24 there is a strong contrast between ἀπιστία
and πιστεύειν as the father of the boy with a dumb spirit cries out in des-
peration to Jesus: "I believe; help my unbelief!"[228] In this instance, as
well as in Mt. 13,58 and Mk. 6,6, ἀπιστία is a decisive factor where miracles of healing are involved.

In the later ending of Mark's gospel, Mk. 16,14, unbelief appears
in the context of the resurrection. Here ἀπιστία means the same as οὐκ
ἐπίστευσαν and is parallel to σκληροκαρδία. Jesus rebukes the unbelief
and hardheartedness of the eleven disciples for not having believed the report of the women concerning the resurrection.[229]

---

[223] προσετίθει δ᾽ ὡς οὔτ᾽ ἂν Οὐεσπασιανὸς ἐνεδρεύων φίλον ἔπεμπεν, ἵνα τοῦ κακίστου πράγματος προστήσηται τὸ κάλλιστον, ἀπιστίας φιλίαν, οὐδ᾽ ἂν αὐτὸς ἀπατήσων ἄνδρα φίλον ὑπήκουσεν ἐλθεῖν.

[224] τῶν δὲ φυλάκων καταλαβεῖν μὲν οὐδεὶς ἴσχυσε, πρὸς δὲ τὴν ἀπιστίαν ἐβλασφήμουν. κἀκεῖνος οὐδὲν ἔφη παραβεβηκέναι τῶν συνθηκῶν· λαβεῖν γὰρ δεξιὰν οὐ τοῦ μένειν παρ᾽ αὐτοῖς ἀλλὰ τοῦ καταβῆναι μόνον καὶ λαβεῖν ὕδωρ, ἅπερ ἀμφότερα πεποιηκὼς πιστὸς ἔδοξεν εἶναι.

[225] Cf. the use of πίστις in *Ant.* 13,411.

[226] Or, perhaps better: 'unbelief'.

[227] καὶ οὐκ ἐποίησεν ἐκεῖ δυνάμεις πολλὰς διὰ τὴν ἀπιστίαν αὐτῶν. Cf. the parallel passage in Mk. 6,6: καὶ ἐθαύμαζεν διὰ τὴν ἀπιστίαν αὐτῶν.

[228] εὐθὺς κράξας ὁ πατὴρ τοῦ παιδίου ἔλεγεν· πιστεύω· βοήθει μου τῇ ἀπιστίᾳ.

[229] Ὕστερον [δὲ] ἀνακειμένοις αὐτοῖς τοῖς ἕνδεκα ἐφανερώθη καὶ ὠνείδισεν τὴν ἀπιστίαν αὐτῶν καὶ σκληροκαρδίαν ὅτι τοῖς θεασαμένοις αὐτὸν ἐγηγερμένον οὐκ ἐπίστευσαν.

4.22 Ἀπιστία as Unfaithfulness

Ἀπιστία in the NT in the sense of 'unbelief', as already noted, often occurs in contrast to the verb πιστεύειν. When ἀπιστία appears in the sense of unfaithfulness, it is used almost exclusively in contrast to the substantive πίστις. This is most obvious in Paul's use of ἀπιστία in Romans. In Rom. 3,3 the unfaithfulness of the Jews is set in direct contrast to the faithfulness of God.[230] Rom. 4,20 states that Abraham did not waver in unfaithfulness concerning God's promise that Sarah would bear a child, but that he grew strong in faith, giving glory to God.[231] And in the parable of the olive tree in Rom. 11,20. 23, the reason for the Jews' being 'cut off' and the Gentiles' being 'grafted in' is the unfaithfulness of the one group over against the faithfulness of the other.[232]

Heb. 3,12. 19 refer likewise to the unfaithfulness of the Israelites in the wilderness as the reason for their being cut off from the promises of God.[233] Indeed, there is no direct contrast to the noun πίστις within the immediate context of these verses, but the emphasis of πίστις is clear enough from the rest of the epistle that one can safely imply the contrast between ἀπιστία and πίστις in these two verses as well.

4.3 Ἀπιστία in Josephus and NT

Ἀπιστία in Josephus is parallel to the NT in its basic meaning. The major difference is that the NT employs the substantive exclusively as a religious term, referring to unbelief in Christ or in the resurrection, or as unfaithfulness towards God. Josephus' use of the substantive does approach the meaning of religious unbelief in a couple of instances,[234] but he primarily understands ἀπιστία in the profane senses of 'incredulity, mistrust, perfidy'.

---

[230] τί γάρ; εἰ ἠπίστησάν τινες, μὴ ἡ ἀπιστία αὐτῶν τὴν πίστιν τοῦ θεοῦ καταργήσει; It is also noteworthy that the substantive ἀπιστία is parallel in meaning to the the verb ἀπιστεῖν.

[231] εἰς δὲ τὴν ἐπαγγελίαν τοῦ θεοῦ οὐ διεκρίθη τῇ ἀπιστίᾳ ἀλλ' ἐνεδυναμώθη τῇ πίστει, δοὺς δόξαν τῷ θεῷ. It is also possible in this passage to take ἀπιστία in the first sense as unbelief. I prefer the above reading because it seems to fit better into Paul's understanding of ἀπιστία and πίστις elsewhere in Romans.

[232] Rom. 11,20: καλῶς· τῇ ἀπιστίᾳ ἐξεκλάσθησαν, σὺ δὲ τῇ πίστει ἕστηκας. μὴ ὑψηλὰ φρόνει ἀλλὰ φοβοῦ· vs. 23: κἀκεῖνοι δέ, ἐὰν μὴ ἐπιμένωσιν τῇ ἀπιστίᾳ, ἐγκεντρισθήσονται· δυνατὸς γάρ ἐστιν ὁ θεὸς πάλιν ἐγκεντρίσαι αὐτούς. Cf. further 1 Tim. 1,13: τὸ πρότερον ὄντα βλάσφημον καὶ διώκτην καὶ ὑβριστήν, ἀλλὰ ἠλεήθην, ὅτι ἀγνοῶν ἐποίησα ἐν ἀπιστίᾳ.

[233] Heb. 3,12: Βλέπετε, ἀδελφοί, μήποτε ἔσται ἔν τινι ὑμῶν καρδία πονηρὰ ἀπιστίας ἐν τῷ ἀποστῆναι ἀπὸ θεοῦ ζῶντος; vs. 19: καὶ βλέπομεν ὅτι οὐκ ἠδυνήθησαν εἰσελθεῖν δι' ἀπιστίαν.

[234] E.g., Ant. 2,327; 10,142.

CHAPTER SIX

ΠΙΣΤΕΥΕΙΝ IN THE WRITINGS OF FLAVIUS JOSEPHUS AND THE
NT

1 GENERAL USE OF ΠΙΣΤΕΥΕΙΝ IN JOSEPHUS

1.1 Introduction

The frequency with which Josephus employs the verb πιστεύειν corresponds to the frequency of the substantive πίστις in his writings. Also
comparable is the proportional use of the verb within a religious context.
Of the 225 times the verb occurs, possibly as many as sixty-six could be
tied in with some sort of religious context. The actual number of times
that πιστεύειν itself is a clearly religious term are much fewer.
Therefore, as with the substantive πίστις , it will be expedient to
establish the normative use of the verb by Josephus before examining the
religious use of πιστεύειν.

Liddell and Scott give two primary definitions of πιστεύειν. First,
it is used in the sense of 'to trust, believe, put faith in, rely upon (a
person, thing, or statement)'. Under this broad category, Liddell and
Scott list a variety of constructions which express this idea with the verb
πιστεύειν. The second meaning of πιστεύειν is 'to entrust'. These basic
definitions correspond to the normative use of πιστεύειν in the writings
of Josephus.

1.2 Πιστεύειν as to Believe, to Trust, to Put Faith In, to Rely Upon

In the sense of 'to believe, trust' πιστεύειν does, in certain instances, oc -
cur in a religious sense as we shall see later. In the majority of instances,
however, it is clearly profane. What is most noteworthy concerning
πιστεύειν in this sense is the variety of syntactical constructions which
Josephus employs to relate various emphases in the act of believing or
trusting.

1.21 Πιστεύειν with the Dative Case Form

Josephus most commonly employs πιστεύειν as a transitive verb with a dative object. Approximately one fourth of all occurrences of πιστεύειν in Josephus appear in this construction. A personal object of πιστεύειν is quite frequent in this construction. For instance, Josephus explains that Apion believed (the reports of) the elders concerning Moses because they supposedly lived at the same time as Moses and knew him.[1] In *Ant.* 10,28 Hezekiah asks Isaiah to perform some sign so that he might believe Isaiah.[2] It is the responsibility of historians, claims Josephus in *Ant.* 14,3, to be conscientious in "speaking the truth to those who must rely upon them[3] in matters of which they themselves have no knowledge". In *Ant.* 20,31 queen Helena was advised by her high nobles and satraps to appoint as trustee of the realm someone whom she greatly trusted.[4] In *Ant.* 6,224 Jonathan pleads with his father Saul not to put trust either in himself, insofar as he had suspicions about David,[5] nor in those who were speaking slanders.

Most common among the impersonal dative objects of πιστεύειν in Josephus are the following things: oral or written reports;[6] charges and slanders;[7] rumors;[8] confessions and statements made under torture;[9] (general) statements;[10] an apology or defense;[11] prophecies or words uttered by a prophet;[12] written documents and scriptures.[13] In *Bel.* 4,94, political pledges (offered by the Romans) are objects of trust.[14] In *Ant.* 18,96 the object of πιστεύειν is a treaty of friendship.[15] Oaths[16] are the object of trust in *Bel.* 4,215. In *Ant.* 12,122 the Macedonian garrison which was occupying the citadel of Jerusalem made light of the assault by the high priest Jonathan because of their confidence in the strength of

---

1 *Ap.* 2,13: πιστεύσας τοῖς διὰ τὴν ἡλικίαν ἐπισταμένοις αὐτὸν καὶ συγγενομένοις.
2 ἵν᾽ αὐτῷ πιστεύσῃ.
3 πιστεύειν αὐτοῖς μέλλουσιν.
4 ᾧ μάλιστα πιστεύει.
5 ἑαυτῷ τοῦθ᾽ ὑπονοοῦντι πιστεύειν.
6 *Ant.* 8,172; *Ap.* 2,14.
7 *Bel.* 1,545; *Ant.* 13,303; 16,121. 251. 254.
8 *Bel.* 1,75.
9 *Bel.* 1,497. 590. 635.
10 *Bel.* 7,56; *Ant.* 5,55; *Ap.* 1,287.
11 *Ant.* 6,259.
12 *Ant.* 9,12. 86; 10,39; *Ap.* 2,286.
13 *Ap.* 1,42 (variant reading). 161; 2,18.
14 ταῖς δεξιαῖς ἐπίστευσαν.
15 φιλίᾳ.
16 τοῖς ὅρκοις.

the place.[17]   In one instance the dative article with an infinitive appears as the object of the verb πιστεύειν. Josephus reports in *Ant.* 2,219 that Amaram [sic], the father of Moses, fearing for his own safety as well as the safety of his infant son, resolved to commit the salvation and protection of the child to God rather than simply relying upon the concealment of the child.[18] Josephus refers once in *Ant.* 8,279 to golden heifers and altars on the mountains[19] as objects of πιστεύειν in the context of what people rely upon for victory in war.[20] *Bel.* 6,288 reports that the residents of Jerusalem neither heeded nor believed the portents[21] that foretold the coming disaster (i.e., the fall of the city).[22]

1.22 Πιστεύειν with the Accusative Case Form

Πιστεύειν commonly appears with the accusative case form in the sense of 'entrusting'. Πιστεύειν in the sense of 'to believe, trust' with a direct object in the accusative case form is, however, quite rare.[23] In Josephus' there are only four instances of this. In each instance it is quite clear that the accusative is not a cognitive accusative, but rather an accusative of respect, an adverbial accusative or simply an accusative of the direct object with πιστεύειν acting as a normal transitive verb.

The most problematic of these instances is *Bel.* 3,328. Reporting the Roman capture of the city of Jotapa, Josephus relates: "At length when the whole (Roman) army had poured in, [the inhabitants of Jotapa] rose up to the realization of the calamity".[24] It is significant that

---

[17] πεπιστευκότες τῇ ὀχυρότητι τοῦ χωρίου; cf. *Ant.* 18,312.

[18] ἢ τῷ λήσεσθαι πεπιστευκώς.

[19] ταῖς χρυσαῖς δαμάλεσι καὶ τοῖς ἐπὶ τῶν ὀρῶν βωμαῖς;

[20] This is very similar to the other things which Philo mentions as improper objects of faith in contrast to faith in God; cf. *de. Abr.* 263; *quis rer. div. heres* 92-93. Especially clear in this passage in Josephus is the fact that this kind of faith is no faith at all, rather superstition.

[21] τέρασιν.

[22] These last two passages are obviously religious in nature. We will return to them later in this chapter.

[23] Liddell and Scott cite only one such reference: Thucydides 5,105: τῆς δὲ ἐς Λακεδαιμονίους δόξης, [ἣν] διὰ τὸ αἰσχρὸν δὴ βοηθήσειν ὑμῖν πιστεύετε αὐτούς, μακαρίσαντες ὑμῶν τὸ ἀπειρόκακον οὐ ζηλοῦμεν τὸ ἄφρον. Liddell and Scott identify this 'problematic' accusative case form (ἣν … πιστεύετε) as a cognate accusative (i.e., = πίστιν πιστεύειν) and suggest the translation: 'entertain a confident opinion'. J. Steup in his edition of the works of Thucydides (Berlin: Weidmann'sche Buchhandlung, 1912, Vol. 5, p. 225) amends the text "nach einer Vermutung von Reiske" from ἣν to the dative ᾗ, expressing in this case a causal relationship. Steup rejects the accusative ἣν on the following basis: "Die Ansicht von Kr., Stahl u.a., daß ἣν (δόξης,[ἣν] πιστεύετε nach Analogie von πίστιν πιστεύειν gesagt sei, ist darum zu verwerfen, weil nach der Wortstellung διὰ τὸ αἰσχρὸν δὴ βοηθήσειν ὑμῖν αὐτούς nicht Epexegese von ἣν (δόξαν) πιστεύετε sein kann".

[24] καὶ τὴν ἅλωσιν ἐπίστευον ἀναιρούμενοι. The last line of this sentence is colorfully translated by Thackeray: "the blade at their throat brought home to them that Jotapa was taken" (*Loeb*

πιστεύειν appears here in the imperfect tense form. From the context πιστεύειν must surely mean 'to realize, become aware of', particularly in order to express the progressive aspect of the imperfect tense form. The accusative ἅλωσιν must then be interpreted either as a simple direct object or as an accusative of respect.

In the other three instances of πιστεύειν with the accusative the idea is clearly that of believing or trusting *in* or *with respect to* something. In *Ant.* 16,125 Herod is urged by Caesar to put away all suspicions concerning his sons and to be reconciled to them, "for it is not right even to believe such things against those of one's own family".[25] Josephus reports in *Ant.* 18,211 that Tiberius was eager to hand the government over to his grandson but wanted to consult the national gods first because he trusted the revelation of the god concerning the future[26] more than his own opinion or desire. In *Ap.* 2,207 Josephus explains that the law does not allow the concealing of things from friends, for there is no (true) friendship which does not trust (in) all things.[27]

1.23 Πιστεύειν with Prepositional Phrases

Only one time in the writings of Josephus, and this only indirectly, does πιστεύειν appear in conjunction with the preposition ἐπί plus a dative case form. In *Bel.* 2,187 Josephus reports that, as Petronius marched against Judea, some of the Jews put no stock in the rumors of war while those who did believe were in no position to defend themselves.[28] Ἐπί plus the dative is directly employed with the verb ἀπιστεῖν and only indirectly with πιστεύειν. Nevertheless, the clear inference is that those who were believing (οἱ πιστεύοντες) were believing ἐπὶ ταῖς φήμαις.

Six times in Josephus the reason or basis for believing or trusting is expressed by the construction πιστεύειν διά plus the accusative case

---

Classical Library). While this translation does bring out the sense of the passage, it ambiguously bypasses any concrete understanding of the relationship between verb and object, between ἐπίστευον and ἅλωσιν. As a translation expressing more clearly these relationships, I would propose the following: "only as they were being taken captive did they begin to realize (the reality of) the conquest".

25 οὐ γὰρ εἶναι δίκαιον οὐδὲ πιστεύειν τὰ τοιαῦτα.

26 πεπιστευκὼς τοῦ θεοῦ τὸ ἐπ' αὐτοῖς ἀποφανούμενον.

27 οὐ γὰρ εἶναι φιλίαν τὴν μὴ πάντα πιστεύουσαν. It is possible that the accusative πάντα is functioning adverbially and that πιστεύειν is to be understood in an absolute sense; i.e., "there is no friendship which does not trust *completely*". This adverbial idea is reflected in the *Loeb Classical Library* translation: "for there is no friendship without absolute confidence". An important NT parallel to this appears in 1 Cor. 13,7: [ἡ ἀγάπη] πάντα στέγει, πάντα πιστεύει, πάντα ἐλπίζει, πάντα ὑπομένει.

28 οἱ μὲν ἠπίστουν ἐπὶ ταῖς τοῦ πολέμου φήμαις, οἱ δὲ πιστεύοντες ἦσαν ἐν ἀμηχάνῳ πρὸς τὴν ἄμυναν.

form[29] or by πιστεύειν ἐκ with the genitive case form.[30] *Bel.* 5,319. 455 have a clearly religious thrust and will be taken up again at a later point.

Πιστεύειν περί plus a genitive occurs eight times in Josephus. This construction commonly signals the idea of 'believing concerning or about something' which is said or heard[31] or written.[32] In *Ant.* 6,263 and 7,178 this construction appears together with a ὅτι clause and a ὡς clause respectively to give emphasis to the content of what is believed or held to be true.

1.24 Πιστεύειν with ὡς and ὅτι

There are eight instances where Josephus indicates the content of what is believed by employing the construction πιστεύειν ὡς or πιστεύειν ὅτι. He writes, for example, in *Ant.* 17,252: "[Sabinus] was confident that he would conquer [the Jews]",[33] and in *Ant.* 16,289: "[Syllaeus] would not have left his country if he had not believed that[34] Caesar was concerned that they should all be at peace with one another".[35]

1.25 Πιστεύειν with Indirect Discourse

A much more common way that Josephus indicates the actual content of what is believed or held to be true is through indirect discourse (accusative plus infinitive) governed by the verb πιστεύειν. This occurs quite frequently in his writings. The construction generally appears with an active form of πιστεύειν, as in *Bel.* 7,354: "So firm and certain have [the Indian people] believed the intercourse to be, which the souls have with one another".[36] This construction also appears in a few instances with πιστεύειν in the passive voice; e.g., *Ant.* 1,270: "...in order that [Jacob], because of the hairiness of the goatskin, might be believed by his father to be Esau".[37] In some passages the infinitive of this

---

29 *Ant.* 4,179; *Bel.* 5,455.
30 *Bel.* 5,319; *Ant.* 8,110; 10,267; 13,167.
31 *Bel.* 3,407; *Ant.* 3,317; 15,83.
32 *Ant.* 14,265. 267; *Vi.* 101.
33 πιστεύων ὡς καὶ περιέσοιτο αὐτῶν. Cf. *Bel.* 4,189; *Ant.* 7,178. 213.
34 μὴ πεπιστευκὼς ὅτι.
35 Cf. *Ant.* 6,263; 10,267; *Ap.* 2,218.
36 οὕτως βεβαίαν καὶ ἀληθεστάτην ταῖς ψυχαῖς τὴν μετ' ἀλλήλων εἶναι δίαιταν πεπιστεύκασιν. It is significant that Josephus employs the adjectives βεβαίαν καὶ ἀληθεστάτην, 'firm and certain (truthful)', both of which express important aspects of the Hebrew root אמן, in the direct context of πιστεύειν as religious belief.
37 ἵνα πιστεύοιτο παρὰ τῷ πατρὶ ... Ἡσαῦς εἶναι.

construction is lacking and εἶναι must be supplied.[38]   This use of
πιστεύειν is virtually synonymous to the meaning of νομίζειν (see
above, Chapter One) and is indicative of a trend in Hellenistic Greek to
use the verbs interchangeably to refer to intellectual belief.

1.26 Πιστεύειν Used Absolutely

Josephus frequently employs πιστεύειν in the absolute sense 'to believe,
to trust, to have faith'. A few examples will suffice for demonstration.
In *Bel.* 1,212 Josephus writes: "The king believed (i.e., the reports
about an impending attack from Herod) but was unable to do anything
about it".[39] Josephus reports in *Ant.* 12,395 that Judas, when he was
being deceitfully dealt with by Bacchides, did not trust[40] (i.e., did not
trust Bacchides).

It is obvious from these examples that an intransitive translation
of 'to believe, trust' is quite awkward. Indeed, in most of these absolute
uses of πιστεύειν the unnamed object is actually to be found in the
immediate preceding context. Grammatically, however, the verb appears
to be absolute and intransitive. It is not surprising therefore that one half
of all these absolute uses of πιστεύειν occur with the verb in the *passive
voice*; i.e., someone or something is believed, trusted.[41]   In a few
instances the passive occurs with the prepositions ὑπό or παρά signifying the agent.[42]

There are some instances, however, where πιστεύειν truly does
have an absolute sense. In *Ant.* 1,23; 3,203 the verb carries the religious
idea of having faith. Further, in *Bel.* 1,482; 7,444 we encounter the
idiom πιστεύειν ῥαδίως in the sense of 'quick to believe' or even
'gullible'. In *Ant.* 3,27 Moses provided grounds (for the Israelites) to
believe (about the manna).[43]

One rather curious use of πιστεύειν appears in *Ant.* 19,54 where
the text reads: ὁ δὲ χάρματι τοῦ λόγου μηδὲν μελλήσας ἠμείβετο
τοῦ Βινουκιανοῦ τὸ ἐπὶ τοιοῖσδε πιστεῦσαν ὁμιλίᾳ χρήσασθαι πρὸς
αὐτόν. Τὸ πιστεῦσαν appears in this passage as neuter aorist active

---

38   E.g., *Ant.* 17,312; 19,138.
39   πιστεύων δ' ὁ βασιλεὺς οὐκ εἶχεν ὅ τι χρὴ δρᾶν.
40   ὁ δ' οὐκ ἐπίστευσεν.
41   Cf. *Ap.* 2,239; *Bel.* 3,130; *Ant.* 10,114.
42   E.g., *Ant.* 13,402; 17,3. 55.
43   καὶ γευομένος τοῦτο αὐτοῖς παρεῖχε πιστεύειν. Cf. *Ant.* 6,289.

substantival participle. Feldman translates this substantival participle as
'trust',[44] making it synonymous with the substantive πίστις.

1.3 Πιστεύειν as to Entrust

Thus far we have seen a number of different syntactical uses of the verb
πιστεύειν, but the basic meaning of the term has remained the same: 'to
believe, to trust, to rely upon, etc'. The second definition given by
Liddell and Scott for πιστεύειν displays a shift in the focus of meaning.
Here the object of πιστεύειν always appears in the accusative case form
and is itself not the object of an act of trusting or believing, but the
object of the act of entrusting. We have shown in Chapter Five that the
noun πίστις in Josephus only occasionally means 'trust' in the sense of
'that which is entrusted'. In contrast to this, Josephus frequently employs
the verb πιστεύειν meaning 'to entrust' or 'to commit'.   This
understanding of πιστεύειν occurs in two different grammatical
constructions, one with an active form and one with a passive form of the
verb πιστεύειν.

1.31 The Active Construction: πιστεύειν τινί τι

The active construction always conveys the idea that someone (τίς)
entrusts (πιστεύει) something (τι) to someone (τινί). Generally this act
of entrusting occurs within a political, governmental or military context.
Among the various things which Josephus names as being entrusted are
the following: positions of power,[45] government,[46] administration,[47]
jurisdiction over a geographical region,[48] treasures and strong cities,[49] the
protection[50] of something, (the administration of) a war,[51] the siege of a
city[52] or even an assassination attempt.[53]

---

[44] *Loeb Classical Library.*
[45] δυναστείαι; *Ant.* 20, 74.
[46] ἀρχή; *Ant.* 20,63.
[47] πρόνοια; *Ant.* 2,104; cf. *Bel.* 4,492.
[48] E.g., ἡ ἀνατολή; *Bel.* 3,3; *Ap.* 2,49.
[49] *Ant.* 8,250.
[50] φυλακή; *Bel.* 4,274; *Ant.* 13,417; cf. *Vi.* 319.
[51] πόλεμον; *Ant.* 7,219.
[52] πολιορκία; *Ant.* 10,135.
[53] [ἐπιχειρήσεως], ἣν μόνοις ἐκείνοις ἐπίστευσε; *Ant.* 9,52.

The idea of entrusting one's own life to someone else is expressed by the formula πιστεύειν τινί with the direct objects σῶμα,[54] αὐτόν,[55] τὸ ζῆν,[56] and σωτηρίαν.[57] There are many more things which are entrusted; e.g., the task of rebuilding city walls,[58] the authority of the high priest over the other priests,[59] the high priesthood itself[60] and the position of a private secretary.[61]

In *Ant.* 4,285 πιστεύειν occurs as the absolute, participial substantive τὸν πεπιστευκότα: 'the entruster'. While there is no grammatical direct or indirect object for this participial form of πιστεύειν, it is clear from the immediate context both what has been entrusted[62] and to whom it has been entrusted.[63]

1.32 The Passive Construction: πιστεύεσθαί τι

Even more frequently than the active construction Josephus employs the passive construction πιστεύεσθαί τι: 'to be entrusted with something'. There is only a shift of emphasis in this construction, with the recipient of the act of entrusting becoming the subject of the verb rather than the indirect object. Occasionally the agent is indicated by the preposition παρά[64] or by ὑπό.[65] In general, the kinds of things which are entrusted are the same as noted above in the active construction.

Of particular interest are two instances where this passive idea of 'being entrusted with' occurs in an absolute sense. In *Ant.* 4,287 ὁ πιστευθείς is a legal term denoting the 'depositary', i.e., the one who has been entrusted with something. What has been entrusted to this person is again clear from the context of the passage. Even more interesting is the participial substantive πεπιστευμένα in *Ant.* 17,158. Literally, this can be translated: 'the things which have been entrusted, the charges, the stewardships'. In this context πεπιστευμένα would be synonymous with

---

54 *Bel.* 1,627.
55 *Ant.* 1,250; cf. 12,396.
56 *Ant.* 9,212.
57 *Bel.* 7,288; *Ant.* 10,167.
58 τὸ τεῖχος ἀνοικοδομῆσαι τῆς πατρίδος; *Bel.* 2,590.
59 *Ap.* 2,185.
60 *Ant.* 20,249.
61 *Vi.* 356.
62 παρακαταθήκη.
63 ὁ παραλαβών.
64 *Bel.* 1,667; *Vi.* 72.
65 *Bel.* 2,309; 5,534; *Ant.* 20,222; *Vi.* 86. 393.

the substantive πίστις[66] when it occurs in the sense of 'that which is entrusted'.

2 RELIGIOUS USE OF ΠΙΣΤΕΥΕΙΝ IN JOSEPHUS

Josephus tends to employ the verb πιστεύειν with religious significance more frequently than the substantive πίστις. His religious understanding of πιστεύειν is almost exclusively[67] that which we have seen as the first major category in Liddell and Scott; i.e., πιστεύειν as 'to believe, trust, put faith in, rely upon'. This religious sense of πιστεύειν appears in almost all the basic syntactical constructions we have considered above in Josephus' general use of πιστεύειν.

The religious uses of πιστεύειν themselves may be subdivided according to the following categories and contexts:
1. πιστεύειν in general creedal formulas
2. πιστεύειν in the context of faith in God
3. πιστεύειν in the context of the person and work of Moses
4. πιστεύειν in the context of the OT prophets
5. πιστεύειν in the context of signs and wonders
6. πιστεύειν in the context of other 'holy persons'
7. πιστεύειν in the context of holy writings

2.1 Πιστεύειν in General Creedal Formulas

Πιστεύειν ὅτι... and πιστεύειν governing indirect discourse commonly appear in Josephus as religious creedal formulas, denoting the content of what is believed. The following creedal statement appears in *Ap.* 2,218: "...but each individual, having a conscience testifying in himself, has believed ... that[68] for those who have kept the laws, and, if it is necessary to die for them, if they have died willingly, to them God has given a new existence and reception of a better life...".[69] The same construction appears in *Ant.* 6,263, where Josephus, in reflecting upon the change in character of King Saul, makes a general creedal statement about God: "...and concerning the Deity, [men] have believed that[70] he is present in

---

[66] Plural, πίστεις.
[67] Πιστεύειν as 'to entrust' is primarily a neutral concept without any religious significance.
[68] πεπίστευκεν ...ὅτι.
[69] This expectation of the 'better life' is different from the 'good life' which Philo connects with faith in God. This 'good life' in Josephus is clearly an eschatological expectation to be realized in 'the revolution of the ages' (ἐκ περιτροπῆς).
[70] περὶ τοῦ θείου πεπιστεύκασιν ὅτι...

all that happens in life and that he not only sees the deeds which are done, but moreover, that he knows beforehand the thoughts from which these deeds come about". This observation is not found in the biblical account of Saul's accession to kingship.[71] It is Josephus' own creedal observation concerning the omnipresence, the omniscience and the foreknowledge of God.

It is interesting here that Josephus uses the more abstract term τὸ θεῖον, 'the divinity', rather than θεός. Also interesting is the fact that the formula πιστεύειν ὅτι is modified further with the preposition περί. On the one hand this περὶ τοῦ θείου is purely superfluous; it is clearly understood from the following creedal statement that a religious belief concerning God is being set forth. On the other hand, the express statement that it is a belief about the Deity makes clear that this is purely a creedal statement and nothing more; i.e., the emphasis here is not upon the *Verbindlichkeit* of faith but upon the *Unverbindlichkeit*.

In a related passage (*Ant.* 4,60) Josephus uses πιστεύειν with the indirect discourse in reporting that the Israelites believed that nothing happens apart from the foreknowledge of God.[72] This passage shows very clearly the *Unverbindlichkeit* of this kind of faith. Although the Israelites believed in God's providence, yet they continued in their sedition against Moses (cf. Num. 16,41 LXX). There is, however, evidence that Josephus himself viewed such creedal statements about God as binding upon the actions of the believers as well. In *Ap.* 2,160 he writes: "Those who believed (have come to believe) that God watches over their lives do not in any way tolerate sin".[73]

2.2 Πιστεύειν *in the Context of Faith in God*

Whereas the creedal formulas πιστεύειν ὅτι and πιστεύειν with indirect discourse express a belief *about* God, θεός also appears often as the dative object of πιστεύειν with the express idea of faith or belief *in* God. Josephus reports in *Ant.* 4,5 that the Israelites, directly after they had disobeyed and had been dissuaded by the reports of the ten spies from going and taking the promised land, changed their minds and thought that they, through faith in God,[74] could still go up and possess the land which had been promised them. This they attempted in spite of Moses'

---

[71] Indeed this kind of creedal statement is itself foreign to the biblical material.
[72] πεπιστευκότες ἤδη μηδὲν γίνεσθαι δίχα τῆς τοῦ θεοῦ προνοίας.
[73] οἱ γὰρ πιστεύσαντες ἐπισκοπεῖν θεὸν τοὺς βίους οὐθὲν ἀνέχονται ἐξαμαρτεῖν.
[74] τῷ θεῷ πιστεύσαντες.

warnings to the contrary.[75]   Similarly in *Ant.* 3,44 Moses encouraged the
Israelites to take heart, "…having believed in the decree of God, by which
they, being roused toward freedom, would utterly conquer those who
withstood them in battle because of this decree".[76]

Πιστεύειν θεῷ is modified in *Ant.* 2,117 by the preposition περί
plus a genitive.   In this passage Josephus relates the preparations of
Jacob's sons to return to Egypt to secure supplies of food.[77] At length
Judah con vinced his father to send Benjamin along (this was the
requirement of their brother Joseph in Egypt whom they did not yet
recognize) by urging Jacob "to trust God concerning [Benjamin] and also
to trust [Judah], that he would bring Benjamin back safely even at the
expense of his own life".[78]   In *Ant.* 8,279 there is a further instance
where this formula πιστεύειν τίνι περί τινος occurs in a religious sense.
Josephus reports here of Abijah's protest to Jereboam's invasion of
Judah.[79] Abijah asks rhetorically: "…in what have you placed your trust
to secure victory? in golden calves and in altars on the mountain tops,
which are proofs of your ungodliness rather than of religious worship?"[80]
Obviously the implication and the accusation in this passage is that
Jereboam was trusting in false gods. Abijah proceeds to point out to him
that the only sure hope of victory over one's adversaries lies in righteous
reverence toward God alone.[81]

In three instances Josephus employs epithets for God in referring
to the placing of faith in God upon the basis of God's help or leadership
or care. In *Ant.* 2,333 he reports that Moses exhorted the Israelites not to

---

75 Cf. *Ant.* 5,37: πιστεύοντας γὰρ ἤδη τῆς γῆς ἐγκρατεῖς εἶναι καὶ σῶον ἕξειν ἐν ταῖς μάχ-
αις τὸν στρατὸν οὕτως τοῦ θεοῦ προϋπεσχημένου, τεθαρρηκότας παραδόξως ἑώρων τοὺς
πολεμίους. In this passage πιστεύειν is referring to the content of what is believed, but this
belief is based upon the earlier promises of God; hence this is an indirect reference to faith in God.

76 παραμυθίας οὖν ὁ Μωυσῆς ἤρχετο καὶ θαρρεῖν παρεκάλει τῇ τοῦ θεοῦ ψήφῳ πεπιστευκότας, ὑφ' ἧς εἰς τὴν ἐλευθερίαν ἡρμένοι κατανικήσειαν τοὺς περὶ αὐτῆς εἰς μάχην
αὐτοῖς καθισταμένους.

77 Cf. Gen. 42,29ff.

78 πιστεῦσαι δὲ περὶ αὐτοῦ τῷ θεῷ παραινοῦντος καὶ αὐτῷ, ὡς ἢ σῶον ἐπανάξοντος αὐτῷ
τὸν υἱὸν ἢ συγκαταστρέψοντος ἅμα ἐκείνῳ τὸν βίον. There is no direct parallel to the use of
πιστεύειν in the context of this narrative in Genesis.

79 Cf. 2 Chr. 13,4.

80 τίνι καὶ πεπιστευκὼς περὶ τῆς νίκης; ἢ ταῖς χρυσαῖς δαμάλεσι καὶ τοῖς ἐπὶ τῶν ὀρῶν
βωμοῖς, ἃ δείγματα τῆς ἀσεβείας ἐστὶν ὑμῶν ἀλλ' οὐχὶ τῆς θρησκείας;

81 *Ant.* 8,280: ἐν γὰρ μόνῳ τῷ δικαίῳ καὶ πρὸς τὸ θεῖον εὐσεβεῖ τὴν βεβαιοτάτην ἐλπίδα
τοῦ κρατεῖν τῶν ἐναντίων ἀποκεῖσθαι συμβέβηκεν. In the biblical account this τίνι πεπιστευκώς has no parallel with reference to Jereboam's misplaced trust. However, in 2 Chr. 13,18
Judah's victory over Jereboam is attributed to the following: ὅτι ἤλπισαν ἐπὶ κύριον θεὸν τῶν
πατέρων αὐτῶν. Here is a hint of what we have already seen in Sirach and in Philo; i.e., faith
or trust placed in anyone or anything other than God is misplaced faith. This is a further
departure of Josephus from OT faith terminology. The Hebrew root אמן never appears in
connection with faith in an idol.

fear the military forces of the Egyptians since their "trust is in such a
[great] helper who has the power to make small things great...".[82]
Similarly in *Ant.* 3,309 Joshua and Caleb tried to encourage the reluctant
Israelites to take possession of the promised land and to march forward
into war without reservation or suspicion, but "by faith in God, our
[political] leader".[83] In a more personal passage in *Bel.* 3,387 Josephus
relates that when he was in peril of his life he did not despair, "but rather,
trusting in the caring God", he ran the risk of his own life.[84]

In *Ant.* 3,203 πιστεύειν is used absolutely. It is clear from the
context, however, that faith in God is assumed. Speaking of God's
selfmanifestation in the sanctuary, Josephus says that God's presence was
made clearly manifest "both to those who were desiring [it] and to those
who had believed".[85]

Josephus employs πιστεύειν in *Ant.* 18,211 within the context of
pagan religion. He reports that Tiberius prayed to his national gods[86] for
some sign concerning his successor to the throne. He was personally eager to leave the kingdom to his grandson, "but more than his own
personal opinion and desire, he put his trust in the revelation of [the] God
concerning these matters".[87] Here it deserves notice that the verb
πιστεύειν appears with an accusative case form.

In almost all of the instances cited, with the exception of *Ant.*
3,203. 204, the formula πιστεύειν θεῷ should be understood as a basic
trusting in God. Trusting in God is, in turn, a prerequisite to further
courses of action taken or to be taken. This is obvious, for example, in
the phrase πιστεύοντες ἤδη, "already believing themselves to be
conquerors",[88] or by the perfect participle πεπιστευκότες, 'having
trusted'.[89] Trust in God is not simply a prerequisite for further action

[82] ὅθεν τοιούτῳ βοηθῷ πεπιστευκότες, ᾧ δύναμις καὶ τὰ μικρὰ ποιῆσαι μεγάλα καὶ τῶν τη-
λικούτων ἀσθένειαν καταψηφίσασθαι, μὴ καταπέπληχθε τὴν Αἰγυπτίων παρασκευήν, μηδ'
ὅτι θάλασσα καὶ κατόπιν ὑμῖν ὄρη φυγῆς ὁδὸν οὐ παρέχοντα διὰ τοῦτ' ἀπογινώσκετε τὴν
σωτηρίαν.
[83] ἴωμεν οὖν," ἔφασαν, "ἐπὶ τοὺς πολεμίους μηδὲν ἔχοντες δι' ὑποψίας ἡγεμόνι τε τῷ θεῷ
πεπιστευκότες καὶ ὁδηγοῦσιν ἡμῖν ἑπόμενοι'.
[84] Ὁ δ' ἐν ταῖς ἀμηχανίαις οὐκ ἠπόρησεν ἐπινοίας, ἀλλὰ πιστεύων τῷ κηδεμόνι θεῷ τὴν
σωτηρίαν παραβάλλεται.
[85] ἡδεῖα δὲ ἀπ' αὐτοῦ δρόσος ἔρρει καὶ θεοῦ δηλοῦσα παρουσίαν τοῖς τοῦτο καὶ βουλομένοις
καὶ πεπιστευκόσι. There are no exact parallels in the LXX to this historical material which
make similar use of πιστεύειν.
[86] εὔχεται τοῖς πατρίοις θεοῖς; cf. Acts 24,14: ὁμολογῶ δὲ τοῦτό σοι ὅτι κατὰ τὴν ὁδὸν ἣν
λέγουσιν αἵρεσιν, οὕτως λατρεύω τῷ πατρῴῳ θεῷ πιστεύων πᾶσι τοῖς κατὰ τὸν νόμον
καὶ τοῖς ἐν τοῖς προφήταις γεγραμμένοις.
[87] μεῖζον δὲ δόξης τε καὶ βουλήσεως τῆς αὐτοῦ πεπιστευκὼς τοῦ θεοῦ τὸ ἐπ' αὐτοῖς ἀποφανούμενον.
[88] *Ant.* 5,37.
[89] *Ant.* 2,333; 3,309; cf. 3,44; 20,48.

according to God's will but, even more, it implies a certain imperative[90] for further action according to God's will. This is particularly clear in *Ant.* 2,333 and 3,309 where, in the first instance, Moses, and in the second instance, Joshua and Caleb, challenge the Israelites to act faithfully *because* of their trust in God. In this understanding of the verb Josephus remains true to the OT concept of faith.

In *Ant.* 20,48 and 3,203, on the other hand, the idea of believing or trusting in God results in a passive benefit for the believer rather than requiring an active response. In one case it was the believer who was privileged to experience the manifestation of God in the sanctuary; in the other instance the reward for the believers is that the fruit of their godliness does not perish when they die.

2.3 Πιστεύειν in the Context of the Person and Work of Moses

In Josephus' reports about Moses the great Jewish lawgiver in *Ant.* and *Ap.*, the verb πιστεύειν always carries some religious significance. In one reference πιστεύειν occurs in connection with the father of Moses, who, while Moses was still an infant, chose to place the responsibility for the child's salvation and safety upon God in an act of trust in God's providence rather than in his own efforts to conceal the baby from Pharaoh's henchmen.[91] Interesting in this instance is that the (dative) infinitive τῷ λήσεσθαι acts as the object of the active participial form πεπιστευκώς.

Ant. 2,276 is the only instance where Moses personally is the subject of the active verb πιστεύειν. Because God performed signs through and for Moses and because whatever Moses asked of God was granted, Moses believed that he would obtain God as a gracious helper in the future.[92] It was, in turn, this firm belief of Moses which stood as the basis for his hope that he would bring salvation to his own kinsmen and bring ruin upon the Egyptians. In this one carefully constructed sentence Josephus links together three important theological terms: signs, faith, and hope.[93] Divine signs provide the basis for firm trust or confidence in

---

90 *Verbindlichkeit!*
91 *Ant.* 2,219: ἔπειτα δὲ δείσας 'Αμαράμης, μὴ κατάφωρος γένηται καὶ πεσὼν ὑπὸ τὴν τοῦ βασιλέως ὀργὴν αὐτός τε ἀπόληται μετὰ τοῦ παιδίου καὶ τοῦ θεοῦ τὴν ἐπαγγελίαν ἀφανίσειεν, ἔγνω μᾶλλον ἐπὶ τούτῳ ποιήσασθαι τὴν τοῦ παιδὸς σωτηρίαν καὶ πρόνοιαν ἢ τῷ λήσεσθαι πεπιστευκώς, τοῦτο δ' ἦν ἄδηλον, ἐναποκινδυνεύειν οὐ τῷ παιδὶ μόνον κρυφαίως τρεφομένῳ ἀλλὰ καὶ αὐτῷ.
92 Μωυσεῖ μέντοι τὰ σημεῖα ταῦτα οὐ τότε μόνον, διὰ παντὸς δὲ ὁπότε δεηθείη συνετύγχανεν· ἐξ ὧν ἁπάντων πλέον περὶ τῆς ἀληθείας τῷ πυρὶ νέμων καὶ τὸν θεὸν εὐμενῆ παραστάτην ἕξειν πιστεύων τούς τε οἰκείους σώσειν ἤλπιζε καὶ τοὺς Αἰγυπτίους κακοῖς περιβαλεῖν.
93 Cf. the role of the signs and wonders (אותת = σημεῖα) which Moses performed in Egypt (Ex. 4,7).

God, which is the basis for hope of a positive outcome in the future. It is probably significant that both verbs πιστεύειν and ἐλπίζειν appear together in this context since πιστεύειν ὅτι expresses here only the content of what is believed;[94] ἐλπίζειν adds to this the idea of *Verbindlichkeit*.

In *Ant.* 3,27 Moses is an example and an agent of faith for the Israelites as they were confused about the initial appearance of the manna in the wilderness. According to Josephus, the Israelites thought that the manna was snow. Moses attempted to convince them that this was for their salvation and for their nourishment. By tasting of the manna himself he brought about 'belief' in the hearts of the Israelites.[95] Πιστεύειν in this instance is employed absolutely.[96] Πιστεύειν appears with an accusative object in *Ant.* 1,23 where Moses is portrayed as the punisher of those (Israelites) who neither took heed of nor believed in [his teachings about God].[97]

Moses is not only an agent of faith but also an object of faith. In *Ant.* 2,274 God explicitly instructs Moses to make use of the divine signs given to him so that he will be believed by all.[98] Important in this passage is the fact that the signs were not meant to bring about some general sense of credibility about Moses personally; rather the belief in Moses was specifically the *belief that* he, being sent by God, was performing all of these things in accordance with God's commands. This is parallel to the tradition about Moses in Ex. 4,5-8.

Josephus records further the words of Moses in his farewell address to the Israelites: "I am worthy to be believed (or trusted) because of my former ambitions on your behalf and because people, when they come to the end of their lives conduct themselves with all virtue in relation to

---

[94] I.e., *Unverbindlichkeit*.

[95] ἀνεδίδασκεν οὐ κατὰ τὴν ἐκείνων ὑπόληψιν ἀπ' οὐρανοῦ καταφέρεσθαι τὴν δρόσον, ἀλλ' ἐπὶ σωτηρίᾳ τῇ αὐτῶν καὶ διατροφῇ, καὶ γευόμενος [variant reading of γευομένοις] τοῦτο αὐτοῖς παρεῖχε πιστεύειν.

[96] It is difficult to say what kind of faith is being expressed here: whether the Israelites simply *believed that* (πιστεύειν ὅτι) the manna was for their nourishment and salvation or whether they *believed in* or *trusted in* (πιστεύειν τῷ...) God and Moses. The former interpretation is probably correct.

[97] ὁ δ' ἡμέτερος νομοθέτης ἀκραιφνῆ τὴν ἀρετὴν ἔχοντα τὸν θεὸν ἀποφήνας ᾠήθη δεῖν τοὺς ἀνθρώπους ἐκείνης πειρᾶσθαι μεταλαμβάνειν καὶ τοὺς μὴ ταῦτα φρονοῦντας μηδὲ μὴν πιστεύοντας ἀπαραιτήτως ἐκόλασε. The accusative object ταῦτα is obviously dependent upon the verb φρονεῖν rather than πιστεύειν. Concerning the idea of punishing or chiding someone because of his or her unbelief, cf. Mk. 16,14 where Jesus chides his disciples for not having believed the eye witnesses of his resurrection: Ὕστερον [δὲ] ἀνακειμένοις αὐτοῖς τοῖς ἕνδεκα ἐφανερώθη καὶ ὠνείδισεν τὴν ἀπιστίαν αὐτῶν καὶ σκληροκαρδίαν ὅτι τοῖς θεασαμένοις αὐτὸν ἐγηγερμένον οὐκ ἐπίστευσαν.

[98] θαυμάζοντα δ' ἐπὶ τούτοις θαρρεῖν παρεκελεύετο καὶ βοηθὸν εἰδέναι μέγιστον αὐτῷ συνεσόμενον καὶ σημείοις πρὸς τὸ πιστεύεσθαι παρὰ πᾶσι χρῆσθαι, "ὅτι πεμφθεὶς ὑπ' ἐμοῦ πάντα κατὰ τὰς ἐμὰς ἐντολὰς ποιεῖς".

others".[99] These are admittedly not strictly religious reasons which
Moses gives as to why he is worthy of the Israelites' faith. Nevertheless
the fact remains that Moses counts himself a worthy object of faith.
More important, since these words of Moses seem to be an interpretation
of Josephus (there is no exact parallel to this use of πιστεύειν in the
narrative of Deuteronomy), this passage shows that Josephus himself
regards Moses as worthy of trust, faith, belief.

    Ant. 3,317 records a summary comment about Moses, that he was
a man admirable in virtue and might, with the end result that he was
believed in everything that he said.[100] This was not simply the case
during Moses' lifetime, says Josephus, but is true even unto today. In
this passage Josephus regards Moses as an object of faith in particular
because of *what Moses said*. This idea recurs in *Ap.* 2,286. Earlier in
2,239 Josephus relates how the Greek sophists found fault with even the
most trusted of the lawgivers[101] because of the ideas about the gods
which they were sowing among the masses. In *Ap.* 2,286 the lawgiver is
Moses, and Josephus includes himself among those who honor their own
Lawgiver and who have believed in the prophecies by him concerning
God.[102] This latter passage shows the importance of faith in connection
with Moses. By including himself as a believer,[103] Josephus confesses
that he views Moses as a prophet of God. It is especially upon the basis
of Moses' prophetic function that he is viewed as an object of religious
faith.

2.4 *Πιστεύειν in the Context of the OT Prophets*

In *Ant.* 8 - 11, where Josephus relates the history of Israel during the
time of the prophets, πιστεύειν appears frequently in connection with the
prophets of God. Among the prophets named by Josephus in connection
with πιστεύειν are Jadon, [104] Jazielos,[105] Elisha,[106] Jonah,[107] Isaiah,[108]

---

[99] *Ant.* 4,179: πιστεύεσθαι δὲ ἄξιός εἰμι διά τε τὰς πρότερον ὑπὲρ ὑμῶν φιλοτιμίας καὶ διὰ τὸ τὰς ψυχὰς ἐπὶ τελευτῇ γιγνομένας μετ' ἀρετῆς πάσης ὁμιλεῖν.

[100] Θαυμαστὸς δὲ τῆς ἀρετῆς ὁ ἀνὴρ καὶ τῆς ἰσχύος τῆς τοῦ πιστεύεσθαι περὶ ὧν ἂν εἴπειεν οὐ παρ' ὃν ἔζη χρόνον ὑπῆρξε μόνον, ἀλλὰ καὶ νῦν.

[101] τοῖςπεπιστευμένοις.

[102] οὐδὲ γὰρ ἐπιφθόνου τινὸς ἀντιποιούμεθα πράγματος τὸν αὐτῶν τιμῶντες νομοθέτην καὶ τοῖς ὑπ' ἐκείνου προφητευθεῖσι περὶ τοῦ θεοῦ πεπιστευκότες.

[103] The first person plural verb ἀντιποιούμεθα governs the participles which follow.

[104] *Ant.* 8,232; cf. 1 Ki. 13,1ff.

[105] *Ant.* 9,12; cf. Jahazael the Levite in 2 Chr. 20,14.

[106] *Ant.* 9,72. 86.

[107] *Ant.* 9,212.

[108] *Ant.* 10,28.

the unnamed prophets sent to Manasseh,[109] Jeremiah,[110] Daniel,[111] the
prophets Haggai and Zechariah[112] and David (whom Josephus regards as a
prophet).[113] With the exception of the reference to Jonah in *Ant.* 9,212
as "a man who had entrusted his life to [the sailors on the ship]",[114] all of
these occurrences of πιστεύειν are religiously significant.   In most
instances it is either the prophets themselves[115] or the messages spoken
by these prophets[116] which are believed or not believed. Indeed it is
impossible, for the most part, to distinguish between the prophet and the
message of the prophet as the object of πιστεύειν.[117]

In the passages where Daniel is mentioned in the context of faith
the emphasis is upon the content of what is believed.   Πιστεύειν
expresses a belief—even an opinion—concerning Daniel himself. The
creedal formula is quite obvious in *Ant.* 10,267: "We have believed
[from his writings] that Daniel used to converse with God".[118] In *Ant.*
10,250 Daniel is believed to possess in himself 'the Divine'.[119]

In this latter instance there is a passive form of πιστεύειν rather
than an active form.   Quite similar to the previously noted use of
πιστεύειν in the passive, referring to faith in Moses, is a statement
about Jeremiah in *Ant.* 10,114. Josephus writes that Jeremiah, after fore-
telling the fall of Jerusalem, was believed by the majority of the people
but ridiculed by the leaders and the impious men.[120] Similarly in *Ant.*
10,124 Jeremiah, when consulted secretly by king Zedekiah for counsel
from God, replied that he indeed had something to say, but he knew he
would not be believed if he said it.[121]

In contrast to the use of πιστεύειν in the context of faith in
Moses, where the passive voice of the verb dominates the usage, the

---

[109] *Ant.* 10,39; cf. 2 Ki. 21,10.
[110] *Ant.* 10,104. 105. 114. 119. 124. 178.
[111] *Ant.* 10,250. 267.
[112] *Ant.* 11,96.
[113] *Ant.* 8,110.
[114] οἱ δὲ τὸ μὲν πρῶτον οὐκ ἐτόλμων, κρίναντες ἀσέβημα εἶναι ξένον ἄνθρωπον καὶ πεπιστευκότα αὐτοῖς τὸ ζῆν εἰς φανερὰν οὕτως ἀπώλειαν ἐκρῖψαι.
[115] *Ant.* 9,72; 10,28. 105. 114. 124. 178; 11,96.
[116] *Ant.* 8,232; 9,12. 86; 10,39.
[117] Cf. Isa. 53,1: "Who has believed our message?"
[118] πεπιστεύκαμεν ἐξ αὐτῶν ὅτι Δανίηλος ὡμίλει τῷ θεῷ.
[119] ὡς ἂν ἔχων τὸ θεῖον πεπιστευμένος ἐν αὐτῷ.
[120] ταῦτα λέγων ὁ Ἱερεμίας ὑπὸ μὲν τῶν πλειόνων ἐπιστεύετο, οἱ δὲ ἡγεμόνες καὶ οἱ ἀσεβεῖς
ὡς ἐξεστηκότα τῶν φρενῶν αὐτὸν οὕτως ἐξεφαύλιζον.
[121] μεταπεμψαμένου δ' αὐτὸν κρύφα τοῦ βασιλέως καὶ τί δύναται φράζειν αὐτῷ παρὰ τοῦ
θεοῦ καὶ πρὸς τὰ παρόντα σημαίνειν ἐρομένου, ἔχειν μὲν ἔλεγεν, οὐ πιστευθήσεσθαι δ'
εἰπὼν οὐδὲ παραινέσας ἀκουσθήσεσθαι. For the use of πιστεύειν in the passive cf. also *Ant.*
10,178.

active voice of the verb dominates usage in connection with faith in the prophets. Outside of the four instances just mentioned, every other reference by Josephus to faith in the prophets employs an active form of πιστεύειν, generally followed by a dative case form. In *Ant.* 10,104, for instance, Jeremiah warns Zedekiah not to believe the false prophets and their deceitful message.[122]

Sometimes the faith or trust that was (or was not) directed toward the prophets of God concerns matters of prophetic counsel in which God indicated through the prophet a course of action which should or should not be pursued. In *Ant.* 9,12 Jehoshaphat instructs the people to trust in the words of the prophet Jazielos. They are not to draw themselves up for battle against the Ammonites but to wait upon the Lord's provision of salvation.[123] Similarly in *Ant.* 11,96 the people returning from the Exile trusted (the counsel of) the prophets Haggai and Zechariah and continued steadfastly in the rebuilding of Jerusalem.[124] In each of these instances the faith or the trust in the prophetic utterances had a direct effect upon the actions of those who believed.[125] This kind of faith, true to the OT tradition, involved personal commitment to the prophetic utterances.

Faith in the prophets can indicate belief in the predictive utterances of the prophets as well as belief in sayings of prophetic counsel. In *Ant.* 9,72, for example, Joram believes the prophet Elisha who predicted that there would be a great abundance of food in Jerusalem on the very next day, even though the people were presently starving and there was no concrete basis for such hope. Joram believed this, having been convinced of Elisha's truthfulness by earlier experiences.[126] Again in this instance the action of the verb πιστεύειν must be understood not simply as an intellectual assent to the validity of a statement but, even more, as a confident and faithful reliance upon the truth of the prophetic message.[127]

---

[122] διὸ καὶ ὁ προφήτης Ἰερεμίας πρὸς αὐτὸν ἐλθὼν πολλάκις ἐμαρτύρατο, κελεύων ... προσανέχειν μήτε τοῖς ψευδοπροφήταις ἀπατῶσιν αὐτὸν πεπιστευκέναι, ὡς οὐκέτι πολεμήσει τὴν πόλιν ὁ Βαβυλώνιος καὶ ὡς Αἰγύπτιοι στρατεύσουσιν ἐπ᾽ αὐτὸν καὶ νικήσουσι· ταῦτα γὰρ οὐκ ἀληθῆ λέγειν οὐδ᾽ οὕτως ὀφείλοντα γενέσθαι. This passage clearly places a distinct emphasis upon the content of what is believed as marked by the double occurrence of ὡς.

[123] Ἅμα δ᾽ ἡμέρᾳ προελθὼν ὁ βασιλεὺς εἰς τὴν ἔρημον τὴν ὑποκάτω Θεκώας πόλεως ἔλεγε πρὸς τὸ πλῆθος, ὡς δεῖ πιστεύειν τοῖς ὑπὸ τοῦ προφήτου εἰρημένοις καὶ μὴ παρατάσσεσθαι μὲν αὐτοὺς εἰς μάχην, προστησαμένους δὲ τοὺς ἱερεῖς μετὰ τῶν σαλπίγγων καὶ Ληουίτας μετὰ τῶν ὑμνούντων εὐχαριστεῖν ὡς ἤδη ῥυσαμένῳ τὴν χώραν ἡμῶν παρὰ τῶν πολεμίων.

[124] πιστεύοντες δὲ τοῖς προφήταις ἐντεταμένως εἴχοντο τῆς οἰκοδομίας, μηδεμίαν ἡμέραν ἀνιέμενοι.

[125] Cf. *Ant.* 10,124. 178.

[126] πιστεύειν γὰρ τῷ προφήτῃ διὰ τὴν ἐπὶ τοῖς προπεπειραμένοις ἀλήθειαν οὐκ ὤκνουν.

[127] Cf. *Ant.* 9,86; also 10,39. 104. 105. 114. 119.

This further reflects the type of faith in God displayed by Abraham in Gen. 15,6. It is significant, however, that the faith of Abraham plays no role whatsoever in Josephus' use of the πιστ- word group!

Πιστεύειν appears once in *Ant.* 10,28f in connection with the healing of a disease. Isaiah had prophesied to king Hezekiah that he would be cured of his illness within three days and would live yet another fifteen years. Hezekiah did not believe Isaiah at once because of the severity of his disease and because the prophecy seemed to him to be so incredible. He requested that Isaiah perform some sign or portent, that he might believe confidently in Isaiah when he spoke these things as in one who came from God; "For", said Hezekiah, "things of an incredible nature and things beyond hope are *confirmed* by acts of a similar nature".[128] It is further significant that the king was immediately freed from his illness as soon as he *saw* the sign which was intended to produce faith.[129]

Sight or experience as the basis for belief is a thought also present in the absolute use of the verb πιστεύειν in *Ant.* 8,110. With regard to David's prophecy, Solomon urged the people not to doubt that any of the promised good fortunes would indeed come to pass; their faith in the certainty of these prophecies of David should arise from their already having seen the fulfillment of certain parts of this prophecy.[130] One other absolute usage of πιστεύειν occurs in *Ant.* 10,119, where the prophet Jeremiah and his message constitute the object of the rulers' unbelief.[131]

2.5 Πιστεύειν *in the Context of Signs and Wonders*

We have already seen instances in the context of faith in Moses and the OT prophets where signs and wonders[132] play a significant role in connection with faith. The fact that Moses was given signs in order to produce faith in himself[133] is firmly rooted in the tradition of Ex. 4,5. 8.

---

[128] Note the difference here between the verbs πιστεύειν and πιστοῦν: ταῦτα τοῦ προφήτου φήσαντος κατ᾽ ἐντολὴν τοῦ θεοῦ, διὰ τὴν ὑπερβολὴν τῆς νόσου καὶ τὸ παράδοξον τῶν ἀπηγγελμένων ἀπιστῶν σημεῖόν τι καὶ τεράστιον ἠξίου ποιῆσαι τὸν Ἡσαΐαν, ἵν᾽ αὐτῷ πιστεύσῃ λέγοντι ταῦτα ἥκοντι παρὰ τοῦ θεοῦ· τὰ γὰρ παράλογα καὶ μείζω τῆς ἐλπίδος τοῖς ὁμοίοις πιστοῦται πράγμασιν. Cf. also the sign of the prophet Jadon in *Ant.* 8,232: ἵνα μέντοι γε πιστεύσωσιν οὗτοι τοῦθ᾽ οὕτως ἕξειν, σημεῖον αὐτοῖς προερῶ γενησόμενον.

[129] *Ant.* 10,29.

[130] ἃ βλέποντας κατὰ τὴν ἐκείνου προφητείαν ἐπιτελῆ τὸν θεὸν εὐλογεῖν ἠξίου καὶ περὶ μηδενὸς ἀπογινώσκειν ὧν ὑπέσχηται πρὸς εὐδαιμονίαν ὡς οὐκ ἐσομένου, πιστεύοντας ἐκ τῶν ἤδη βλεπομένων.

[131] οὐδὲ ἐν αὐτοῖς δὲ ὄντες τοῖς δεινοῖς ἐπίστευον οἱ ταῦτ᾽ ἀκούοντες τῶν ἡγεμόνων. Note the use of the imperfect tense form!

[132] Normally σημεῖα, τέρατα.

[133] *Ant.* 2,273. 276.

9. 31.[134] Likewise Isaiah provided a sign[135] so that Hezekiah would believe his prophecy of the king's healing. According to *Ant.* 8,232 the prophet Jadon[136] gave Jereboam a sign[137] so that his prophecy against Jereboam would be believed.[138]

Reporting the history of the later Jewish war in *Bel.* 6,288, Josephus tells how the portents of the coming destruction upon Jerusalem, although they came from messengers of God, were not being taken seriously nor believed.[139] In *Ant.* 18,211, a pagan religious setting, Josephus reports that Tiberius asked of his national gods some sign[140] concerning the choice of his successor, because he trusted the oracle of the god with respect to this matter more than his own opinion or desire.[141]

Outside of Ex. 4 and Num. 14,11 one other very important OT passage linking the verb πιστεύειν with σημεῖον is Isa. 7,9-11ff. In this prophecy to Ahaz Isaiah adds a warning against unbelief: καὶ ἐὰν μὴ πιστεύσητε, οὐδὲ μὴ συνῆτε. In the following verses Ahaz is instructed to ask for a σημεῖον as a guarantee of the certainty of Isaiah's prophecy.[142]

2.6 *Πιστεύειν in the Context of Other 'Holy Persons'*

In addition to the OT prophets, Josephus employs πιστεύειν in connection with other 'holy persons'. In *Ant.* 3,308 Joshua and Caleb entreat the Israelites not to trust those who were frightening them with false reports about the Canaanites, but rather to trust them, who were rousing the people toward good fortune and toward the possession of good things.[143] *Ant.* 5,215 reports that Gideon was believed by some of the

---

[134] Cf. Num. 14,11.

[135] σημεῖον; *Ant.* 10,28; cf. 2 Ki. 20,8.

[136] The prophet is not mentioned by name in the biblical account.

[137] Josephus: σημεῖον; cf. 1 Ki. 13,3: τέρας.

[138] ἵνα πιστεύσωσιν οὗτοι τοῦθ' οὕτως ἕξειν; πιστεύειν does not appear in the LXX text of 1 Ki. 13,1ff.

[139] τοῖς δ' ἐναργέσι καὶ προσημαίνουσι τὴν μέλλουσαν ἐρημίαν τέρασιν οὔτε προσεῖχον οὔτ' ἐπίστευον.

[140] σημεῖόν τι.

[141] μεῖζον δὲ δόξης τε καὶ βουλήσεως τῆς αὑτοῦ πεπιστευκὼς τοῦ θεοῦ τὸ ἐπ' αὐτοῖς ἀποφανούμενον.

[142] Cf. Isaiah's sign to Hezekiah concerning his healing; *Ant.* 10,28; par. 2 Ki. 20,8.

[143] θαρσεῖν δεόμενοι καὶ μήτε ψευδολογίαν κατακρίνειν τοῦ θεοῦ μήτε πιστεύειν τοῖς ἐκ τοῦ μὴ τἀληθῆ περὶ τῶν Χαναναίων εἰρηκέναι καταπληξαμένοις, ἀλλὰ τοῖς ἐπὶ τὴν εὐδαιμονίαν καὶ τὴν κτῆσιν αὐτοὺς τῶν ἀγαθῶν παρορμῶσιν. In this passage is a hint of the utilitarian nature of faith which we have noted in Philo's concept of faith. Trust in Joshua and Caleb would lead toward the inheritance of good fortune and the possession of good things.

young men[144] after he had revealed God's instructions, and suddenly there
was an army of ten thousand ready for battle. In an unrelated passage in
Ant. 4,219 Josephus repeats the commandment from Dt. 17,6 and Dt.
19,15 that the testimony of a single witness is not to be trusted.[145] Four
times Josephus connects the action of the verb πιστεύειν with the person
or office of the [high] priest.[146] In all of these instances, however,
πιστεύειν carries the profane meaning 'to entrust'.[147]

In a more religious vein, πιστεύειν appears three times with reference to the Pharisees. In *Ant.* 17,43, concerning the ability of the
Pharisees to foretell the future, Josephus adds parenthetically that they
were entrusted with foreknowledge by periodic visits of God.[148] In *Ant.*
13,288 Josephus relates that the Pharisees had such an influence over the
masses that even when they spoke out against the king or against the
high priest they were immediately believed.[149]

In another isolated instance Josephus reports that Herod was
believed by all to be a 'friend of God' when the roof of his house fell in.
He and all who were with him in the house escaped physical harm in this
great and incredible disaster.[150] The holy city of Jerusalem is called "the
[city] which is believed by us to have God as her founder".[151] These
latter uses of πιστεύειν are much more characteristic of Hellenistic
Greek, lacking the element of personal commitment. For these
occurrences of πιστεύειν in connection with the Pharisees, Herod or
Jerusalem, there are no clear parallels in the OT or in the NT.

2.7 *Πιστεύειν in the Context of Holy Writings*

In three instances Josephus employs πιστεύειν in connection with the
writings[152] of the Greeks and the Phoenicians. Quite neutrally he writes
in *Ap.* 2,18: "If it is possible (or necessary) to believe the writings of

---

[144]   ὁ Γεδεὼν τισὶ τῶν νέων ἐπιστεύετο.

[145]   Εἷς δὲ μὴ πιστευέσθω μάρτυς, ἀλλὰ τρεῖς ἢ τὸ τελευταῖον δύο, ὧν τὴν μαρτυρίαν ἀληθῆ
        ποιήσει τὰ προβεβαιωμένα.   ...ἂν δέ τις ψευδομαρτυρήσας πιστευθῇ, πασχέτω ταῦτ'
        ἐλεγχθεὶς ὅσα ὁ καταμαρτυρηθεὶς πάσχειν ἔμελλεν.

[146]   *Ant.* 20,249. 251; *Ap.* 2,185. 188.

[147]   Cf. *Ant.* 17,158-59; also Rom. 3,2 where the Jews are entrusted with the word of God; cf. further,
        Tit. 1,3.

[148]   πρόγνωσιν δὲ ἐπεπίστευντο ἐπιφοιτήσει τοῦ θεοῦ.

[149]   τοσαύτην δὲ ἔχουσι τὴν ἰσχὺν παρὰ τῷ πλήθει ὡς καὶ κατὰ βασιλέως τι λέγοντες καὶ
        κατ' ἀρχιερέως εὐθὺς πιστεύεσθαι. Cf. *Ant.* 13,402.

[150]   *Ant.* 14,455: πίπτει μὲν γὰρ ἡ στέγη τοῦ οἰκήματος, οὐδένα δὲ ἀπολαβοῦσα διέφθειρεν,
        ὥστε πάντας πιστεῦσαι τὸν Ἡρώδην εἶναι θεοφιλῆ, μέγαν οὕτω καὶ παράδοξον
        διαφυγόντα κίνδυνον.

[151]   *Bel.* 7,376: ποῦ γέγονεν ἡμῖν ἡ τὸν θεὸν ἔχειν οἰκιστὴν πεπιστευμένη;

[152]   ἀναγραφαί.

the Phoenicians, it is recorded there that...".[153]   In *Ap.* 1,161 Josephus finds it necessary to answer the challenge of those who disbelieve all of the writings among the barbarians and who deem only the writings of the Greeks worthy of credibility.[154]   And in *Ap.* 1,14 Josephus points out that even the Greeks are skeptical about the authenticity of their oldest writings.[155]   In these three passages Josephus himself challenges the credibility and the reliability of the non-Jewish writings.

On the other hand, Josephus employs πιστεύειν much more positively with regard to the Jewish writings—particularly with regard to the Hebrew scriptures. In *Ant.* 10,267 Josephus states that the belief that Daniel conversed with God arose out of the books[156] that Daniel had written and left behind: πεπιστεύκαμεν ἐξ αὐτῶν ὅτι Δανίηλος ὡμίλει τῷ θεῷ.

In *Ap.* the belief of the Jewish people in their holy scriptures becomes an important theme for Josephus. In *Ap.* 1,38 he argues: "We do not have a myriad of books which are inharmonious and contradictory to one another; but rather there are only twenty-two books containing the record of all time, which are justly believed".[157]

In *Ap.* 2,233 Josephus speculates that the reason why Jews were constantly being persecuted was not because of hatred on the part of the persecutors; rather the persecutors were simply curious and fascinated to see if there were people who actually believed that the only evil that could come upon them would be if they were compelled to do something against their own laws or to speak a word against them.[158]

---

[153] εἰ γὰρ πιστεύειν δεῖ ταῖς Φοινίκων ἀναγραφαῖς, ἐν ἐκείναις Εἴρωμος ὁ βασιλεὺς γέγραπται πρεσβύτερος τῆς Καρχηδόνος κτίσεως ἔτρεσι πλείοσι πρὸς τοῖς πεντήκοντα καὶ ἑκατόν, περὶ οὗ τὰς πίστεις ἀνωτέρω παρέσχον ἐκ τῶν Φοινίκων ἀναγραφῶν.

[154] Δεῖ δ' ἄρα καὶ τῶν ἀπιστούντων μὲν ταῖς ἐν τοῖς βαρβάροις ἀναγραφαῖς μόνοις δὲ τοῖς Ἕλλησι πιστεύειν ἀξιούντων ἀποπληρῶσαι τὴν ἐπιζήτησιν.

[155] καὶ ταῦτα τοῖς Ἕλλησιν εἶναι δοκεῖ πάντων ἀρχαιότατα καὶ μόλις αὐτὰ πιστεύουσιν ὑπ' ἐκείνων γεγράφθαι.

[156] τὰ βιβλία.

[157] οὐ μυριάδες βιβλίων εἰσὶ παρ' ἡμῖν ἀσυμφώνων καὶ μαχομένων, δύο δὲ μόνα πρὸς τοῖς εἴκοσι βιβλία τοῦ παντὸς ἔχοντα χρόνου τὴν ἀναγραφήν, τὰ δικαίως πεπιστευμένα.

[158] ...ἀλλ' ὡς θαυμαστόν τι θέαμα βουλομένους ἰδεῖν, εἴ τινές εἰσιν ἄνθρωποι οἱ μόνον εἶναι κακὸν αὐτοῖς πεπιστευκότες, εἰ ἢ πράξαί τι παρὰ τοὺς ἑαυτῶν νόμους ἢ λόγον εἰπεῖν παρ' ἐκείνους παραβιασθεῖεν.

3 ΠΙΣΤΕΥΕΙΝ IN JOSEPHUS AND THE NEW TESTAMENT

3.1 Similarities in Use

3.11 Profane Use

The various profane meanings of πιστεύειν dominate the use of the verb
by Josephus. In the NT a profane understanding of πιστεύειν occurs in
only two senses: 1) 'to believe' (in the sense of intellectual assent); and
2) 'to entrust'.

Three times in the NT πιστεύειν means 'to believe in a general
fact or opinion'; i.e., to consider something to be true. In Jn. 9,18, for
instance, following the healing of the man who had been born blind, it is
reported: "The Jews did not believe that he had been blind and had
received his sight, until they called the parents of the man who had
received his sight".[159] This passage brings to mind Josephus' version of
the OT commandment in Dt. 17,6 and 19,15: Εἶς δὲ μὴ πιστευέσθω
μάρτυς.[160] Also noteworthy is Josephus' similar use of the construction: πιστεύειν περί [τινος] ὅτι/ὡς...[161]

Acts 9,26 reports similarly the reason why Paul was not readily
trusted by the Jerusalem disciples after his conversion: καὶ πάντες
ἐφοβοῦντο αὐτὸν μὴ πιστεύοντες ὅτι ἐστὶν μαθητής.[162] In this
instance even πιστεύειν in a profane sense implies a certain degree of
personal commitment, of *Verbindlichkeit*. The Jerusalem disciples'
[lack of] trust in Paul corresponds directly to their [lack of] belief that
Paul himself was truly a disciple.[163]

Paul also implements πιστεύειν once in 1 Cor. 11,18 in the
general profane sense: He considers a report he had heard about the
Corinthian church to be true: ἀκούω σχίσματα ἐν ὑμῖν ὑπάρχειν καὶ
μέρος τι πιστεύω.[164] All of these uses of πιστεύειν are normal in
Greek and have direct parallels in Josephus' profane use of the verb.

The second kind of profane use of πιστεύειν in the NT occurs in
the sense: 'to entrust'. The verb has this meaning in eight instances —
primarily in the Pauline corpus—and then always in the passive

---

[159] Οὐκ ἐπίστευσαν οὖν οἱ Ἰουδαῖοι περὶ αὐτοῦ ὅτι ἦν τυφλὸς καὶ ἀνέβλεψεν ἕως ὅτου
ἐφώνησαν τοὺς γονεῖς αὐτοῦ τοῦ ἀναβλέψαντος.
[160] *Ant.* 4,219.
[161] See esp. *Ant.* 6,263; 7,178.
[162] Cf. Josephus, *Ant.* 6,263; 7,178. 213; 10,267; *Ap.* 2,218.
[163] Cf. in Josephus the case of Judas and Bacchides in *Ant.* 12,395.
[164] Cf. Josephus, *Bel.* 1,212. 482; 7,444; *Ant.* 6,289.

construction: πιστεύεσθαί τι. Paul writes in Rom. 3,2 that [the Jews] were entrusted with the oracles of God.[165] Elsewhere Paul maintains that he himself was entrusted with certain things: He was entrusted with his office[166] or with the gospel.[167] As already noted, the formula πιστεύεσθαί τι appears frequently in Josephus.[168] Especially akin to Paul's use of the formula is Josephus' report in *Ant.* 17,43 that the Pharisees were from time to time entrusted by God with a knowledge of the future.[169]

Although these occurrences of πιστεύεσθαί τι in the Pauline corpus, as well as in *Ant.* 17,43, in the sense of 'to be entrusted with' technically represent a profane understanding of the verb, it must be admitted that there is also a religious element involved. In each instance God is the 'One who entrusts', and the deposit or trust[170] is always of a religious or spiritual nature.

The same principle can be seen in Lk. 16,11, where πιστεύειν in the sense of 'entrust' appears in the active voice: "If then you have not been faithful in the unrighteous mammon, who will entrust to you the true riches?"[171] The use of the verb is profane but the passage does not deal simply with the entrusting of profane earthly goods. The larger context reveals that 'the true riches'[172] will be entrusted by God to the one who has proven himself or herself faithful.[173]

Jn. 2,24f. reports about Jesus: "But Jesus did not [en]trust himself to them, because he knew all men and needed no one to bear witness of man; for he himself knew what was in man".[174] Here again 'entrusting' is very closely related to 'trusting'. Jesus did not *entrust himself* to [the people in Jerusalem] because he "knew what was in man"; i.e., he did not *trust* them. There is a clear parallel to this in *Ant.* 12,396. In this passage Josephus reports the incidents of 1 Macc. 7,8ff. where Bacchides was

---

[165] ἐπιστεύθησαν τὰ λόγια τοῦ θεοῦ.

[166] οἰκονομίαν πεπίστευμαι; 1 Cor. 9,17.

[167] πεπίστευμαι τὸ εὐαγγέλιον τῆς ἀκροβυστίας καθὼς Πέτρος τῆς περιτομῆς; Gal. 2,7; cf. 1 Thes. 2,4; 1 Tim. 1,11; also Tit. 1,3: ἐφανέρωσεν δὲ καιροῖς ἰδίοις τὸν λόγον αὐτοῦ ἐν κηρύγματι, ὃ ἐπιστεύθην ἐγὼ κατ᾽ ἐπιταγὴν τοῦ σωτῆρος ἡμῶν θεοῦ.

[168] E.g., *Bel.* 1,224, 667; *Ant.* 2,227; 20,15; *Vi.* 72. 137.

[169] πρόγνωσιν δὲ ἐπεπίστευντο ἐπιφοιτήσει τοῦ θεοῦ. Cf. also *Ant.* 17,158; *Ap.* 2,188.

[170] I.e., the Oracles of God, the office, the gospel, the kerygma, foreknowledge.

[171] εἰ οὖν ἐν τῷ ἀδίκῳ μαμωνᾷ πιστοὶ οὐκ ἐγένεσθε, τὸ ἀληθινὸν τίς ὑμῖν πιστεύσει; For the active construction πιστεύειν τινί τι in Josephus, cf. *Bel.* 2,590; 4,274; *Ant.* 9,212; *Vi.* 319; *Ap.* 2,185.

[172] τὸ ἀληθινόν.

[173] πιστός.

[174] αὐτὸς δὲ Ἰησοῦς οὐκ ἐπίστευεν αὐτὸν αὐτοῖς διὰ τὸ αὐτὸν γινώσκειν πάντας (25) καὶ ὅτι οὐ χρείαν εἶχεν ἵνα τις μαρτυρήσῃ περὶ τοῦ ἀνθρώπου· αὐτὸς γὰρ ἐγίνωσκεν τί ἦν ἐν τῷ ἀνθρώπῳ. ἐπίστευεν αὐτόν in vs. 24 should read with the other MSS ἐπίστευεν ἑαυτόν.

sent by Demetrius to Judea to kill Judas and his followers. Bacchides, coming with a force of soldiers, plotted to deceive Judas with offers of peace and friendship. Judas himself was not taken in, but some of the citizens, thinking they would suffer no harm, went over to Bacchides and Alcimus (whom Demetrius had appointed high priest). After receiving oaths of safety, these citizens put themselves in the hands of Bacchides and Alcimus: καὶ λαβόντες ὅρκους παρ᾽ ἀμφοτέρων μήτε αὐτοί τι παθεῖν μήτε τοὺς ἐκ τῆς αὐτῆς ὄντας προαιρέσεως, ἐπίστευσαν αὐτοὺς ἐκείνοις. The trust of these citizens was not rewarded however. Bacchides did not keep his pledge,[175] but made light of his oaths and killed sixty of them.

There are other passages where Josephus employs πιστεύειν in the sense of someone entrusting of himself to someone else. The prophet Jonah had entrusted his life to the foreigners on the ship from Joppa.[176] In *Bel.* 1,262 Mariamme, the daughter of Hyrcanus, implored Herod not to entrust himself to the barbarians who were openly plotting his ruin.[177] In *Bel.* 1,627 σῶμα is substituted for the reflexive ἑαυτόν: οὗτός ἐστιν ὁ παραινῶν ἐμοί ποτε φυλάττεσθαι ζῶντα ᾽Αλέξανδρον καὶ μὴ πᾶσιν πιστεύειν τὸ σῶμα.[178]

In contrast to these passages in Josephus, Jesus' mistrust of 'all men' in Jn. 2,24f. is embedded in a deeply religious context so that even this profane use of πιστεύειν as 'entrust' probably cannot be understood in a purely profane sense. In the immediate and larger context of Jn. 2,24 the verb πιστεύειν plays a very important theological role. Particularly significant is the contrast between the two occurrences of πιστεύειν in Jn. 2,24 and in 2,23. In vs. 23 the verb signifies faith in Jesus: As Jesus was in Jerusalem for the Passover feast many people believed in his name, seeing the signs he was performing.[179] Vs. 24 on the other hand stresses Jesus' own lack of trust, even in these people who had put their trust in him: αὐτὸς δὲ ᾽Ιησοῦς οὐκ ἐπίστευεν [ἑ]αυτὸν αὐτοῖς. While it is difficult to assign a religious meaning to πιστεύειν in the translation of vs. 24, it is nonetheless striking that author chose to insert a profane use of the verb at this very point, especially when πιστεύειν is found nowhere else in the Johannine corpus in a profane sense.

---

[175] τὴν πίστιν μὴ φυλάξας.

[176] πεπιστευκότα αὐτοῖς τὸ ζῆν; *Ant.* 9,212; cf. 10,167.

[177] μηδ᾽ ἐμπιστεύειν ἑαυτὸν ... τοῖς βαρβάροις.

[178] Cf. also *Bel.* 7,288.

[179] πολλοὶ ἐπίστευσαν εἰς τὸ ὄνομα αὐτοῦ. Cf. also Jn. 2,22.

It is obvious that the NT knows and employs the verb πιστεύειν in the general, profane sense of 'to believe', 'to hold something to be true' or 'to entrust'. These profane senses of the verb are parallel to the profane usages of the verb in Josephus' writings. Nonetheless, it must be pointed out that a profane understanding of πιστεύειν occurs very seldom in the NT, and then only within a religious context. This is not the case with Josephus.

3.12 Adolf Schlatter's Register of Parallels

Adolf Schlatter lists a number of parallel uses of πιστεύειν in the NT and Josephus.[180] The most important parallels from his list are the following:

> πιστεύετε ὅτι δύναμαι Mt. 9,28. πεπιστεύκαμεν ἐξ αὐτῶν (den Büchern Daniels) ὅτι Δανίηλος ὡμίλει τῷ θεῷ Ant. 10,267. αὐτὸς ἕκαστος αὐτῷ τὸ συνειδὸς ἔχων μαρτυροῦν πεπίστευκεν, τοῦ μὲν νομοθέτου προφητεύσαντος, τοῦ δὲ θεοῦ τὴν πίστιν ἰσχυρὰν παρεσχηκότος, ὅτι τοῖς τοὺς νόμους διαφυλάξασι—ἔδωκεν ὁ θεὸς γενέσθαι τε πάλιν καὶ βίον ἀμείνω λαβεῖν ἐκ περιτροπῆς Ap. 2,218. Zur Stützung des Glaubens auf die Kraft des Angerufenen vgl. Israel am Roten Meer τοιούτῳ βοηθῷ πεπιστευκότες ᾧ δύναμις καὶ τὰ μικρὰ ποιῆσαι μεγάλα Ant. 2,333. Statt des mit ὅτι begonnenen Satzes gibt Josefus auch den Akkusativ mit dem Infinitiv; Israel in der Wüste πεπιστευκότες ἤδη μηδὲν γίνεσθαι δίχα τῆς τοῦ θεοῦ προνοίας Ant. 4,60. οἱ πιστεύσαντες ἐπισκοπεῖν θεὸν τοὺς ἑαυτῶν βίους οὐδὲν ἀνέχονται ἐξαμαρτεῖν Ap. 2,160. ἄνθρωποι μόνον εἶναι κακὸν αὐτοῖς πεπιστευκότες, εἰ πρᾶξαί τι παρὰ τοὺς ἑαυτῶν νόμους ἢ λόγον εἰπεῖν παρ' ἐκείνους παραβιασθεῖεν Ap. 2,233.
>
> οὐκ ἐπιστεύσατε αὐτῷ Mt. 21,25. τῶν μόνοις τοῖς Ἕλλησιν πιστεύειν ἀξιούντων Ap. 1,161.
>
> πιστεύεις τοῖς προφήταις Acts 26,27. τοῖς ὑπ' ἐκείνου προφητευθεῖσι περὶ τοῦ θεοῦ πεπιστευκότες Ap. 2,286. ψευδοπροφήταις ἀπατῶσιν αὐτὸν πεπιστευκέναι ὡς Ant. 10,104.
>
> οὐκ ἐπίστευσας τοῖς λόγοις μου Lk. 1,20. δεῖ πιστεύειν τοῖς ὑπὸ τοῦ προφήτου εἰρημένοις Ant. 9,12. τοῖς ὑπ' αὐτοῦ (Elisa) λεγομένοις οὐκ ἐπίστευσεν Ant. 9,86. οἱ δὲ τοῖς μὲν λόγοις οὐκ ἐπίστευσαν—τοῖς δ' ἔργοις ἔμαθον ἀληθῆ τὰ παρὰ τῶν προφητῶν Ant. 10,39.
>
> πιστεύοντες τῷ Κυρίῳ Acts 5,14. πιστεύων κηδεμόνι θεῷ τὴν σωτηρίαν παραβάλλεται, Josefus in Jotapata Vi. 63. 387. τοῖς εἰς αὐτὸν ἀποβλέπουσιν καὶ μόνῳ πεπιστευκόσιν ὁ καρπὸς οὐκ

---

180   Schlatter, *Glaube im NT*, pp. 582-83.

ἀπόλλυται τῆς εὐσεβείας *Ant.* 20,48; Glaube, der allein auf Gott
vertraut, ist die richtige Weise der Verehrung Gottes. Jakob soll
πιστεῦσαι περὶ αὐτοῦ (Benjamin) τῷ θεῷ *Ant.* 2,117. Israel soll trotz
des Berichts der Kundschafter nach Kanaan ziehen ἡγεμόνι τῷ θεῷ
πεπιστευκότες *Ant.* 3,309. Vor dem Kampf mit Amalek fordert Mose
Israel auf θαρρεῖν τῇ τοῦ θεοῦ ψήφῳ πεπιστευκότας *Ant.* 3,44.

ἵνα ἴδωμεν καὶ πιστεύσωμεν Mk. 15,32. περὶ μηδενὸς
ἀπογινώσκειν ὧν ὑπέσχηται πρὸς εὐδαιμονίαν ὡς οὐκ ἐσομένου
πιστεύοντας ἐκ τῶν ἤδη βλεπόμενων *Ant.* 8,110.

μὴ πιστεύσητε Mt. 24,3. πολλάκις κατηγορηθέντος (Josefus) οὐκ
ἐπίστευσεν (Titus) *Vi.* 428.

αὐτὸς δὲ Ἰησοῦς οὐκ ἐπίστευσεν αὐτὸν αὐτοῖς Jn. 2,24. Die
Frommen ἐπίστευσαν αὐτοὺς ἐκείνοις (Bakchides und Alkimus) *Ant.*
12,396.

ἐπιστεύθησαν τὰ λόγια Röm. 3,2. διὰ τὸ καὶ τὴν ἐξουσίαν τῶν
ἐκεῖ πραγμάτων αὐτὸς παρὰ τοῦ κοινοῦ τῶν Ἱεροσολυμιτῶν
πεπιστεῦσθαι *Vi.* 72. τοῖς τῆς Τιβεριάδος τὴν διοίκησιν ὑπ' ἐμοῦ
πεπιστευμένοις *Vi.* 86.

ἐπιστεύθη 1 Tim. 3,16. πιστευθεὶς οὖν Παῖτος *Bel.* 7,224. ὑπὸ
μὲν τῶν πλειόνων ἐπιστεύετο *Ant.* 10,114. ὅρκους καὶ ἀρὰς δι' ὧν
ᾤετο πιστευθήσεσθαι περὶ ὧν ἐπέστειλε *Vi.* 101. 22 biblische Bücher
τὰ δικαίως πεπιστευμένα *Ap.* 1,38.

3.13 Religious Use

Creedal formulas employing the verb πιστεύειν, and particularly the
formula πιστεύειν ὅτι as it occurs in Josephus to express some belief
about God, are not foreign to the OT or NT. In Isa. 43,10, for example,
the LXX reads: "You be my witnesses, and I too am a witness, says the
Lord God, and my servant whom I have chosen, in order that you may
know and believe and understand that I am [He]".[181]

4 Macc. 7,18. 19 uses the religious formula πιστεύειν ὅτι in
much the same way as Josephus: "But they who have meditated upon
religion with their whole heart, they alone are able to master the passions
of the flesh: they who believe that to God they die not; for as also our
forefathers, Abraham, Isaac, Jacob, they [did not die] but live to God".[182]

---

[181] ἵνα γνῶτε καὶ πιστεύσητε καὶ συνῆτε ὅτι ἐγώ εἰμι. Cf. Heb. 11,6.
[182] πιστεύοντες ὅτι θεῷ οὐκ ἀποθνήσκουσιν, ὥσπερ οὐδὲ οἱ πατριάρχαι ἡμῶν Ἀβραὰμ καὶ
Ἰσαὰκ καὶ Ἰακώβ, ἀλλὰ ζῶσιν τῷ θεῷ. Cf. esp. *Ap.* 2,160. 218. This belief in life after
death in connection with the patriarchs Abraham, Isaac and Jacob is taken up by Jesus in Mk.
12,18-27 in his discussion with the Sadducees concerning the resurrection of the dead. Jesus
quotes Ex. 3,16 where God says: ἐγὼ ὁ θεὸς Ἀβραὰμ καὶ [ὁ] θεὸς Ἰσαὰκ καὶ [ὁ] θεὸς
Ἰακώβ (Mk. 12,26), and drives home his point about the reality of the resurrection in vs. 27:
οὐκ ἔστιν θεὸς νεκρῶν ἀλλὰ ζώντων. In this Markan passage the verb πιστεύειν does not
appear in connection with this creedal statement concerning the resurrection of the dead. Rather

Also in the NT there are examples of πιστεύειν ὅτι… as a creedal formula. In Rom. 10,9 the fact that God raises the dead is presented as a (Christian) creedal statement: ὅτι ἐὰν ὁμολογήσῃς ἐν τῷ στόματί σου κύριον Ἰησοῦν καὶ πιστεύσῃς ἐν τῇ καρδίᾳ σου ὅτι ὁ θεὸς αὐτὸν ἤγειρεν ἐκ νεκρῶν, σωθήσῃ. Likewise in 1 Jn. 5,5: Τίς [δέ] ἐστιν ὁ νικῶν τὸν κόσμον εἰ μὴ ὁ πιστεύων ὅτι Ἰησοῦς ἐστιν ὁ υἱὸς τοῦ θεοῦ;[183]

Πιστεύειν governing indirect discourse also appears in the NT as a creedal formula. A clear example is the statement of the Ethiopian in Acts 8,37: πιστεύω τὸν υἱὸν τοῦ θεοῦ εἶναι τὸν Ἰησοῦν Χριστόν. This is admittedly a later addition to the the text of the narrative, but a similar construction is found also in Acts 15,11: ἀλλὰ διὰ τῆς χάριτος τοῦ κυρίου Ἰησοῦ πιστεύομεν σωθῆναι καθ' ὃν τρόπον κἀκεῖνοι.[184] As indicated above, Josephus also frequently uses πιστεύειν with indirect discourse, more often in the profane sense of 'believing [something] to be the case',[185] but also in the sense of a creedal formula.[186]

In Rom. 4,17 πιστεύειν appears in connection with a genitive absolute, indicating the content of Abraham's faith in God; i.e., that God is the one "who gives life to the dead and calls into existence the things that do not exist".[187] This creedal formula is unique at this point in the NT and is not found in Josephus at all. Nevertheless it *is* a creedal formula and is, as such, comparable to creedal formulas elsewhere in the NT and in Josephus.

Josephus occasionally has the formula πιστεύειν ὡς indicating the content of what is believed. This formula is very similar to πιστεύειν ὅτι. On three occasions the formula occurs in a religious sense, referring to belief in the message of a prophet, with ὡς marking the content of that message.[188] Πιστεύειν ὡς does not occur in the NT. The closest parallel is οὕτως πιστεύειν in 1 Cor. 15,11. This passage refers to belief in the *kerygma* of Paul and the other apostles. Paul writes to the

---

the verb λέγειν appears in vs. 18: Καὶ ἔρχονται Σαδδουκαῖοι πρὸς αὐτόν, οἵτινες λέγουσιν ἀνάστασιν μὴ εἶναι.

[183] Cf. Mt. 9,28; Mk. 11,23. 24; Lk. 1,45; Jn. 6, 69; 8,24; 11,27. 42; 13,19; 14,10. 11; 16,27. 30; 17,8. 21; 20,31; Acts 27,25; Rom. 6,8; 1 Thes. 4,14; Heb. 11,6; Jas. 2,19; 1 Jn. 5,1; in a purely secular sense, Jn. 9,18; Acts 9,26; πέπεισμαι ὅτι, 2 Tim. 1,12.

[184] For further instances in the NT of πιστεύειν with indirect discourse, cf. Rom. 4,18; 14,2.

[185] E.g., Ant. 5,37; 16,190; 19,72; 20,255; Bel. 1,112.

[186] See esp. Ant. 2,276; 4,60; 8,232; 12,304; Ap. 2,160; cf. also Ant. 14,455; Bel. 7,354; Ap. 1,14; 2,233. 279.

[187] καθὼς γέγραπται ὅτι πατέρα πολλῶν ἐθνῶν τέθεικά σε, κατέναντι οὗ ἐπίστευσεν θεοῦ τοῦ ζῳοποιοῦντος τοὺς νεκροὺς καὶ καλοῦντος τὰ μὴ ὄντα ὡς ὄντα.

[188] Ant. 10,104. 178. 250.

Corinthian church: εἴτε οὖν ἐγὼ εἴτε ἐκεῖνοι, οὕτως κηρύσσομεν καὶ οὕτωςἐπιστεύσατε.189

Josephus' use of πιστεύειν in creedal formulas is therefore essentially the same as that of the LXX and the NT. Both Josephus and the NT writers—particularly the evangelist John—have adopted this religious use of the verb πιστεύειν from the normal religious use of the verb in secular Greek. In Josephus it is important to note that, with only one minor ex ception, this religious creedal formula occurs exclusively within the con text of Jewish religion.190 This kind of faith normally includes the element of personal commitment as it does in the NT and in the LXX.191

Josephus' use of πιστεύειν in reference to faith or trust in God is not foreign to OT and NT. In *Ant.* 2,333 Moses calls God a great helper192 and urges the Israelites to trust him as such in their flight from the Egyptian army. After the miraculous crossing of the Red Sea and the defeat of the Egyptian army, Ex. 14,31 reports that the people feared the Lord and ἐπίστευσαν τῷ θεῷ καὶ τῷ Μωυσῇ θεράποντι αὐτοῦ. Two verses later in the song of Moses, the Lord is called 'helper': βοηθὸς καὶ σκεπαστὴς ἐγένετό μοι εἰς σωτηρίαν.193 It is clear in these instances that God the Helper is also God the Savior. These themes194 are brought together once again in Ps. 78(77), especially in verses 22, 32, 35.195

22— ὅτι οὐκ ἐπίστευσαν ἐν τῷ θεῷ οὐδὲ ἤλπισαν ἐπὶ τὸ σωτήριον αὐτοῦ.

32—ἐν πᾶσιν τούτοις ἥμαρτον ἔτι καὶ οὐκ ἐπίστευσαν ἐν τοῖς θαυμασίοις αὐτοῦ.

35—καὶ ἐμνήσθησαν ὅτι ὁ θεὸς βοηθὸς αὐτῶν ἐστιν καὶ ὁ θεὸς ὁ ὕψιστος λυτρωτὴς αὐτῶν ἐστιν.

Also in the NT God's help is a recurring theme.196 In Mk. 9,22-24 the ideas of help and faith are tied closely together. In this passage the fa ther

---

189 The use of οὕτως in this passage is, however, different from the use of πιστεύειν ὡς i n Josephus. In 1 Cor. 15,11 the content of faith is primary and prerequisite!

190 In *Bel.* 7,354 Josephus reports the following concerning the Indian belief in the intercourse of souls after death: οὕτως βεβαίαν καὶ ἀληθεστάτην ταῖς ψυχαῖς τὴν μετ' ἀλλήλων εἶναι δίαιταν πεπιστεύκασιν. While this passage may be considered religious in nature, it is clearly different from the other creedal statements we have seen in Josephus. Faith in this instance is not tied to a statement about God.

191 Important exceptions in Josephus are: *Ant,* 4,60; 6,263.

192 τοιοῦτοςβοηθός.

193 Ex. 15,2; cf. Ex. 18,4; Dt. 33,7. 26. 29.

194 πιστεύειν; θεός = βοηθός; σωτηρία.

195 Cf. Ps. 118(117),7; Heb. 13,6.

196 E.g., Mt. 15,25; 2 Cor. 6,2; Heb. 2,18; 4,16.

of a demon-possessed boy pleads with Jesus to help his son if he is able to do anything.[197]   Jesus replies that all things are possible τῷ πιστεύοντι; at this the father cries out: πιστεύω· βοήθει μου τῇ ἀπιστία.

Faith in God as ἡγεμών is not common in the biblical material. In *Ant.* 3,309 Joshua and Caleb urged the Israelites to go with them and to take possession of the promised land, placing their trust in ἡγεμόνι τῷ θεῷ. In the corresponding biblical account at Num. 14,8ff. neither the verb πιστεύειν nor the reference to God as 'leader' appears; rather these negative commands appear: μὴ φοβηθῆτε and μὴ ἀποστάται γίνεσθε. In vs. 11, however, God's charge against the Israelites in their refusal to go up and take the promised land is formulated thus: οὐ πιστεύουσίν μοι ἐν πᾶσιν τοῖς σημείοις.[198]   Also in other contexts within the Exodus story, God is pictured as the one who was leading or would lead the Israelites.[199] Only in Mt. 2,6 is there a close NT parallel to this concept of God as ἡγεμών. Matthew echoes the prophecy from Mic. 5,1f. that out of Bethlehem would come the leader[200] who would shepherd God's people Israel. There is no use of πιστεύειν in this passage.

There are many more instances of πιστεύειν τῷ θεῷ in both OT and NT. In Num. 14,11 and Dt. 1,33; 9,23 Israel is charged with lack of faith in God.[201]   The teaching of Prov. 30,1 is directed toward τοῖς πιστεύουσιν θεῷ. In Wis. Sol. 16,26 it is the word[202] of God that preserves those who put their trust in God.[203] The admonition to trust in the Lord[204] appears in Sir. 2,6. 8. (10). In Jon. 3,5 the men of Nineveh responded to Jonah's message in faith and repentance.[205] Dan. 6,24 reports that Daniel was kept safe from the lions ὅτι ἐπίστευσεν ἐν τῷ θεῷ αὐτοῦ. And, of course, the classic OT example of faith in God is the faith of Abraham in Gen. 15,6: καὶ ἐπίστευσεν Ἀβραὰμ τῷ θεῷ, καὶ ἐλογίσθη αὐτῷ εἰς δικαιοσύνην.

---

[197] ἀλλ' εἴ τι δύνῃ, βοήθησον ἡμῖν σπλαγχνισθεὶς ἐφ' ἡμᾶς.

[198] Cf. the Jewish leaders' disbelief in the σημεῖα of Jesus in Jn. 12,37ff.

[199] E.g., Ex. 13,21: ὁ θεὸς ἡγεῖτο αὐτῶν; cf. Ex. 23,23.

[200] ἡγούμενος.

[201] οὐκ ἐπιστεύσατε αὐτῷ; cf. Jer. 25,8.

[202] ῥῆμα.

[203] τοὺς σοὶ πιστεύοντας.

[204] πίστευσον αὐτῷ.

[205] καὶ ἐνεπίστευσαν οἱ ἄνδρες Νίνευη τῷ θεῷ καὶ ἐκήρυξαν νηστείαν καὶ ἐνεδύσαντο σάκκους. Cf. Mt. 12,38ff.

Also in the NT there is an important connection between πιστεύειν τῷ θεῷ and the concept of faithfulness. In Tit. 3,8 those who have believed in God are to apply themselves to good deeds.[206] 1 Pet. 2,6 quotes Isa. 28,16, saying that the one who believes in him will not be put to shame.[207] Rom. 4,3; Gal. 3,6 and Jas. 2,23 all echo the faith of Abraham in Gen. 15,6 with emphasis upon his faithfulness.

In these instances faith in God is an active faithfulness (or lack of faithfulness) to God rather than simply a *fides quae creditur* with its focus upon the content of what is believed. This is also true of Josephus' use of the formula πιστεύειν τῷ θεῷ.[208] It is the OT concept of πιστεύειν τῷ θεῷ in the sense of 'active faithfulness toward God', as is also reflected in the NT, which lays the foundation for and which is further reflected in Josephus' use of πιστεύειν τῷ θεῷ.

Faith in Moses is a recurring theme in the OT, particularly in the Exodus material. The phrase πιστεύσωσίν μοι/σοι[209] occurs five times in Ex. 4,1. 5. 8. 9. Moses' concern in these passages is that the Israelites may not believe him when he returns to deliver them from Egypt. God gives Moses the σημεῖα in order that the children of Israel will believe him. Ex. 14,31 reports that the Israelites believed in God and in his servant Moses as a result of the miraculous deliverance from the Egyptians at the Red Sea. In Ex. 19,9 God appears to Moses in the thick cloud: ...ἵνα ἀκούσῃ ὁ λαὸς λαλοῦντός μου πρὸς σὲ καὶ σοὶ πιστεύσωσιν εἰς τὸν αἰῶνα.[210]

Num. 12,7 emphasizes the fact that Moses was faithful in all of God's house.[211] This tradition could very well form the basis for Josephus' report in *Ant.* 4,179 where Moses claims: πιστεύεσθαι δὲ ἄξιός εἰμι. Num. 12,7 is reflected in Sir. 45,4 and then again even more clearly in the NT in Heb. 3,2. 5.[212] In addition, Heb. 11,23-24 speaks about the faith of Moses. But only once in the NT, in Jn. 5,46, is Moses explicitly presented as the cbject of πιστεύειν. Here Jesus challenges the Jewish leaders: εἰ γὰρ ἐπιστεύετε Μωϋσεῖ, ἐπιστεύετε

---

[206] ἵνα φροντίζωσιν καλῶν ἔργων προΐστασθαι οἱ πεπιστευκότες θεῷ.

[207] ἰδοὺ τίθημι ἐν Σιὼν λίθον ἀκρογωνιαῖον ἐκλεκτὸν ἔντιμον καὶ ὁ πιστεύων ἐπ' αὐτῷ οὐ μὴ καταισχυνθῇ.

[208] Nonetheless it is significant that Josephus never mentions Abraham in connection with the verb πιστεύειν or with the substantive πίστις.

[209] Referring to Moses.

[210] Cf. Ps. 106(105), 12. 24.

[211] ἐν ὅλῳ τῷ οἴκῳ μου πιστός ἐστιν.

[212] Vs. 2: πιστὸν ὄντα τῷ ποιήσαντι αὐτὸν ὡς καὶ Μωϋσῆς ἐν [ὅλῳ] τῷ οἴκῳ αὐτοῦ. vs. 5: καὶ Μωϋσῆς μὲν πιστὸς ἐν ὅλῳ τῷ οἴκῳ αὐτοῦ ὡς θεράπων εἰς μαρτύριον τῶν λαληθη-σομένων.

ἂν ἐμοί. It is clear that Jesus is referring to belief in the writings of Moses[213] as well as faith in the person of Moses, for he goes on to pose the question in vs. 47: εἰ δὲ τοῖς ἐκείνου γράμμασιν οὐ πιστεύετε, πῶς τοῖς ἐμοῖς ῥήμασιν πιστεύσετε; Important here is that faith in Moses appears once again in in the context of Moses' prophetic office.[214] It is especially upon the basis of Moses' *prophetic function* that Josephus views him as an object of faith. This is important since Josephus' most common religious use of πιστεύειν occurs within the context of the OT prophets.

Before leaving this discussion of Moses as an object of religious faith, it should be noted that there is a significant difference between faith in Moses and what we have earlier noted in Josephus with regard to faith in God. When referring to faith in God, Josephus commonly employs the active construction πιστεύειν θεῷ. With regard to Moses the OT and the NT writers can use this same active construction.[215] Nowhere in Josephus does the active construction occur with regard to faith in Moses, not even in a profane use of the verb πιστεύειν. Rather that which occurs repeatedly is the passive construction [Μωϋσῆς] πιστεύεσθαι.

Thus Josephus distinguishes between faith in God and faith in Moses in that faith in Moses is always less direct. In the one instance where Josephus expresses this faith with an active form of the verb πιστεύειν,[216] the dative object is not Μωϋσεῖ but rather τοῖς ὑπ' ἐκείνου προφητευθεῖσι περὶ τοῦ θεοῦ. Moses himself is only indirectly, and at best secondarily, the object of faith.[217]

There are a few similarities between Josephus' use of πιστεύειν in the context of the prophets and the corresponding accounts in the LXX. The conversation between Jeremiah and Zedekiah recorded by Josephus in *Ant.* 10,124 takes up the tradition of Jer. 38(45),15 where the king asks Jeremiah for counsel from the Lord. Jeremiah replies (LXX): καὶ ἐὰν συμβουλεύσω σοι, οὐ μὴ ἀκούσῃς μου. Josephus has expanded this to include the verb πιστεύειν: οὐ πιστευθήσεσθαι δ' εἰπὼν οὐδὲ παραινέσας ἀκουσθήσεσθαι.

---

[213] I.e., in his messianic testimony.
[214] περὶ γὰρ ἐμοῦ ἐκεῖνος ἔγραψεν; cf. Lk. 16,29: ἔχουσιν Μωϋσέα καὶ τοὺς προφήτας· ἀκουσάτωσαν αὐτῶν.
[215] Cf. Ex. 14,31; Jn. 5,46.
[216] *Ap.* 2,286.
[217] It is not clear how much should be made of this distinction between passive and active expressions of faith. We shall see presently that, with regard to the OT prophets, Josephus uses the active construction πιστεύειν προφήταις more frequently than he does the passive construction.

Similarly, with regard to the king, leaders and people of Jerusalem who did not believe Jeremiah's predictions of destruction and exile,[218] Jer. 43(50),4 reports: οὐκ ἤκουσεν ... τῆς φωνῆς κυρίου. Even closer to Josephus' terminology Lam. 4,12 reads: οὐκ ἐπίστευσαν βασιλεῖς γῆς ... ὅτι εἰσελεύσεται ἐχθρὸς καὶ ἐκθλίβων διὰ τῶν πυλῶν Ἱερουσαλήμ. Concerning Manasseh and the people of Judah who did not believe the message of the prophets of God,[219] 2 Chr. 33,10 reports: καὶ ἐλάλησεν κύριος ἐπὶ Μανάσση καὶ ἐπὶ τὸν λαὸν αὐτοῦ, καὶ οὐκ ἐπήκουσαν.

From these parallel instances it would seem that the LXX uses πιστεύειν more in the sense of intellectual assent to the message of the prophets whereas (ἐπ)ακούειν signifies an active and faithful commitment[220] to the message of the prophet. 2 Chr. 20,20ff., however, shows clearly that Josephus' understanding of πιστεύειν τοῖς ὑπὸ προφήτου εἰρημένοις in *Ant.* 9,12 as both an intellectual assent to and an active confidence in the prophetic utterance is also present in the LXX use of πιστεύειν. The account here concerns the prophecy of Jehaziel the Levite. Upon hearing the prophecy, Jehoshaphat urged the people to follow the counsel of Jehaziel: ἐμπιστεύσατε ἐν κυρίῳ θεῷ ὑμῶν, καὶ ἐμπιστευθήσεσθε· ἐμπιστεύσατε ἐν προφήτῃ αὐτοῦ, καὶ εὐοδωθήσεσθε. The same use of πιστεύειν occurs in Isa. 7,9 with reference to the prophetic utterance of Isaiah to Ahaz: (LXX) ἐὰν μὴ πιστεύσητε, οὐδὲ μὴ συνῆτε.[221]

The fact that Josephus' use of πιστεύειν with reference to the prophets of God is parallel to the LXX use is clear from other OT passages as well. In Isa. 53,1, with reference to the prophetic message, Isaiah asks: Κύριε, τίς ἐπίστευσεν τῇ ἀκοῇ ἡμῶν; Samuel the prophet is described in 1 Sam. 3,20 as: πιστὸς εἰς προφήτην τῷ κυρίῳ.[222] The LXX carries this tradition even further than the MT in vs. 21: καὶ ἐπιστεύθη Σαμουηλ προφήτης γενέσθαι τῷ κυρίῳ εἰς πάντα Ἰσραήλ.

In Ms. '*S*' of Tobit this faith in the prophetic message is once again spelled out along with the required actions consistent with faith. Tobit urges his son in this passage: "[Take your child and flee to

---

[218] Cf. *Ant.* 10,119. 178.
[219] *Ant.* 10,39.
[220] I.e., obedience.
[221] The Hebrew of the MT shows much more clearly the parallelism between Isa. 7,9 and 2 Chron. 20,20. See above, Chapter Two.
[222] Cf. the similar observation about the prophet Isaiah in Sir. 46,15; 48,22.

Midian,] ...ὅτι πιστεύω ἐγὼ τῷ ῥήματι τοῦ θεοῦ ἐπὶ Νινευή, ἃ
ἐλάλησεν Ναουμ... διὸ γινώσκω ἐγὼ καὶ πιστεύω ὅτι πάντα, ἃ
εἶπεν ὁ θεός, συντελεσθήσεται καὶ ἔσται" (Tobit 14,4).

The connection of πιστεύειν with the OT prophets is even more
prominent in the NT. In his defense before Felix in Acts 24,14 Paul
declares himself a believer in all that is written in the law and
prophets.[223] Likewise in his defense before Agrippa in Acts 26,27 he
asks the king: πιστεύεις, βασιλεῦ 'Αγρίππα, τοῖς προφήταις; οἶδα
ὅτι πιστεύεις. In Mk. 11,31[224] the scribes and elders of the Jewish
people, in their deliberation about Jesus' question concerning the
authority of John the Baptist, realized that if they recognized John's
authority as having come from heaven—i.e., if they admitted that John
was indeed a prophet—then they would open themselves up to the
legitimate charge of unbelief: ἐὰν εἴπωμεν· ἐξ οὐρανοῦ, ἐρεῖ· διὰ τί
[οὖν] οὐκ ἐπιστεύσατε αὐτῷ; In the same way Jesus scolds the two
disciples on the road to Emmaus for being slow of heart ... τοῦ
πιστεύειν ἐπὶ πᾶσιν οἷς ἐλάλησαν οἱ προφῆται (Lk. 24,25).

Jn. 12,38 claims that Isa. 53,1 has been fulfilled in the unbelief of
the Jewish leaders toward Jesus.[225] This connection of faith in Jesus as,
at least in some sense, a prophet is further seen in Jn. 13,19 and 14,29,
where Jesus informs his disciples beforehand of what is to come so that
when it happens they will believe.[226]

One of the most striking similarities, however, between Josephus
and the NT in the use of πιστεύειν with the prophets is in the way Jer.
38(45),15 is reflected in Ant. 10,124 and in Lk. 22,67.[227] When asked
for counsel by Zedekiah, Jeremiah replied: "If I tell you, will you not
put me to death? And if I give you counsel, you will not listen to
me".[228] Josephus adds the verb πιστεύειν in his account of this narrative. In Lk. 22,67ff. Jesus is being tried before the Jewish Sanhedrin.
His examiners ask him to tell them plainly if he is the Christ. Jesus' answer reflects the style of Jer. 38,15 but also uses the verb πιστεύειν:
ἐὰν ὑμῖν εἴπω, οὐ μὴ πιστεύσητε.

---

[223] οὕτως λατρεύω τῷ πατρῴῳ θεῷ πιστεύων πᾶσι τοῖς κατὰ τὸν νόμον καὶ τοῖς ἐν τοῖς
προφήταις γεγραμμένοις.

[224] Par. Mt. 21,25ff.; Lk. 20,5.

[225] Rom. 10,16 sees the fulfillment of this prophecy in the Jews' lack of obedience to the gospel: οὐ
πάντες ὑπήκουσαν τῷ εὐαγγελίῳ. See Otto Betz, "Jesu Evangelium vom Gottesreich", *Das
Evangelium und die Evangelien,* ed. Peter Stuhlmacher (Tübingen: J. C. B. Mohr, 1983),
pp.70f., 76f.

[226] ἵνα πιστεύσητε. See Isa. 41,26-29; 43,10; 45,21!

[227] Cf. also Jn. 3,12.

[228] LXX: οὐ μὴ ἀκούσῃς μου.

It is clear from this evidence that Josephus, when speaking of faith in the OT prophets and in their prophetic utterances, shares the tradition of a use of πιστεύειν that is common with the NT use. This is a tradition which has its roots firmly planted in the OT!

In the NT there is an important relationship between signs and faith, as also in Josephus. On the negative side, in Jn. 4,48, Jesus makes this charge against the ruler who asked him to heal his son: ἐὰν μὴ σημεῖα καὶ τέρατα ἴδητε, οὐ μὴ πιστεύσητε.[229] The same thought appears again in Jn. 6,30 where the Jews asked Jesus: τί οὖν ποιεῖς σὺ σημεῖον, ἵνα ἴδωμεν καὶ πιστεύσωμέν σοι; τί ἐργάζῃ;[230] With a somewhat different emphasis the later ending of Mark's gospel talks about the signs and wonders which will accompany the believers: σημεῖα δὲ τοῖς πιστεύσασιν ταῦτα παρακολουθήσει.[231] Again, on the basis of this evidence, we must conclude that Josephus' understanding of the relationship between πιστεύειν and σημεῖα is one which he shares with the NT (and OT).[232]

The words of the prophets (spoken or written) appear as the object of πιστεύειν in the OT and NT alike.[233] References to faith in the scriptures, such as occur in Josephus, are far more rare in the biblical material. Ps. 119(118),66 reads: ταῖς ἐντολαῖς σου ἐπίστευσα. But this is not precisely the same idea conveyed by Josephus. A little closer to his use is the reference in Jn. 2,22: "When Jesus arose from the dead his disciples remembered that he said this, καὶ ἐπίστευσαν τῇ γραφῇ[234] καὶ τῷ λόγῳ ὃν εἶπεν ὁ Ἰησοῦς".

Much closer to Josephus' use of πιστεύειν referring to faith in the scriptures are apocryphal statements such as in 4 Macc. 5,25: "Therefore we do not eat unclean things, for believing that the Law was set down by God,[235] we are convinced that the creator of the world, in giving his laws, sympathizes with our nature". Similar to this is the statement in Sir.

---

[229] Cf. 1 Cor. 1,22; Acts 13,12. This brings to mind once again Hezekiah's request of a sign from Isaiah in *Ant.* 10,28.

[230] Cf. Jn. 6,37; 7,31; note also the taunts of the crowd at the crucifixion: ὁ χριστὸς ὁ βασιλεὺς Ἰσραὴλ καταβάτω νῦν ἀπὸ τοῦ σταυροῦ, ἵνα ἴδωμεν καὶ πιστεύσωμεν; Mk. 15,32; par. Mt. 27,42.

[231] Mk. 16,17; cf. 1 Cor. 14,22-23.

[232] Axel von Dobbeler (*Glaube als Teilhabe* (Tübingen: J. C. B. Mohr (Paul Siebeck), 1987), pp. 291-92) indicates that the πιστ- words were employed in connection with faith in signs and wonders in Greek literature from the 5th century B.C.E. on. Such references are particularly common in Lucian.

[233] E.g., Isa. 53,1; Lk. 24,25.

[234] This refers to the OT in its entirety!

[235] πιστεύοντες γὰρ θεοῦ καθεστάναι τὸν νόμον.

32,24: "The one who believes the Law[236] keeps the commandments" (cf. Sir. 33,3). Here, as in Josephus, πιστεύειν indicates faithfulness to the Law.

In addition to the contextual similarities there are also important syntactical parallels between Josephus' use of πιστεύειν and the use in the NT. One similarity is the use of πιστεύειν with an accusative case form. This construction occurs three times in Josephus[237] and four times in the NT.[238] Although this syntactical construction is relatively rare in both sources, the parallels between the NT and Josephus are striking.

Jesus' question to Martha in Jn. 11,26: πιστεύεις τοῦτο;[239] is directly parallel to Josephus' statement in *Ant.* 1,23: ὁ δ' ἡμέτερος νομοθέτης[240] ... τοὺς μὴ ταῦτα φρονοῦντας μηδὲ μὴν πιστεύοντας ἀπαραιτήτως ἐκόλασε. In both instances the forms of the demonstrative neuter pronoun τοῦτο refer to religious [creedal] statements which are objects of πιστεύειν.[241] Likewise in *Ant.* 18,211 τὸ ἀποφανούμενον, referring to a revelation or an oracle of God, is the object of the participle πεπιστευκώς.[242]

In 1 Jn. 4,16 τὴν ἀγάπην ἣν ἔχει ὁ θεὸς ἐν ἡμῖν is the object of the verbs ἐγνώκαμεν καὶ πεπιστεύκαμεν. Acts 13,41 quotes the LXX of Hab. 1,5 where the object of πιστεύειν is the accusative relative pronoun ὅ, referring to the noun ἔργον: ὅτι ἐργάζομαι ἐγὼ ἐν ταῖς ἡμέραις ὑμῶν, ἔργον ὃ οὐ μὴ πιστεύσητε ἐάν τις ἐκδιηγῆται ὑμῖν.

But the most striking parallel between Josephus and the NT in the use of an accusative with πιστεύειν appears in *Ap.* 2,207 and in 1 Cor. 13,7 where in both cases the neuter plural πάντα is the object of πιστεύειν. In the latter instance the noun ἀγάπη is the subject of the four main verbs which occur in sequence: πάντα στέγει, πάντα πιστεύει, πάντα ἐλπίζει, πάντα ὑπομένει. In *Ap.* 2,207 the context is similar to 1 Cor. 13,7, but φιλία rather than ἀγάπη is the matter at hand: οὐ γὰρ εἶναι φιλίαν τὴν μὴ πάντα πιστεύουσαν.

The formula δεῖ πιστεύειν occurs once in the NT and twice in Josephus. In Heb. 11,6 it appears as a part of a creedal imperative:

---

[236] ὁ πιστεύων νόμῳ.
[237] *Ant.* 1,23; 18,211; *Ap.* 2,207.
[238] Jn. 11,26; Acts 13,41 (= Hab. 1,5 LXX); 1 Cor. 13,7; 1 Jn. 4,16; (perhaps also 1 Cor. 11,18).
[239] I.e., "do you believe that every one who lives and believes in me will never die"?
[240] I.e., Moses.
[241] There is, however an important difference. Josephus is referring to faith in the Law and the passage in John has reference to faith in the promise.
[242] μεῖζον δὲ δόξης τε καὶ βουλήσεως τῆς αὐτοῦ πεπιστευκὼς τοῦ θεοῦ τὸ ἐπ' αὐτοῖς ἀποφανούμενον.

πιστεῦσαι γὰρ δεῖ τὸν προσερχόμενον τῷ θεῷ ὅτι ἔστιν καὶ τοῖς
ἐκζητοῦσιν αὐτὸν μισθαποδότης γίνεται. In Josephus this imperative
occurs in *Ant.* 9,12 in connection with belief in the words of a prophet:
ἔλεγε πρὸς τὸ πλῆθος ὡς δεῖ πιστεύειν τοῖς ὑπὸ τοῦ προφήτου
εἰρημένοις. The formula also occurs in *Ap.* 2,18 in a (profane) reference
to the writings of the Phoenicians: εἰ γὰρ πιστεύειν δεῖ ταῖς Φοινίκων
ἀναγραφαῖς.

3.2 Differences in Use

3.21 Uses in Josephus Lacking in the NT

As is the case with the substantive πίστις, the major difference between
Josephus and the NT is that Josephus' use of the verb πιστεύειν is
primarily profane and the NT use is primarily religious. Practically all
specifically religious occurrences of πιστεύειν in Josephus find some
parallel in the NT. The only exception to this is Josephus' use of
πιστεύειν in the context of certain 'holy persons', e.g., the Pharisees.[243]
There is no parallel to this in the NT. More important for the present
discussion, however, are the religious uses of πιστεύειν in the NT which
do not appear in Josephus.

3.22 Uses in the NT Lacking in Josephus

The NT frequently employs the constructions: πιστεύειν εἰς plus
accusative (58 times), πιστεύειν ἐπί plus accusative (six times) or dative
(five times)[244] and πιστεύειν ἐν plus dative (two times). These
prepositions serve to mark the object of faith, belief or trust. In each
instance it is obviously an attempt to reproduce the Hebrew preposition
ב from the formula האמין־ב. This is purely a syntactical difference
between the NT and Josephus. Josephus can also speak of trusting in
God[245] or believing in the words of the prophets,[246] but he always avoids
the above Hebraisms and uses the simple Greek construction of
πιστεύειν with the dative case form.[247]

The command 'Believe!', or 'Have faith!' (with πιστεύειν in the
imperative mode) appears often in the Synoptics and John. This impera-

---

[243] Cf. *Ant.* 13,288. 402.
[244] Of the instances employing πιστεύειν ἐπί plus dative, three are direct quotations of Isa. 28,16.
[245] *Ant.* 2,117. 333; 3,309; 4,5; *Bel.* 3,387.
[246] *Ant.* 9,12. 86; 10,39.
[247] The NT also employs πιστεύειν with the simple dative 46 times.

tive appears five times as in the negative: μὴ πιστεύσητε.[248] But in most instances the imperative of πιστεύειν represents the positive command to have faith or to believe in God,[249] in Jesus,[250] in the light,[251] in the works of Jesus[252] or in the gospel.[253] Three times the imperative occurs with the absolute sense 'have faith'.[254] In 1 Jn. 3,23 the subjunctive ἵνα πιστεύσωμεν appears also with the force of an imperative. In fact, ἐντολή is expressly mentioned in this passage: καὶ αὕτη ἐστὶν ἡ ἐντολὴ αὐτοῦ, ἵνα πιστεύσωμεν τῷ ὀνόματι τοῦ υἱοῦ αὐτοῦ Ἰησοῦ Χριστοῦ καὶ ἀγαπῶμεν ἀλλήλους, καθὼς ἔδωκεν ἐντολὴν ἡμῖν.

It is interesting that πιστεύειν in the imperative mode is completely lacking in the Pauline corpus and, with the exception of 1 Jn. 4,1, in the other NT epistles. The occurrence of the imperative in Acts 16,31 shows very clearly, however, that the command to have faith or to believe was an important part of the early Christian missionary activity. In this account of the conversion of the Philippian jailer, when the jailer asked Paul and Silas what he must do to be saved, they replied: πίστευσον ἐπὶ τὸν κύριον Ἰησοῦν καὶ σωθήσῃ σὺ καὶ ὁ οἶκός σου.

In Josephus' writings the active imperative of πιστεύειν occurs only once, and then only in a profane sense.[255] In Bel. 4,189 Ananus, in a speech inciting the citizens of Jerusalem to attack the Zealots, states: "But, believe [me], if we mount to the attack, conscience will humble them and the advantage of superior height will be neutralized by reflection".[256] This is obviously something quite other than a command to believe in God, in the Lord or in the gospel. Indeed, as noted above,[257] there is no missionary element in Josephus' use of the πιστ-word group.

---

[248] In Mt. 24,23. 26 and Mk. 13,21 with reference to false reports about the messiah being in the wilderness; in 1 Jn. 4,1 with reference to 'every spirit' and in Jn. 10,37 with reference to Jesus himself: εἰ οὐ ποιῶ τὰ ἔργα τοῦ πατρός μου, μὴ πιστεύετέ μοι.

[249] E.g., Jn. 14,1: πιστεύετε εἰς τὸν θεόν.

[250] E.g., Jn. 14,1: καὶ εἰς ἐμὲ πιστεύετε. Cf. Jn. 4,21; 14,11. (Note: Πιστεύετε in Jn. 14,1 could also be interpreted as an indicative.)

[251] Jn. 12,36: πιστεύετε εἰς τὸ φῶς.

[252] Jn 10,38: τοῖς ἔργοις πιστεύετε.

[253] Mk. 1,15: μετανοεῖτε καὶ πιστεύετε ἐν τῷ εὐαγγελίῳ.

[254] Mk. 5,36; Lk. 8,50; Jn. 14,11.

[255] The passive imperative also occurs once in Ant. 4,219: Εἷς δὲ μὴ πιστευέσθω μάρτυς, ἀλλὰ τρεῖς ἢ τὸ τελευταῖον δύο.

[256] πιστεύσατε δ' ὡς, ἐὰν προσβαίνωμεν ἐπ' αὐτούς, ἔσονται τῇ συνειδήσει ταπεινότεροι, καὶ τὸ πλεονέκτημα τοῦ ὕψους ὁ λογισμὸς ἀπολεῖ.

[257] See the comparison of the use of πίστις in Josephus and the NT in Chapter Five above.

Harold W. Attridge[258] confirms this observation. Although the reader of Josephus' ancient history of the Jews was supposed to learn about the providence of God and the proper way to relate to God, Attridge points out that Josephus knows no "explicit call to 'conversion' or even to reliance upon this God". Attridge does maintain, however, that there is a "type of implicit paraenesis which appears throughout [the Antiquities]".[259] In support of this he cites Moses' speech to the Israelites in *Ant.* 2,333. As the Israelites were hemmed in by the Egyptians on the banks of the Red Sea, Moses urged them to trust in God who had been their standby in the past and not to fear the Egyptian host.[260]

Josephus does use δεῖ πιστεύειν in *Ant.* 9,12 referring to a necessity or even an obligation (but perhaps also an imperative) to believe in or to trust in the words of the prophet. Similarly Josephus can speak of Moses encouraging[261] the Israelites to believe, of Joshua and Caleb pleading[262] with the Israelites to believe and of Moses providing grounds for[263] the Israelites to believe. But these concepts are still quite different from the missionary message of Paul and Silas in Acts 16,31 or the *kerygma* of Jesus in Mk. 1,15. As a general rule in Josephus, religious faith is something which a person either has or does not have. Josephus does not employ πιστεύειν in the NT sense of a command to believe in God.

The relatively frequent construction ἵνα πιστεύ(ειν) (subjunctive) in the NT reflects further the missionary element in the NT. This formula, '[in order] that [someone] might believe', occurs regularly in the Johannine corpus,[264] but also appears once in Mk. 15,32; and once in Acts 19,4. In Mk. 15,32 the mockers standing by at the crucifixion taunt Jesus with these words: ὁ χριστὸς ὁ βασιλεὺς Ἰσραὴλ καταβάτω νῦν ἀπὸ τοῦ σταυροῦ, ἵνα ἴδωμεν καὶ πιστεύσωμεν. Likewise in Jn. 6,30 the Jewish leaders ask Jesus: τί οὖν ποιεῖς σὺ σημεῖον, ἵνα ἴδωμεν καὶ πιστεύσωμέν σοι; Directly parallel to this is

---

258 Harold W. Atteridge, *The Interpretation of Biblical History in the Antiquitates Judaicae of Flavius Josephus,* Harvard Theological Review, Harvard Dissertations in Religion, No. 7 (Missoula, Montana: Scholars Press, 1976), p. 104.

259 Ibid., p. 105.

260 Ibid. It should be noted, however, that τοιούτῳ βοηθῷ πεπιστευκότες in the text of *Ant.* 2,333 can hardly be translated as an imperative. Rather faith in God is already a given (ὅθεν...) upon which Moses' further advice is based.

261 παρακαλεῖν; *Ant.* 3,44.

262 δεόμενοι ... πιστεύειν; *Ant.* 3,308.

263 παρεῖχε πιστεύειν; *Ant.* 3,27.

264 Eleven times in John's Gospel; once in 1 Jn. 3,23.

Ant. 10,28 where Hezekiah asks Isaiah for some sign in order that he might believe the prophet's message.[265]

Again, It is not the formula ἵνα πιστεύ(ειν) (subj.) which is missing in Josephus but rather the missionary element. In the NT every occurrence of this construction appears in connection with faith in Jesus.[266] Jn. 1,7 and Acts 19,4 point out that the purpose of the ministry of John the Baptist was that the people who heard him *might be - lieve* in Jesus. The purpose of the raising of Lazarus from the dead was, at least in part, so that the disciples would believe.[267] Jesus predicted coming events for his disciples, in order that when these things came to pass the disciples would believe.[268] One petition of Jesus' high priestly prayer in Jn. 17,21 was "that the world might believe that you have sent me". But the missionary emphasis of the construction ἵνα πιστεύ(ειν) (subj.) is most clearly seen in Jn. 19,35; 20,31 where the author states the express purpose of his testimony and written account of Jesus' earthly ministry:

> Jn. 19,35—καὶ ὁ ἑωρακὼς μεμαρτύρηκεν, καὶ ἀληθινὴ αὐτοῦ ἐστιν ἡ μαρτυρία, καὶ ἐκεῖνος οἶδεν ὅτι ἀληθῆ λέγει, ἵνα καὶ ὑμεῖς πιστεύ[σ]ητε.
>
> Jn. 20,31—ταῦτα δὲ γέγραπται ἵνα πιστεύ[σ]ητε ὅτι Ἰησοῦς ἐστιν ὁ χριστὸς ὁ υἱὸς τοῦ θεοῦ, καὶ ἵνα πιστεύοντες ζωὴν ἔχητε ἐν τῷ ὀνόματι αὐτοῦ.

Josephus has no parallel for this understanding and use of πιστεύειν.

The NT employs substantival participles of πιστεύειν a total of 62 times.[269] The substantival participle, referring to 'the one(s) who believe(s)' or 'the believer(s)', commonly occurs in the regular syntactical structures already noted above; i.e., [ὁ πιστεύων] εἰς,[270] [ὁ πιστεύων] ἐν,[271] [ὁ πιστεύων] ἐπί,[272] [ὁ πιστεύων] plus dative[273] and [ὁ

---

[265] σημεῖόν τι καὶ τεράστιον ἠξίου ποιῆσαι τὸν Ἡσαΐαν, ἵν' αὐτῷ πιστεύσῃ λέγοντι ταῦτα ἥκοντι παρὰ τοῦ θεοῦ. Cf. also *Ant.* 8,232: ἵνα μέντοι γε πιστεύσωσιν οὗτοι τοῦθ' οὕτως ἕξειν, σημεῖον αὐτοῖς προερῶ γενησόμενον.

[266] Even in Jn. 11,15; 14,29, where πιστεύειν is used absolutely, the context clearly shows that faith in Christ is the matter at hand.

[267] Jn. 11,15; cf. 11,42.

[268] Jn. 13,19; 14,29.

[269] In Rom. 9,33; 10,11; 1 Pet. 2,6 the ὁ πιστεύων is a part of a direct quotation from Isa. 28,16 (LXX).

[270] Jn. 1,12; 3,16. 36; 6,35. 40; 7,38. 39; 11,25. 26; 12,44. 46; 14,12; 17,20; Acts 10,43; 1 Jn. 5,10. 13.

[271] Jn. 3,15.

[272] Acts 22,19; Rom. 4,24; [9,33]; [10,11]; [1 Pet. 2,6].

[273] Jn. 5,24; 8,31; Acts 5,14; 2 Thes. 2,12; Tit. 3,8; 1 Jn. 5,10.

πιστεύων] ὅτι.²⁷⁴ But in thirty instances the substantival participle of
πιστεύειν occurs absolutely, meaning: 'the believer(s)'. This absolute
usage appears consistently in Acts and in the Pauline corpus where the
believers are the believers in Christ, i.e., Christians, members of the
community of faith.²⁷⁵ Acts 2,44, for example, reads thus: πάντες δὲ
οἱ πιστεύοντες ἦσαν ἐπὶ τὸ αὐτὸ καὶ εἶχον ἅπαντα κοινά.²⁷⁶ The
same use occurs in Rom. 3,22: δικαιοσύνη δὲ θεοῦ διὰ πίστεως
Ἰησοῦ Χριστοῦ εἰς πάντας τοὺς πιστεύοντας.²⁷⁷ But also in Mark's
gospel,²⁷⁸ in John's gospel²⁷⁹ and elsewhere²⁸⁰ substantival participles of
πιστεύειν appear, referring to 'the one(s) who believe(s)'.

The substantival participle of πιστεύειν is not foreign to
Josephus, but it does not occur frequently. In *Ant.* 1,23 Josephus writes
that Moses punished those [Israelites] who did not hold with or believe
the doctrines which he taught.²⁸¹ Here the substantival participle appears
with an accusative object.²⁸² The only absolute use of the substantival
participle of πιστεύειν by Josephus appears in *Bel.* 2,187: Ἰουδαίων δὲ
οἱ μὲν ἠπίστουν ἐπὶ ταῖς τοῦ πολέμου φήμαις, οἱ δὲ πιστεύοντες
ἦσαν ἐν ἀμηχάνῳ πρὸς τὴν ἄμυναν.²⁸³

Otherwise, Josephus does not employ the participle of πιστεύειν
substantivally. Moreover, in none of the instances mentioned is the
substantival participle of πιστεύειν in Josephus parallel to the use in the
NT, where 'the believers' constitute the community of the faithful (i.e.,
the Church) or where 'the one who believes' is an individual member of
that community.²⁸⁴

²⁷⁴ Lk. 1,45; 1 Jn. 5,1. 10.
²⁷⁵ In this sense οἱ πιστεύοντες is synonymous to οἱ πιστοί; see below, Chapter Seven; cf. also the LXX, Ps. 100(101),6.
²⁷⁶ Cf. also Acts 4,32; 15,5; 18,27; 19,18; 21,20.
²⁷⁷ Cf. Rom. 4,ll; 10,4; 1 Cor. 1,21; 14,22; Gal. 3,22.
²⁷⁸ Mk. 9,23; 16,16. 17.
²⁷⁹ Jn. 3,18; 6,47. 64; 20,29.
²⁸⁰ E.g., Heb. 4,3; Jude 5.
²⁸¹ τοὺς μὴ ταῦτα φρονοῦντας μηδὲ μὴν πιστεύοντας ἀπαραιτήτως ἐκόλασε.
²⁸² Cf. also *Ant.* 3,203: ἡδεῖα δὲ ἀπ' αὐτοῦ δρόσος ἔρρει καὶ θεοῦ δηλοῦσα παρουσίαν τοῖς τοῦτο καὶ βουλομένοις καὶ πεπιστευκόσι.
²⁸³ This is not, however, truly an absolute use of πιστεύειν. The object of the verb ἀπιστεῖν should also be understood as the object of πιστεύειν.
²⁸⁴ Cf. Josephus' lack of substantival use of πιστός to refer to the same (see below, Chapter Seven).

4 THE VERB ΑΠΙΣΤΕΙΝ

4.1 Ἀπιστεῖν in Josephus

4.11 General Use

Ἀπιστεῖν appears forty-one times in Josephus, and almost exclusively with the profane meaning: 'to disbelieve, to be incredulous'. Normally the verb occurs either in an absolute sense[285] or in connection with an impersonal dative object. In most cases the object of disbelief has to do with words,[286] either spoken[287] or written.[288] In one instance the 'greatness of [someone's] boldness' is the object of disbelief.[289] Twice, in *Ant.* 2,330 and *Bel.* 2,187, Josephus marks the object of ἀπιστεῖν with the preposition ἐπί plus a dative case form. In this profane sense of 'to disbelieve' ἀπιστεῖν is clearly being employed as an opposite of πιστεύειν.[290]

In just a few instances ἀπιστεῖν in Josephus means 'to distrust, to mistrust'. Generally the verb has this sense when construed with a personal dative object.[291] In one instance the dative object is impersonal.[292] Ἀπιστεῖν appears once absolutely with the meaning: 'to mistrust'.[293]

4.12 Religious Use

Ἀπιστεῖν in a religious sense occurs relatively seldom in Josephus in comparison to the total occurrences of the verb. When a religious use does appear, however, it appears in one of two contexts: in connection with the narrative about Moses or the narrative about the prophets. Concerning Moses himself, Josephus reports in *Ant.* 2,275 that "Moses was unable to doubt the promises of the Deity, having seen and heard such confirmation of them".[294] Likewise Moses, after rehearsing the

---

285 E.g., *Ant.* 2,58. 111; 5,101; 7,4; 17,332. 354; 18,76; *Bel.* 2,135; 3,403; et al. In these absolute uses of ἀπιστεῖν, however, the immediate context reveals the object of disbelief.
286 λόγοις, *Ant.* 14,13; also 'promises', ταῖς ὑποσχέσιν, *Bel.* 2,54.
287 τοῖςλεγομένοις; e.g., *Ant.* 8,182; *Bel.* 1,72; [4,388]; *Ap.* 2,284.
288 τοῖς γεγραμμένοις; *Ant.* 14,187; *Ap.* 1,2.
289 τῷ μεγέθει τοῦ τολμήματος, *Bel.* 7,405.
290 Cf. *Ant.* 10,28; *Ap.* 1,161.
291 Cf. *Ant.* 2,330; 12,177; *Ap.* 1,6.
292 τῷ βεβαίῳ τῆς φορᾶς, *Bel.* 7,139.
293 *Bel.* 5,278.
294 Μωυσῆς δ' οὐκ ἔχων ἀπιστεῖν οἷς ἐπηγγέλλετο τὸ θεῖον θεατής γε τοιούτων βεβαιωμάτων καὶ ἀκροατὴς γενόμενος.

message of God and the divine signs before the king of Egypt, entreated Pharaoh not to disbelieve these things and by so doing obstruct the purpose of God.[295] In three other passages Moses is only indirectly the object of ἀπιστεῖν.[296]

In the context of prophetic utterances, *Ant.* 8,420 reports that Achab [sic] disbelieved those who foretold his defeat, while he was persuaded by those who prophesied things that pleased him.[297] So also Hezekiah in *Ant.* 10,28 was unbelieving[298] when Isaiah prophesied the miraculous cure of his illness. Similarly, Zedekiah disbelieved the prophecies of Ezekiel and Jeremiah, who were predicting the misfortunes which would come upon Jerusalem.[299]

4.2 Ἀπιστεῖν in the NT

In comparison to Josephus, the NT employs the verb ἀπιστεῖν relatively seldom, a total of only eight times. Syntactically the use of ἀπιστεῖν in the NT is parallel to Josephus. The verb appears only in an absolute sense or (one time) with a simple dative object. Generally, as in Josephus, ἀπιστεῖν means 'to disbelieve'. In the NT, however, this is always religious disbelief. In Lk. 24,11. 41 and Mk. 16,11 ἀπιστεῖν refers to the disbelief of the disciples in the resurrection of Jesus. Acts 28,24 reports the disbelief of some of the Jews in Rome after their audience with Paul.[300] In 1 Pet. 2,7 and Mk. 16,16 active substantival participles of ἀπιστεῖν refer to '[the] unbeliever(s)'.

The NT does not employ ἀπιστεῖν with the meaning 'to mistrust' as Josephus does. Twice, however, the verb has the sense 'to be unfaithful'—a sense lacking in Josephus. In Rom. 3,3 the ἀπιστία of some, expressed also in the verb ἀπιστεῖν, is viewed in direct contrast to the faithfulness of God.[301] Likewise in 2 Tim. 2,13 'our' unfaithfulness stands in direct contrast to God's faithfulness.[302]

---

[295] *Ant.* 2,283: παρεκάλει τε μὴ ἀπιστοῦντα τούτοις ἐμποδὼν ἵστασθαι τῇ τοῦ θεοῦ γνώμῃ.

[296] Cf. *Ant.* 2,330; 3,298. 316.

[297] φαίνεται οὖν καὶ Ἄχαβος ὑπὸ τούτου τὴν διάνοιαν ἀπατηθείς, ὥστε ἀπιστῆσαι μὲν τοῖς προλέγουσι τὴν ἧτταν, τοῖς δὲ τὰ πρὸς χάριν προφητεύσασι πεισθεὶς ἀποθανεῖν.

[298] ἀπιστῶν.

[299] ταῖς δὲ προφητείαις αὐτῶν Σαχχίας ἠπίστησεν; *Ant.* 10,106; cf. 10,107.

[300] οἱ δὲ ἠπίστουν.

[301] πίστις τοῦ θεοῦ.

[302] εἰ ἀπιστοῦμεν, ἐκεῖνος πιστὸς μένει.

5 SUMMARY

Josephus, in his use of the verb πιστεύειν as a religious term, shares a great deal of common ground with the OT and the NT. Only in two con-texts, in the context of certain 'holy persons' or in the context of holy scriptures, does Josephus employ the verb in a way that the biblical material does not. But even in these instances it is quite clear that Josephus bases his use of πιστεύειν upon his Jewish religious heritage. The fact that Josephus' use of πιστεύειν in a religious sense is to be understood primarily upon the basis of Jewish religious usage is indicated further by the fact that the vast majority of these instances come from *Antiquities* or *Contra Apionem*, with only a couple such references from *Bellum Judaicum*.

We must once again be careful to point out, however, that these re-ligious uses of πιστεύειν account for only a scant twenty-five percent of the total occurrences of the verb in Josephus' writings. Josephus' primary understanding of πιστεύειν is the purely profane sense of 'trusting, believing or entrusting'. Therefore it is not possible to force a religious meaning upon the verb every time it appears, even within a passage that is theological in nature or content. In the instances where the verb does have a religious significance, it appears that this religious significance arises from Josephus' own Jewish religious background and not from any Hellenistic religious use of the word group.

Πιστεύειν as faith terminology in Josephus is comparable to his use of πίστις, although πίστις occurs less frequently as a term for faith. Just as πιστεύειν appears in creedal formulas, so also does πίστις.[303] Πίστις is also used (as is πιστεύειν) in the context of an active confidence or faith in God,[304] in the context of the person and work of Moses,[305] in the context of the prophets,[306] in the context of signs and wonders[307] and in the context of faithfulness to the Law and the scriptures.[308]

---

[303] E.g., *Ant.* 18,14; *Ap.* 2,163. 169.
[304] *Bel.* 3,404; *Ant.* 2,218; 12,147.
[305] *Ant.* 2,218. 272. 283.
[306] *Ant.* 10,268; *Bel.* 2,261. 586.
[307] *Ant.* 2,283.
[308] *Ap.* 1,41; *Ant.* 9,153.

CHAPTER SEVEN

ΠΙΣΤΟΣ IN THE WRITINGS OF FLAVIUS JOSEPHUS AND THE NEW TESTAMENT

1 ΠΙΣΤΟΣ IN JOSEPHUS

The adjective πιστός always occurs in a profane sense in Josephus' writings.[1] In almost every instance πιστός simply means 'faithful, loyal, trustworthy'. This designation is primarily a personal designation reserved for human relationships. Πιστός occurs quite frequently in heirarchichal relationships, e.g., the faithful servant,[2] the faithful soldier[3] and other military or political personnel.[4] In other instances πιστός designates a faithful friend,[5] and sometimes specific persons are described as faithful or loyal.[6]

In a few passages Josephus employs πιστός as an attribute for an impersonal noun, generally a spoken word or report. Πιστὸς λόγος indicates a word or report that is credible and, therefore, trustworthy.[7] The same is true when πιστός refers to things spoken,[8] inquiries made under torture,[9] apologies[10] and accusations.[11] In one instance πιστός modifies the noun 'deeds'. In a parenthetical statement in *Ant.* 7,29 Josephus remarks: πιστότερα γὰρ τῶν δι' ἄλλου πραττομένων ὅσα δι' αὐτῶν

---

[1] The adjective appears 77 times in Josephus' works (including one instance of the compound form ἀξιόπιστος). In *Ant.* 19,9 and in *Bel.* 2,140 πιστός appears within a semi-religious context, but in neither instance is there any justification for a religious interpretation of the adjective itself.

[2] There are a variety words for 'servant' to which Josephus attributes the adjective πιστός. 1) (the most common) οἰκέτης, *Ant.* 2,252; 6,205. 330; 8,384; 9,88; 2) δοῦλος, *Ant.* 6,256; 18,182; 3) διάκονος, *Ant.* 7,201. 224; 4) θεράπαινα , *Ant.* 7,223.

[3] 1) ὁπλίτης, *Ant.* 9,137; *Vi.* 95; 228; 240; 242; 253; 2) (σωματα-)φύλαξ , *Ant.* 18,325; *Bel.* 4,493.

[4] 1) ἔπαρχος, *Ant.* 19,317; 2) ὕπαρχος, *Bel.* 5,534; 3) χιλίαρχος , *Ant.* 6,256.

[5] *Ant.* 7,5. 211; 12,402; 16,180. 256; 20,163; *Vi.* 163; 228; 234; 378; cf. *Ant.* 17,31.

[6] E.g., Dositheus, *Ant.* 15,170; Josephus and Soemus, *Ant.* 15,185. 205. 228; Ptolemy and Sapinnius, *Ant.* 16,257; Apion, *Ap.* 2,17.

[7] Cf. *Ant.* 16,100; 17,62; 19,132.

[8] τὰ εἰρημένα , *Ant.* 18,188.

[9] βάσανοι, *Ant.* 17,119.

[10] ἀπολογία, *Bel.* 1,633.

[11] κατηγορούμενα, *Ant.* 18,252.

ἕκαστοι ποιοῦμεν εἶναι δοκεῖ.[12]   In a semi-religious context πιστός appears in *Ant.* 19,9 referring to portents which were not to be discredited.[13]

The substantival use of the neuter τὸ πιστόν in *Vi.* 380 also merits attention, where τὸ πιστόν simply refers to the credibility or believability of a rumor.[14] A similar use of the substantive πίστις occurs in *Bel.* 1,485 and *Ant.* 19,135. Elsewhere τὸ πιστόν can refer to a 'pledge' or 'assurance'. In *Ant.* 19,144 τὸ πιστὸν τοῦ περιεῖναι refers to an assurance [of someone's] survival.[15] *Bel.* 2,486 employs the neuter plural τὰ πιστά in reference to [military] pledges of safety.[16] In three instances τὸ πιστόν simply refers to the good faith (='good will, loyalty') displayed by one person to another.[17]

2 ΠΙΣΤΟΣ IN THE NT

2.1 *Profane Use*

The intertwining of a profane understanding with religious nuances, which has been apparent to some degree in the NT use of the noun πίστις and the verb πιστεύειν, is even more obvious in the its use of the adjective πιστός. The πιστὸς δοῦλος in passages such as Mt. 24,45 and 25,21. 23[18] and ὁ πιστός in Lk. 16,10-12 appear on the surface to be normal profane uses of the adjective πιστός. The πιστὸς δοῦλος is simply a trustworthy servant; ὁ πιστός is a trustworthy person.

Precisely this understanding of πιστός is very common in Josephus. 'Faithful' or 'trustworthy' is the normal definition of πιστός. When Jesus poses the question in Mt. 24,45: Τίς ἄρα ἐστὶν ὁ πιστὸς δοῦλος καὶ φρόνιμος; the obvious answer is: "the servant who does what was commanded by his master". Faithfulness and trustworthiness, even on a profane level, are only displayed in the relationship of one

---

[12] This was spoken of Abner, who, rather than sending envoys, met personally with David at Hebron to receive his oath of security. The nature of this statement is proverbial.

[13] λέγεται δὲ Μέμμιον διὰ ταῦτα καὶ σημείων μειζόνων γενομένων, ἢ ὡς ἄν τινα μὴ πιστὰ ἡγεῖσθαι, ὑπερβαλέσθαι τὴν ἀναίρεσιν. (Memmion had been ordered by Caligula to transport the statue of Zeus from Olympia to Rome. Memmius was advised by one of the technicians that the statue would be ruined in the move. Because of this and because of the portents he disobeyed orders and postponed the action.)

[14] πρὸς γὰρ τὸ πιστὸν τῆς φήμης ἐσκηπτόμην ὁμοίως αὐτοῖς διατίθεσθαι.

[15] Cf. πίστις, e.g., *Bel.* 3,334; *Ant.* 12,396.

[16] Cf. Josephus' use of the plural πίστεις, e.g., *Bel.* 3,345; 4,61; *Ant.* 5,131.

[17] *Bel.* 2,140. 467; 3,320; cf. *Ant.* 17,329. This substantival use of the adjective πιστός is comparable to Josephus' similar use of πίστις, e.g., in *Ant.* 7,43; 15,134; 17,246f.

[18] Par. Lk. 12,42; 19,17; et al.

person to another. This profane use of πιστός in the NT is thus parallel to Josephus' use.

Πιστός in the NT passages cited above, however, cannot be interpreted in a purely profane sense. When Jesus speaks of the πιστὸς δοῦλος in Mt. 24,45 (et al.), he is speaking in parables. Ὁ κύριος is God and ὁ δοῦλος is a man or woman. The profane relationship of an earthly servant to an earthly master is parallel to the sacred relationship of humankind to God. Πιστός thus takes on a religious significance in addition to the non-religious sense.

2.2 Religious Use

It may actually be accurate to say that the NT knows πιστός only as a religious term, for all other instances of the adjective in the NT are clearly religious in nature. The NT use of πιστός is clearly parallel to the LXX use, where πιστός generally represents the niphal (participle) of אמן and means 'faithfulness, trustworthiness', either on a divine or on a human level.

2.21 Πιστός as a Divine Attribute

God is often described in the NT as 'faithful, trustworthy' in his dealings with humankind. The formula πιστὸς ὁ θεός occurs three times.[19] This is clearly an OT formula, finding its classic expression in Dt. 7,9; 32,4.[20] But the characteristic faithfulness of God is not limited to this formula in the NT. God is also described as 'faithful' in certain divine activities such as calling[21] and promising.[22] God's word is regularly described as faithful[23] — a tradition stemming from the OT.[24]

Faithfulness is also an attribute of Jesus. In Heb. 2,17 Jesus is called the "faithful high priest".[25] In Heb. 3,2 Jesus, the faithful high priest, is likened to Moses, who was faithful in all of God's household (Num. 12,7). In Rev. 1,5 Jesus is called "the witness, the faithful one,

---

[19] 1 Cor. 1,9; 10,13; 2 Cor. 1,18; cf. 2 Thes. 3,3; 1 Jn. 1,9.

[20] In the latter of these Deuteronomy passages the direct opposite of πιστός is ἀδικία. These opposites appear again in Lk. 16,10-11, where the 'the faithful one' (ὁ πιστός) is presented in contrast to 'the unrighteous one' (ὁ ἄδικος).

[21] 1 Thes. 5,24: πιστὸς ὁ καλῶν ὑμᾶς.

[22] Heb. 10,23: πιστὸς γὰρ ὁ ἐπαγγειλάμενος; cf. Heb. 11,11.

[23] 1 Tim. 1,15; 3,1; 4,9; 2 Tim. 2,11; Tit. 1,9; 3,8; Rev. 21,5; 22,6.

[24] Cf. Ps. 19,7(18,8); 111(110),7; 145(144),13.

[25] πιστὸς ἀρχιερεύς. This is clearly a reference to 1 Sam. 2,35, where God promises to raise up for himself a faithful high priest.

the firstborn of the dead and the ruler over the kings of the earth",[26] and in Rev. 19,11 he is called "the faithful and true one".[27]

2.22 Πιστός as a Human Attribute

'Faithful' is also the (proper) attribute of a man or woman in his or her relationship to God. The 'faithful servant' of Mt. 24,45 (et al.) is, as noted above, a metaphorical presentation of this proper relationship to God. Those who possess this proper relationship to God are called πιστοί.[28] This use of the adjective in the NT is also parallel to OT use.[29]

So important is this attribute for men and women in their relation-ship to God that πιστός can be viewed as the 'mark of a Christian'. This is especially clear in Acts 16,15, where Lydia, following her baptism, entreated Paul and his company to come and stay in her home, if indeed they judged her to be faithful to the Lord.[30] Likewise Thomas is in-structed by Jesus in Jn. 20,27 not to be unbelieving but to be believing.[31] In this same sense πιστός commonly appears substantivally referring to Christian(s) as 'believer(s), the faithful one(s), the saint(s)'.[32]

3 THE ADJECTIVE ΑΠΙΣΤΟΣ

3.1 Ἄπιστος in Josephus

3.11 Profane Use

The adjective ἄπιστος appears nineteen times in Josephus' writings. Its use is primarily profane. Josephus employs ἄπιστος in two senses: 1) 'incredible, unbelievable', and 2) 'unfaithful, not to be trusted'.[33]

---

[26] ὁ μάρτυς, ὁ πιστός, ὁ πρωτότοκος τῶν νεκρῶν καὶ ὁ ἄρχων τῶν βασιλέων τῆς γῆς. Cf. Ps. 89, 28. 38 (88,29. 38); Jer. 42(49),5.

[27] πιστὸς καὶ ἀληθινός. It is significant here that the ideas of faithfulness and truth are linked to-gether, since both elements are present in the Hebrew root אמן; cf. also Rev. 21,5; 22,6.

[28] E.g., Timothy, 1 Cor. 4,17; Paul, 1 Cor. 7,25; Abraham, Gal. 3,9 (cf. Gen. 15,6; 1 Macc. 2,52); Tychicus, Eph. 6,21; the 'brethren' in Colossae, Col. 1,2; Epaphras, Col. 1,7; Onesimus, Col. 4,9; 'the women', 1 Tim. 3,11; Silvanus, 1 Pet. 5,12; Antipas, Rev. 2,13.

[29] E.g., Moses, Num. 12,7; Samuel, 1 Sam. 3,20; David, 1 Sam. 22,14; the city of Zion, Isa. 1,21. 26; etc.

[30] εἰ κεκρίκατέ με πιστὴν τῷ κυρίῳ εἶναι. Cf. 1 Cor. 4,2; 1 Tim. 1,12; 6,2; 2 Tim. 2,2; also Neh. 9,8; 13,13.

[31] μὴ γίνου ἄπιστος ἀλλὰ πιστός.

[32] E.g., Acts 10,45; 16,1; 2 Cor. 6,15; Eph. 1,1; 1 Tim. 4,3. 10. 12; 5,16; 1 Pet. 1,21; Rev. 17,14; cf. Ps. 101(100),6; 1 Macc. 3,13.

[33] I.e., the true opposite of πιστός.

In the first sense Josephus describes a variety of things as incredible: a report,[34] a deed,[35] swiftness,[36] a promise,[37] the architecture and decoration of a building,[38] a general fact[39] or an event of history.[40] In this sense ἄπιστος can also be used substantivally, referring to the incredibility or unlikelihood[41] of a hope[42] or of a slander against someone.[43] The neuter plural substantive τὰ ἄπιστα means 'incredible things'.[44]

In the sense 'not to be trusted', ἄπιστος generally refers to persons; e.g., women,[45] barbarians,[46] foreigners[47] or one who does not deal responsibly with a deposit or trust.[48] In *Bel.* 5,536 ἄπιστος as a designation for a certain man named Simon probably has the extended meaning 'treacherous'. Twice the neuter substantive τὸ ἄπιστον has the meaning 'untrustworthiness, perfidy'.[49]

3.12 Religious Use

In contrast to the adjective πιστός, there are at least two instances in Josephus where ἄπιστος is clearly used within a religious context and probably has some religious significance. Ἄπιστος appears in *Ant.* 9,73 in the sense of 'incredible, unbelievable'. The prophet Elisha had prophesied to King Jehoram that the famine in Samaria would come to an end and that food would be plentiful on the very next day. The commander of Jehoram's third division did not believe this prophecy of Elisha, but replied: "Incredible are the things you are saying, O prophet.[50] And, as impossible as it is for God to rain down from heaven

---

34   *Ant.* 2,169; 15,425; 18,76.
35   *Ant.* 6,198.
36   *Ant.* 7,16.
37   *Ant.* 14,31.
38   *Ant.* 15,416.
39   *Ant.* 19,167.
40   *Bel.* 6,199.
41   τὸ ἄπιστον.
42   τὸ μὲν τῆς ἐλπίδος ἄπιστον, *Ant.* 15,388.
43   *Ant.* 16,122.
44   *Ant.* 9,73.
45   *Ant.* 17,352.
46   *Bel.* 1,255.
47   *Bel.* 2,472.
48   *Bel.* 3,372.
49   *Ant.* 14,341; *Bel.* 1,260. This is clearly the opposite of τὸ πιστόν when used in the sense of 'good faith'.
50   ἄπιστα, εἶπε, ζ λέγεις, ὦ προφῆτα.

torrents of barley or fine flour, just so impossible is it for the things of which you have now spoken to happen". *Ant.* 2,169 relates Jacob's reaction upon hearing the report from his sons that Joseph was alive and held a high position in the Egyptian government. Josephus writes: "[Jacob] could deem none of these reports incredible, when he reflected on God's mighty power and his benevolence towards him, albeit for a while suspended; and he straightway sped forth to go to Joseph".[51] In *Ant.* 15,425 Josephus recalls the fact that, during the rebuilding of the temple, no rain fell during the day, but only at night, so that there was no interruption of the work. This story, he says, is not at all incredible if one considers the other manifestations of God's power.[52]

In the religious sense of 'unfaithful, untrustworthy' ἄπιστος appears in *Bel.* 3,372. Josephus condemns the practice of suicide in this passage, referring to the soul as a portion of the Deity housed in our [mortal] bodies. It is a trust, a deposit from God. Josephus reasons: "If, then, one who makes away with or misapplies a deposit entrusted to him by a fellow-man is considered wicked and unfaithful, how can he who casts out from his own body the deposit which God has placed there, hope to elude Him whom he has thus wronged?"[53]

3.2 Ἄπιστος in the NT

The adjective ἄπιστος in the NT always appears as a religious term. There is little or no precedent for the use of the adjective in the OT,[54] so that the occurrence of ἄπιστος as a religious term in the NT seems to be an innovation. The meaning of ἄπιστος in most instances is the true opposite of πιστός as it appears in the NT; i.e., 'unfaithful, unbelieving', or substantively, 'the non-believer'.

Ἄπιστος in the sense of 'not to be trusted', as it occasionally appears in Josephus, is missing in NT use. Only in Acts 26,8 does ἄπιστος occur in the sense of 'incredible, unbelievable'. Here, in his speech before Agrippa, Paul asks: "Why is it thought incredible by any

---

[51] ἄπιστον μὲν οὐδὲν ἐδόκει τῶν ἠγγελμένων λογιζόμενος τοῦ θεοῦ τὴν μεγαλουργίαν καὶ τὴν πρὸς αὐτὸν εὔνοιαν, εἰ καὶ τῷ μεταξὺ χρόνῳ διέλιπεν, ὥρμητο δ' εὐθὺς πρὸς τὸν Ἰώσηπον. Thackeray rightly points out in a footnote (*Loeb Classical Library*, "Josephus", vol. 4, p. 237, note *a*): "Josephus omits, or deliberately contradicts, the mention of his first incredulity: 'his heart fainted, for he believed not', Gen. 45,26".

[52] καὶ τοῦτον τὸν λόγον οἱ πατέρες ἡμῖν παρέδωκαν, οὐδ' ἔστιν ἄπιστον, εἰ καὶ πρὸς τὰς ἄλλας ἀπίδοι τις ἐμφανείας τοῦ θεοῦ.

[53] εἶτ' ἐὰν μὲν ἀφανίσῃ τις ἀνθρώπου παρακαταθήκην ἢ διαθῆται κακῶς, πονηρὸς εἶναι δοκεῖ καὶ ἄπιστος, εἰ δέ τις τοῦ σφετέρου σώματος ἐκβάλλει τὴν παρακαταθήκην τοῦ θεοῦ, λεληθέναι δοκεῖ τὸν ἀδικούμενον;

[54] In the LXX ἄπιστος appears only in Prov. 17,6 and Isa. 17,10 (and as a textual variant in Prov. 28,25); the idea of unfaithfulness is, however, completely absent.

of you that God raises the dead?"[55] Strictly speaking, ἄπιστος in this passage is not a religious concept. Rather the definition 'incredible' is the normal profane meaning of ἄπιστος.   This is directly parallel to Josephus' use of the adjective in *Ant.* 9,73 (et al).

Normally ἄπιστος in the NT means 'unfaithful, unbelieving'.   In Mk. 9,19 Jesus cries out against the 'unfaithful generation'.[56]   In Lk. 12,46 the reward for the servant who does not act in accordance with the instructions of his master is to have his portion with the 'unfaithful'.[57] It is obvious in this passage that such a servant is an 'unfaithful servant', even though the designation δοῦλος ἄπιστος does not occur as such. Ὁ πιστὸς οἰκονόμος does, however, appear in Lk. 12,42 as the positive counterpart to this evil servant. Therefore ἄπιστος in vs. 46 should be seen as the direct opposite of πιστός in vs. 42.

In the Pauline corpus ἄπιστος appears exclusively as a *terminus technicus* for 'non-believer(s)' (i.e., non-Christians). In 1 Cor. 7,12-15 Paul gives counsel to Christian spouses of 'non-Christian' husbands and wives.[58] Generally ἄπιστος in this sense occurs substantivally, and then almost always in the plural.[59] Again this definition of ἄπιστος is the true opposite of πιστός when employed substantivally in the sense of 'the believer, the Christian'.

4 SUMMARY

Although the adjective πιστός has the same basic meaning in Josephus and in the NT, i.e., 'faithful, trustworthy', there is nonetheless an important difference in usage. In the NT the adjective should almost exclusively be interpreted in a religious sense, referring to God's faithfulness to humankind or vice versa. This religious understanding of πιστός is directly influenced by and thus directly parallel to the use of πιστός in the LXX, especially as a translation for the niphal (participle) of אמן.

---

[55] τί ἄπιστον κρίνεται παρ' ὑμῖν εἰ ὁ θεὸς νεκροὺς ἐγείρει;

[56] γενεὰ ἄπιστος; parallels: Mt. 17,17; Lk. 9,41.

[57] ἥξει ὁ κύριος τοῦ δούλου ἐκείνου ἐν ἡμέρᾳ ᾗ οὐ προσδοκᾷ καὶ ἐν ὥρᾳ ᾗ οὐ γινώσκει, καὶ διχοτομήσει αὐτὸν καὶ τὸ μέρος αὐτοῦ μετὰ τῶν ἀπίστων θήσει. The parallel passage in Mt. has ὑποκριταί instead of ἄπιστοι. Otto Betz maintains, however, that Luke reproduces the correct sense with his use of ἄπιστοι. See Otto Betz, "The Dichotomized Servant and the End of Judas Iscariot", *Jesus: Der Messias Israels* Vol. 1 (Tübingen: JCB Mohr [Paul Siebeck], 1987), pp. 169ff.

[58] Cf. also 2 Cor. 6,15.

[59] E.g., 1 Cor. 10,27; 14,22-24; 2 Cor. 4,4; 6,14-15; 1 Tim. 5,8; Tit. 1,15; also Rev. 21,8.

In Josephus, on the other hand, πιστός almost always denotes faithfulness or trustworthiness in profane relationships. Josephus does not view the attribute of faithfulness or trustworthiness to be a religious attribute, either of God in God's relationship toward humankind or of humankind in its relationship toward God. This indicates further that there is something missing in Josephus' concept of religious faith(fulness) which is an integral part of the OT and NT understanding of faith. That which is missing is the aspect of personal commitment *(Verbindlichkeit),* and Josephus' concept of faith shows itself in this point to be much more a Hellenistic than a Hebrew concept of faith.

Josephus' understanding and use of ἄπιστος is primarily profane. Even in the passages where the context is religious, ἄπιστος has at best only a religious *flavor*. It is not a theological term as it is in the NT, designating unfaithfulness to God or referring substantivally to 'the unfaithful ones'. This omission in Josephus demonstrates once again the missing *(verbindliche)* element in his understanding of faith. The NT forms its religious understanding of ἄπιστος based upon its own (OT!) religious understanding of πιστός. Since the latter is missing in Josephus, it is also natural that Josephus does not employ the adjective ἄπιστος as a religious term.

CONCLUSION

TWO TYPES OF FAITH

1 MARTIN BUBER: JEWISH FAITH VERSUS CHRISTIAN FAITH

> There are two, and in the end only two, types of faith. To be sure there
> are very many contents of faith, but we only know faith itself in two basic
> forms. Both can be understood from the simple data of our life: the one
> from the fact that I trust someone, without being able to offer sufficient
> reasons for my trust in him; the other from the fact that, likewise without
> being able to give a sufficient reason, I acknowledge a thing to be true.[1]

In his monograph entitled *Two Types of Faith*, Martin Buber places over
against one another the אֱמוּנָה of the OT-Jewish tradition and the πίστις of
the NT-Christian tradition (or more precisely the πίστις of the Christian
Church in later interpretation[2] as two distinct kinds of faith. The 'classic
example' of the first kind of faith is found, according to Buber, in the
early history of Israel. Israel as a people was 'the people of faith'[3] and
actually came into existence as a 'community of faith'.[4] The example of
the second kind of faith comes from the early period of Christianity. This
second kind of faith, maintains Buber, was an innovation which arose
from "the death of a great son of Israel and the subsequent belief in his
resurrection" at a time when the settled state of Israel and the nations and
faith communities of the ancient East were crumbling.[5]

The various difficulties and strengths of Buber's designations of
Jewish faith and Christian faith may appear at once to some to be
obvious. Here, however, we shall seek first of all to summarize Buber's
understanding of these two types of faith, reserving our response and
critique of Buber for the end of this summary.

---

[1] Martin Buber, *Two Types of Faith*, p. 7.

[2] Cf. Emil Brunner, *The Christian Doctrine of the Church, Faith, and the Consummation;
Dogmatics: Vol. III,* trans. by David Cairns (Philadelphia: The Westminster Press, 1962), p.
162.

[3] *Ein Glaubensvolk.*

[4] *Glaubensgemeinschaft.* Cf. Buber, pp. 9f. Buber's terminology is absolutely foreign to the OT.
Nowhere is Israel designated as a 'people of faith' or a 'community of faith'.

[5] Ibid.

1.1 אֱמוּנָה *in Jewish Tradition*

Is Buber correct when he identifies the faith of Abraham in Gen. 15 as 'an immovable steadfastness'?[6] He draws an analogy between the use of הֶאֱמִן in Gen. 15,6 with the purely non-religious use of the noun אֱמוּנָה in Ex. 17,12, where, during the battle with Amalek, Aaron and Hur supported Moses' hands so that his hands were 'steady'[7] until the going down of the sun. But in Gen. 15 the faith of Abraham is kindled by God's promise, by God's word. Buber interprets the verb form in Gen. 15,6 accordingly: "'…and [Abraham] let remain firm to JHVH' (no object is required here), whereby however no special action is meant but only as it were a supply of strength in relation to an existent essential relationship of trust and faithfulness together".[8]   The nature of Abraham's faith is not that he believed *in* God, but rather quite simply that he *believed God*.   Buber calls this kind of faith "an act of the soul".[9]

The use of the hiphil and niphal forms of the verb in Isa. 7,9 provides further substantiation for this OT understanding of faith. Buber maintains correctly that the hiphil and niphal forms of אמן in this passage indicate something much more significant than simply a play on words.

> The two different meanings of the verb in the passage go back to one
> original: stand firm. The prophet is saying (to put it in our language):
> only if you stand firm in the fundamental relationship of your life do you
> have an essential stability.[10]

There is further a reciprocal relationship between faithfulness and trust inherent in this OT concept of faith. The aspect of trust, unlike that of faithfulness, is not to be understood completely as an attitude or function of the human soul. The soul is indeed involved in both aspects of this re-ciprocal relationship between faithfulness and trust.

> The soul is as fundamentally concerned in the one as in the other, but it is
> decisive for both that the disposition of the soul should become an attitude
> of life. Both, fidelity and trust, exist in the actual realm of relationship
> between two persons. Only in the full actuality of such a relationship can
> one be both loyal and trusting.[11]

---

6   Ibid., p. 44.
7   Literally, "his hands were *steadfastness*": יָדָיו אֱמוּנָה; LXX: αἱ χεῖρες … ἐστηριγμέναι.
8   Buber, p. 45.
9   Ibid., p. 46.
10   Ibid., p. 28.
11   Ibid., p. 29.

Most of what Buber writes about אֱמוּנָה is essentially the same as what we have shown above in Chapter Two. As Emil Brunner points out, Buber's portrayal of faith in the OT is one that can be readily accepted by the Christian OT scholar and is one that can be valued as a contribution to the understanding of the OT; however "with one very important qualification".[12] It is rather what Buber maintains about πίστις in the NT and in Christian tradition which requires a closer, more critical examination.

1.2 Πίστις in Christian Tradition

1.21 Jesus and the Synoptics

In the Foreword of his book Buber refers to Jesus as his 'great brother' and confesses that his own open brotherly relationship to Jesus has become ever stronger and clearer.[13] It is therefore not surprising that Buber, himself a Jew, wishes to pull Jesus out of the light of Christian theological interpretation and view him purely in his Jewish environment. In this light Buber identifies Jesus' own concept of faith as identical with that of the OT. He makes a careful distinction here between what he labels 'the Christian type of faith' and the teachings of Jesus himself.

> By the 'Christian' type of faith therefore is meant here a principle which was joined in the early history of Christianity with the genuine Jewish one; but it must be borne in mind, as I have pointed out, that in the teaching of Jesus himself, as we know it from the early texts of the gospels, the genuine Jewish principle is manifest.[14]

In Jesus' encounter with the father of the demon-possessed boy in Mk. 9,14-27, Buber sees important evidence for his stance. After the disciples were not able to cast the unclean spirit out of the boy, the father appealed to Jesus to do something if he was able (vs. 22). Jesus replied (vs. 23): "What do you mean *if* you are able? All things are possible to the one who believes".[15] Buber argues correctly that Jesus was not simply maintaining that he could heal the boy because of his own faith. Faith is not an 'inner certainty' in the sense: 'I believe that I can heal'. Indeed, it is evident from human experience that 'inner certainty' alone cannot produce the desired ability to heal.[16]

---

12   Brunner, p. 159.
13   Buber, p. 12.
14   Ibid., p. 12.
15   πάντα δυνατὰ τῷ πιστεύοντι.
16   Buber, p. 19.

Jesus' answer that all things are possible for the one who believes
is parallel to his statement that all things are possible with God (Mk.
10,27; Mt. 19,26) and should be interpreted in this light.

> The words 'possible with God' and 'possible to him that believes' do not
> really coincide. 'With God all things are possible' does not mean what the
> disciples who heard it knew very well, that God is able to do all things,
> however much this is also associated with it, but, transcending this, that
> with God, in His realm, in His nearness and fellowship, there exists a
> universal possibility, that therefore all things otherwise impossible
> become and are possible here. This applies also to the person who has
> entered into His realm: the 'one who believes'. But it applies to him in
> virtue of his having been taken into the realm of God. He does not
> possess the power of God; rather the power possesses him....[17]

This concept of 'the believer' is no Hellenistic invention but a Hebrew
one. Buber maintains that the only occurrence of this concept in
preChristian writing is in the OT. The passage he cites in support of this
is Isa. 28,16: "Behold, I am laying in Zion for a foundation a stone, a
tested stone, a precious cornerstone, of a sure foundation: 'He who
believes will not be in haste'".[18] Also in this passage Buber sees a
connection between the believer and the possibility of doing all things:

> For what is possible to the man who believes, therefore also hastening, is
> here likewise possible to him only as to one who believes; but all through
> the Old Testament to believe means to follow in the will of God, even in
> regard to the temporal realization of His will: the man who believes acts
> in God's tempo. ...So the 'passive' in Isaiah and the 'active' in the Gospels
> are combined. This person acts because God's time commands him to act,
> the fact that illness meets him on his way indicates the Divine call to heal;
> even he can only act in God's tempo.[19]

In addition, Buber notes the common ground shared by Jesus' statement in
Mk. 9, 23 and Isaiah's prophecy in 28,16 in that both use the substantival
participle 'the believer' in an absolute sense.[20]
    Also important for Buber's understanding of Jesus' concept of faith
is the statement in Mk. 1,15: "Believe in the gospel".[21] From the

---

[17] Ibid., p. 21.
[18] RSV. Buber offers the following translation: "'He that believeth will not make haste', which includes the thought: 'he will not want to make haste'" (ibid., p. 22). A better English translation
is: "He who believes will not yield, will not flee" The verb יָחִישׁ is intransitive, as is the niphal
of אמן in Isa. 7,9. Since 'faith' itself indicates a 'standing firm', then 'yield, flee' is the correct
understanding in this instance.
[19] Buber, p. 22.
[20] Ibid., p. 23.
[21] Cf. Ibid., pp. 24ff. It should be noted, however, that Buber considers τῷ εὐαγγελίῳ in this passage to be a later addition to the text.

preaching of Jesus he identifies three important principles: "realization of the kingship, the effecting of turning to God, a relationship of faith to - wards Him". [22] Faith is particularly important in this process, considering the nature of the the the radical repentance and turning to God which is required.

> Nevertheless the individual as an individual cannot perceive this event in its course; he must 'believe', more correctly, 'trust'. But this is not merely an attitude of soul, which is required for the accomplishment of turning; the most decisive turning does not yet achieve sufficient human reality, but still requires something which is effective not only in the soul but in the whole corporeality of life; it requires Pistis, more correctly, Emunah. [23]

These three principles of Jesus' preaching are the heritage of Israelite re - ligion. [24] Again, this is most clearly seen in comparison with Isaiah — particularly Isa. 6-8:

> Therefore for Isaiah the principles are apportioned to three moments which closely follow one another in his 'I'-narrative about the beginnings of his effective work (chap. 6 - 8): when he sees 'the King' (Isa. 6,5), when he gives his son the name 'a remnant remains' (implicit in Isa. 7,3), and when he calls upon the unfaithful viceroy of God to trust (Isa. 7,9); for Jesus they are blended in the first proclamation of his preaching in Galilee. [25]

These two examples are not the only ones drawn by Buber to show that Jesus' understanding of faith was the same as the OT understanding, [26] but they are the most important for his argument. Again, Brunner maintains that the Christian scholar can agree with most of what Buber has to say about Jesus' concept of faith as drawn from the text of the synoptics, "though here indeed with an even more important qualification". [27] But, as noted above, Buber intends to drive a wedge between Jesus' teaching concerning faith and what he labels as the 'Christian kind of faith'. [28] Gerhard Ebeling sees this as the most provocative viewpoint presented by Buber on this theme: "Jesus gehört ganz auf die Seite der jüdischen

---

[22] Ibid., p. 25.
[23] Ibid., p. 26.
[24] Ibid., p. 27.
[25] Ibid., p. 29. Also in the LXX version of Ps. 106(105),12 Buber finds a parallel to Jesus' mes- sage: "Believe in the Gospel". Here, as in Mk. 1,15, he suggests the translation: "Trust the message!" (ibid., p. 24; cf. also Ps. 106(105),24).
[26] Cf. ibid., p. 116 where Buber comments on Jesus' conversation with the rich young ruler: "It is truly an instance here of Emunah"; also p. 58: "For the actuality of the faith of Biblical and post- Biblical Judaism, and also for the Jesus of the Sermon on the Mount, fulfilment of the Torah means to extend the hearing of the Word to the whole dimension of human existence".
[27] Brunner, p. 159f.
[28] Cf. Buber, p. 12.

Glaubensweise. Die christliche Glaubensweise, der Glaube an ihn, widerspricht dem Glauben Jesu selbst".[29] According to Buber, 'Christian faith' has its roots and its foundation in the Johannine and Pauline writings of the NT. And it is here where we come into conflict with Buber's teaching of 'two types of faith'.

1.22 The Apostles John and Paul

Emil Brunner identifies and clarifies a threefold aim and a threefold theme in Buber's *Two Types of Faith:*

> ...to make the religious message of Judaism understandable in the light of the Old Testament, to illuminate the message of Jesus as a phenomenon belonging to this world of faith, and to prove the theology of the Apostles—above all the theology of Paul and John...—to be an alien thing, separated from that world of faith by a great gulf.[30]

Buber maintains that there is a radical shift in the Johannine and Pauline understanding of faith away from the Jewish *'emunah*, which is still apparent in Jesus' understanding of faith. This shift formed the foundation of Christianity and marked the beginning of Christian theology. Therefore, for Buber, Christian faith is a second kind of faith.

This radical shift in John is particularly to be seen in the differing accounts of the Petrine confession in the synoptics (Mk. 8,27-30; par.) and John (Jn. 6,66-71).[31] In the synoptic accounts Jesus asks quite pointedly whom the disciples say (believe!) that he is. Peter answers for the other disciples: "You are the Christ (the Son of the Living God)". The formulation in John is different. Here Jesus does not ask whom the disciples believe him to be; rather he asks if the disciples also want to forsake him because of embarrassment at his teaching. Again Peter acts as spokesperson and replies: "Lord, to whom would we go? You have the words of eternal life, and we have believed and have known that[32] you are the Holy One of God".

Buber capitalizes on this difference:

> The direct statements about the master in the synoptics have in this case become one about the disciples. In the synoptics, Peter in answer to the question as to 'who' Jesus is in the opinion of the disciples, makes a

---

[29] Gerhard Ebeling, "Jesus und Glaube", *Wort und Glaube,* vol. 3 (Tübingen: J.C.B. Möhr [Paul Siebeck], 1975), p. 242.

[30] Brunner, p. 159.

[31] Cf. also Buber, pp. 127f. concerning the faith of Thomas as reported in John's Gospel.

[32] πεπιστεύκαμεν καὶ ἐγνώκαμεν ὅτι....

declaration about this nature, but in this case he confesses his faith in an *asserting sentence* (*that...*).[33]

> The difference between this 'It is true' and the other 'We believe and know' is not that of two expressions of faith, but of two kinds of faith. For the first, faith is a position in which one stands, for the second it is an event which has occurred to one, or an act which one has effected or effects, or rather both at once.[34]

It is now very clear what Buber views as the second kind of faith: It is an 'asserting sentence' (*ein Glauben, daß...*), whereby a fact, not a person, is the object of one's commitment. In John's gospel it is the fact that Jesus is the Holy One of God which signifies for Buber John's concept, and consequently the Christian concept, of faith.

Of course Buber admits that a 'Glauben, daß...' is not foreign to the synoptics or, for that matter, even to the OT. He cites Ex. 4,5 as an OT example where faith is brought to expression in this formula. He maintains nonetheless that the OT and synoptic concept of faith in such a formula is essentially different from John's use and understanding of the formula.[35]

Buber views the synoptic and the Johannine accounts of Peter's confession as two stages of a development in which something important is gained and something important is lost in the understanding of faith.

> The gain was the most sublime of all theologies; it was procured at the expense of the plain, concrete and situation-bound dialogicism of the original man of the Bible, who found eternity, not in the super-temporal spirit, but in the depth of the actual moment. The Jesus of the genuine tradition still belongs to that, but the Jesus of theology does so no longer.[36]

Just as much, if indeed not more than the Apostle John, does the Apostle Paul in his epistles represent the second kind of faith. Buber points out that the center of Paul's preaching and of Christian faith is the resurrection of Christ (1 Cor. 15,4. 14).[37] In order to grasp the nature of the faith for which Paul makes his plea, the starting point is belief in the resurrection of Jesus from the dead.[38] It is precisely here that Buber differentiates between Jewish faith and Pauline (Christian) faith.

---

[33] Buber, p. 33 (italics mine).
[34] Ibid., p. 35.
[35] "...but where it occurs it concerns predominantly, or at least in the main, trust"; ibid., p. 33.
[36] Ibid., p. 34.
[37] This not entirely accurate, however. The cross also plays a very important role in Paul's preaching; cf. 1 Cor. 1,18; 2,2f.
[38] Buber, pp. 97f.

> And this faith [in Jesus' resurrection] is a 'belief that' in the pregnant sense
> of the word, which is essentially different from the faith of the Jews that
> on Sinai a divine revelation took place, as it signifies the acceptance of the
> reality of an event, which is not destined, like the former, to confirm and
> strengthen the hereditary actuality of faith of the Jewish person who hears
> about it, but fundamentally to change it.[39]

Buber finds the greatest conflict between Pauline and Jewish faith in
Paul's teachings on faith versus the Law in relation to justification. This
issue is much too complex for us to treat fully in just a few paragraphs.
In essence Buber argues that Paul's view of justification by faith rules out
the possibility of justification for any Jews before the coming of
Christ,[40] since faith itself has to do with the fact that Jesus, the Christ,
was crucified and arose from the dead.

> The faith, which Paul indicates in his distinction between it and the law, is
> not one which could have been held in the pre-Christian era. 'The
> righteousness of God', by which he means His declaration of man as
> righteous, is that which is through faith in Christ (Rom. 3,22; Gal. 2,16),
> which means faith in one who has come, died on the cross and risen.[41]

The Law and its mandates were, according to Paul, unable to bring justification for mankind. Indeed Paul viewed the Law to be unfulfillable.[42] Of
course, Paul would say that there were indeed certain ones who, before the
coming of Christ, were justified by their faith in God, the classic example
being Abraham in Gen. 15,6 (cf. Gal. 3,6ff). But Buber argues that Paul
has altered the original understanding of Abrahamic faith.

> With its assumption by Paul however [Gen. 15,6] is penetrated by the
> principles of the Pauline faith and justification doctrine, and its import is
> changed: faith, as the divine activity in man, gives rise to the condition of
> being righteous, which the 'works', proceeding from men alone, the mere
> fulfilment of the 'law', are not able to bring about.[43]

This pitting of faith against works in Paul's theology is, according to
Buber, irreconcilable with the Jewish teaching of the relationship between
faith and works; i.e., "fulfilment of the divine commandment is valid
when it takes place in conformity with the full capacity of the person and

---

[39] Ibid.
[40] Precisely the same as for Jews after the coming of Christ who did not believe in the resurrection
of Christ from the dead.
[41] Buber, p. 51.
[42] Rom. 3,20; Gal. 2,16; 3,10. Cf. ibid., pp. 53-54.
[43] Ibid., pp. 46f.

from the whole intention of faith".[44]   But, more important, it is irreconcilable with the teaching of Jesus: "Fulfilment of the divne commandment is valid if it takes place in conformity with the full intention of the revelation and from the whole intention of faith—in which however the conception of the intention of faith receives an eschatological character".[45]

This then becomes the crucial point for Buber in his argument for two kinds of faith. He wants to show the radical difference between Jesus and Paul, as he has set it up, to be the radical turning point in the understanding of faith—the difference between Jewish faith and Christian faith, between *'emunah* and *pistis*.

> The answer which Paul gave to the life-question of the man who came from the world of 'law' and wanted to attain to true life in the revealed will of God and the answer with which he anticipated this question was the summons to have faith in Christ. In this way he did precisely what Jesus, in so far as we know him from the synoptic tradition, did not do, and whatever was the case with his 'messianic consciousness', obviously did not wish to do. ...Jesus does indeed ask whom he is considered to be, but he does not desire that a man should hold him to be anyone in particular. The situation for Paul is that a man shall recognize Jesus with all the strength of faith to be the one whom he proclaims as the door to salvation. This is indeed "the word of faith wich we preach" and that to which "the word is nigh to thee" from the Torah is referred (Rom. 10,9): "If thou shalt confess with thy mouth that Jesus is Lord and believe in thy heart that God has raised him from the dead, thou shalt be saved".[46]

1.3 A Response to the Critical Thesis of Martin Buber

It is not my purpose here to provide a comprehensive rebuttal to Buber but rather to expose some of the weaknesses of his argument with regard to Jewish faith versus Christian faith.[47] I shall then proceed to clarify a direction in which his 'two types of faith' may indeed be a helpful category for the understanding of πίστις and πιστεύειν in the writings of Josephus and in the NT.

---

[44]   Ibid., p. 56.
[45]   Ibid.
[46]   Buber, pp. 96f.
[47]   For a further response to Buber's *Two Types of Faith*, see Sung-Jeung Oh, *Der Gerechte wird durch den Glauben leben* (Tübingen Dissertation, 1992).

1.31 Weaknesses of Buber's *Two Types of Faith.*

In an excursus over "Martin Buber's Teaching on the Apostles'
Misunderstanding of Faith",[48] Emil Brunner formulates a cogent response
to the far-reaching and unsettling implications posed by Buber's *Two
Types of Faith* for the Christian teaching on faith. Brunner criticizes the
fact that Buber's guiding presupposition and point of departure for the
distinction which he makes between Jewish faith and the faith of
Johannine and Pauline tradition actually stems from the "'liberal theology'
of the nineteenth century which conceived that there was a radical conflict
between the faith of Jesus and the teaching of Paul".[49] Clearly evident in
Buber's portrayal of Jesus' concept of faith is the Bultmannian thesis that
the teaching of the synoptic Jesus actually belongs to the OT.[50] It is
further clear that Buber was following other NT scholars of his time "who
believed that Paul and John must be understood as radically influenced by
Gnosticism".[51] Buber openly acknowledges this heritage, citing four
Christian theologians to whom he owed much of the substance of his
book: Rudolf Bultmann, Albert Schweitzer, Rudolf Otto and Leonhard
Ragaz.[52]

      Starting from this presupposition, it is not difficult to see how
Buber could portray Christian faith as radically different from—and even
opposed to—Jewish faith. Brunner maintains, however, that Buber's
presupposition has a major flaw:

> When the historians whose theme is primitive Christianity so often played
> off Jesus against Paul, they forgot that Paul was continually surrounded by
> men who had seen Jesus in his lifetime, and who had been with Him day
> by day. How could they have accepted the Pauline Christology and given
> Paul the right hand of fellowship if his teaching had been something
> incompatible with their own picture of Jesus, or even if it had merely
> seemed to them something unfamiliar? Their judgment was rather "Yes,
> this is what He was, this was why He had to suffer death on the Cross,
> this is why He rose again". The unity of the teaching about 'Christ, the
> Son of God' with the narrative about Jesus, as they had experienced Him
> was *the* decisive thing about the *kerygma* concerning Christ. John found
> the most perfect expression for this: "The Word became flesh". With this
> formula, too, he built a bridge between the Old Testament self-

---

[48] Brunner, pp. 159-162.
[49] Ibid., p. 160.
[50] This thesis Bultmann took over from J. Wellhausen.
[51] Brunner, p. 160.
[52] Cf. Buber, pp. 13-15.

manifestation of God and God's self-communication in Jesus the Son of God. [53]

Brunner explains Buber's understandıng of 'fact' [54] to be 'the historical event of Christ': "That this *fact* is the content of faith makes—in Buber's opinion—the Christian faith a faith in facts, a *fides historica*. But a faith in facts is not a faith of trust; it is a 'belief that..'". [55] This 'fact' is then further interpreted by a (gnostic) theology, and the end result is the proposition: "This Jesus is the Christ, the Redeemer".

> Thus in [Buber's] opinion the Christian Faith becomes faith in a mythical gnostic doctrine. Through both, through the relation to historical event and through this dogmatic content, the structure of faith is completely altered. The place of personal surrender in trust and obedience is taken by a theoretical 'conviction that'. [56]

It is this distinction, indeed *contradiction* (according to Buber!), between a faith of trust and a faith in facts, which Buber sees as the distinction and contradiction between Jewish faith and Christian faith. [57] Brunner challenges the idea that there is a contradiction here in the sense of distinction between the faith of trust and the 'belief that...'. Turning the tables on Buber, Brunner *affirms* a distinction between Jewish faith and Christian faith: "Put in another way, here is decided whether one acknowledges Christ as God's plenipotentiary, trusts Him and obeys Him, or whether one is 'offended at Him' (Mt. 11,6)". [58]

The confession of Peter is again an important case in point. Peter was not accepting a theology, "least of all a gnostic theology", when he confessed Jesus as Messiah. Rather, he recognized the person Jesus as "the Only Son and bowed before Him". [59] There was no theological instruction about Jesus as the Christ prior to this confession. "What we here perceive as faith in Jesus", writes Brunner, "stands wholly within what Buber means by faith, security in God, trust and obedience". [60] Moreover, this is precisely the same concept of faith which Paul expresses concerning himself in Gal. 1,16. The authorization for Paul's teaching was the fact that "God revealed His son in me". Brunner

---

[53] Brunner, pp. 182f.
[54] *Tatsache.*
[55] Brunner, p. 161.
[56] Ibid.
[57] Brunner admits that this contradiction is made more pointed by Buber's citation of "certain gnostic doctrines which are in fact to be found in Paul"; ibid., p. 161.
[58] Ibid.
[59] Ibid.
[60] Ibid.

understands this statement as a 'Pauline confession' and, as such, directly parallel to the confession of Peter in the synoptics.[61]

Brunner is willing to accept much of what Buber has to say about the OT concept of faith as well as the concept of faith represented by the teachings of the synoptic Jesus. Nevertheless, he indicates two important qualifications, which he states thus:

> Buber's understanding of faith is not identical with that of the Old Testament, but ... *one* essential element is missing in it. Buber's concept of faith does not make it clear that even Old Testament faith is an answer to God's action in *historical events* and in the prophetic Word. Further ...
> Buber will not admit that Jesus believed Himself to be the bringer of the Kingdom of God (whether one calls Him Messiah, Christ, Son of God or Lord, Kyrios)—and at the same time the suffering servant of Isaiah 53. If Buber has jibbed at the first—as the Jews did—the second, in connection with the event of the Cross, was far more unacceptable to him. But this is the heart of the Pauline Gospel, which is not indeed to be believed as his teaching or theology, but which refers to that event in which God encounters man, and which only he who knows himself to be a sinner can understand in trustful obedience as God's self-communication.[62]

Brunner is correct when he maintains that it is not the *kerygma* about Jesus which constitutes the foundation of Christian faith, but rather Jesus Christ himself.[63] He affirms that Christian faith has precisely the same structure as OT faith with one important modification: "God's rule over history, in which he makes known His own nature, has gained in the his-torical event of Jesus at one and the same time the significance of self-revelation and of self-surrender".[64] This is not, as Buber maintains, a different *type* of faith from the OT faith, but rather a different *content* of faith.

There is a further flaw in Buber's reasoning when he drives a wedge between the Johannine and the synoptic accounts of Peter's confession, maintaining that the former represents faith as an 'event which has occurred to one' (*Begebnis*) and the latter represents faith as a 'position in which one stands' (*Stand*).[65] In fact, the simple syntactical consideration that John uses the perfect tense form of πιστεύειν is sufficient indication that John also has in mind the idea of faith as a 'position in which one stands'. In the Johannine account Peter is not making, as Buber main-

---

61   Ibid., p. 181.
62   Ibid., pp. 161f.
63   Ibid., pp. 179f.
64   Ibid., p. 162.
65   Buber, p. 35.

tains,[66] a statement about the disciples (i.e., "*We* believe that..."), but indeed, just as in the synoptics, a clear statement about who Jesus is (i.e., he is "the Holy One of God").

As a matter of fact there is no real difference between the synoptics and John at this point. The structure of the context is different, but the mode of faith is the same. Mt. 16,16 could also be formulated: "I, Peter, believe that you are the Christ, etc.". The only difference is that in the synoptic accounts Jesus asks his disciples whom they believe him to be, whereas in John's narrative Peter simply makes a confession without answering any question about Jesus' identity.

The OT itself contradicts Buber's thesis about two types of faith. In his attempt to differentiate between faith as trust and faith as the content of what is believed, Buber makes a distinction which the OT does not. On the one hand, Buber does not take into account that the latter element is also present in the OT concept of faith. He does not reckon with the passage Isa. 53,1: "Who has believed *our message*". On the other hand, he actually contradicts himself, when, in one instance referring to Abraham's faith in Gen. 15,6, he rejects the notion that there is a necessary relationship between faith in God and trust in God's word[67] and, in another instance, referring to the faith of Israel in Ex. 14,31, he maintains: "Where it is said of the people (Ex. 4,31; 14,31) that they believed, that simple trust which one has or holds is meant, as in the case of the first pa triarch. When anybody trusts someone he of course also believes what the other says".[68]   In fact, there is not such a clear distinction between these 'two types of faith', as Buber would like to maintain.

Pauline faith does not contradict OT faith.   Buber's (mis)interpretation of Pauline faith as opposed to OT faith is a result both of a misreading of Paul and of a misreading, or better, of a partial reading of the OT. A good example of this is Buber's argument that Paul's teaching of justification by faith contradicts the Jewish (OT) idea of faith. Faith for Paul, according to Buber, is tied together exclusively with the fact that Jesus rose from the dead. And since faith is the only means of justification in the Pauline system, the possibility of justification for any Jews before the coming of Christ must be ruled out.

Of course there is a shift in the faith language of the NT, since faith is now viewed in connection with Christ, and Buber is correct in pointing out this shift. But this shift does not indicate the drastic change

---

[66]   Ibid., p. 33.
[67]   Ibid., p. 46.
[68]   Ibid., p. 35.

which Buber implies. The *content* of faith is indeed new, and Buber is by no means the first to stumble over the NT content of faith; but the *mode* of faith, or the *type* of faith (in Buber's language), is precisely the same as the mode of faith in the OT.

Buber does not take into account, for example, how important the faith of Abraham (Gen. 15,6) is for Paul's theology (cf. Rom. 4). Nor does he see the importance of divine promise in the OT for Paul's understanding of faith.[69] It was the promise of God to Abraham which evoked Abraham's response of faith. In a sense one could even say that this faith of Abraham in Gen. 15,6 was itself the belief in a proposition, a *'Glauben, daß...'*.[70] God promised Abraham that his descendents would be numerous as the stars in the sky, and Abraham *believed*.. Buber's interpretation of Gen. 15,6 fails to take the whole context into consideration.

Buber maintains that Paul has altered the original understanding of Abrahamic faith in Gen. 15,6, that Paul reworked this Abrahamic faith to fit his own system of faith and justification. The proof of this for Buber lies in the fact that Pauline faith, as a divine act within a person, brings about the status of justification, which a person through his or her own works, i.e., through fulfilment of the Law, could not effect.[71] Buber does not recognize this as OT faith. What he fails to see, however, is that this 'Pauline notion' is also deeply embedded in OT tradition (e.g., Ps. 14). Paul's teaching about justification by faith displays not a discrepancy but, rather, a unity with the OT concept of faith. Abraham also was justified by his faith in God (Gen. 15,6).

Buber's faith terminology is problematic. His misinterpretation of Paul in light of the OT is actually one symptom of a much deeper problem. The term 'faith' appears relatively seldom in the OT in comparison with later Jewish and Christian writings. In his interpretation of OT faith, Buber tends to impose his own concept of faith upon the OT texts rather than to proceed from an exegetical starting point. This is particularly clear from the terminology he employs. The language Buber uses to talk about OT faith is not necessarily OT faith language; rather it is his own philosophical, existential language.

A case in point is Buber's reference to ancient Israel as a 'people of faith' or 'community of faith'.[72] Otto Betz writes:

---

[69] Cf. esp. Rom. 4,13. 14. 16. 20.
[70] I.e., the belief that God raises the dead ('the dead' referring to the womb of Sarah!).
[71] Buber, pp. 46f.
[72] Ibid., p. 9.

Die hebräische Konkordanz spricht bisweilen gegen Buber. Nirgends im Alten Testament wird Israel als ein 'Volk des Glaubens' bezeichnet; dagegen findet sich im Sinai-Kontext mehrfach die Wendung 'Volk der Hartnäckigkeit' (Ex. 32,9; 33,3. 5; 34,9; Dt. 9,6. 13), und die Propheten tadeln Israels Herzenshärigkeit (11x).[73]

Another example is Buber's designation of OT faith as 'to follow in the will of God' (*im Willen Gottes gehen*) or his statement that the believer (and also Jesus) 'acts in God's tempo' (*wirkt im Tempo Gottes*).[74] This definition of faith directly contradicts the OT concept of faith. The Hebrew verb הֶאֱמִין does not indicate 'movement', as Buber's language suggests, but rather 'standing firm'. Buber, of course, would not deny the latter,[75] but his own 'faith language' displays an inconsistency with the OT language.

Betz points out further that Buber's translation of אֱמוּנָה as 'trust' is not in line with the OT understanding of the term:

Das von Buber für Israels Glaubenshaltung thematisch gebrauchte Wort Emuna heißt nur selten 'Glauben' (am ehesten in Hab. 2,4) und nie 'Vertrauen'; es bezeichnet meist die Treue Gottes. ...Zwischen 'Glauben' und 'Vertrauen' ist demnach begrifflich zu unterscheiden: Der Glaube ist im Alten Testament in der Regel eben nicht das immer schon bestehende, bleibende und letztlich unerklärliche Vertrauen, sondern ein Akt der Annahmen von Gottes Zusage, die eine Wendung der Dinge bedeutet (vgl. Jes. 7,9; 28,16; Hab. 2,4).[76]

It is interesting at this point that the apostles Paul and John, whom Buber claims have deviated from the OT concept of faith, are the ones who, in contrast to Buber, employ the faith language of the OT. This contradiction is particularly clear in Buber's treatment of Isa. 53. On the one hand, Buber correctly sees the importance of Isa. 53 as background for Jesus' own sense of divine mission; but on the other hand, he completely overlooks the importance of Isa. 53,1 for the NT understanding of faith. Isa. 53,1 also calls for a 'belief that...'; i.e., belief in the fact that God's servant is a *suffering* servant.

In Jes. 53,1 fragt der Prophet fast verzweifelt: "Wer hat unserer Botschaft geglaubt und wem wurde der Arm des Herrn offenbar"? Beide, Paulus und Johannes, haben diese Stelle zitiert (Röm. 10,16; Joh. 12,38); die ersten Christen haben ihr das Nomen und auch den Inhalt des 'Evangeliums' und

---

[73] Otto Betz, "Zwei Wesen der Geschichtsbetrachtung" (unpublished lecture).
[74] Buber, p. 22.
[75] Cf. Buber's translation of Isa. 28,16: "He that believeth will not be in haste"; ibid., pp. 21f.
[76] Otto Betz, "Geschichtsbetrachtung".

natürlich auch ihr Verständnis von Glauben entnommen (vgl. Tg. Jes. 53,1
mit Röm. 1,16f; 1 Kor. 1,18; 15,1-5).[77]

Buber's faith terminology is different from the OT language of faith; indeed it is different from the language of Jesus and Paul and also of the
rabbis. It is his own existential language which does not do justice to the
theological statements of the OT.[78]

1.32 A Strength of Buber's *Two Types of Faith.*

Obviously Buber is not imagining things when he identifies two kinds of
faith—even within the Christian tradition. Brunner grants that the
Christian Church itself is at least in part responsible for giving occasion
for Buber's misunderstanding of Pauline and Johannine faith as a doctrine
to be believed. "Only in most recent times", declares Brunner, "has theology begun to distinguish between the *kerygma* which awakens faith and
the doctrine which is to be believed".[79] Brunner finds in Buber's
'exaggerated' thesis a confirmation of the importance of the task of the
Christian exegete to take a fresh look at the meaning of 'faith'.

This misunderstanding of faith in the Christian tradition was caused
by "the fatal displacement in the interpretation of the word 'believe'".[80]
Brunner identifies four forms of the misunderstanding of πίστις in
Christian tradition:[81]

> 1) The narrative witness to the life of Jesus is conceived of as a report
> of facts which as such are to be believed. Therefore one might call this
> form of misunderstanding of faith 'belief in facts'.
> 2) The case of belief in doctrine is exactly similar. From the
> (doctrinal) witness to Jesus the Christ, the Lord crucified and risen for us,
> in whom we believe because He shatters our autonomy and at the same
> time fills us with trust and obedience, there is isolated the doctrinal
> element which declares "Jesus is God's son—this must be believed".
> 3) In place of the Ekklesia ... we now have the episcopal institution
> which puts forward a doctrine to be believed in; that is, prescribes it to
> man as a law of faith.
> 4) In orthodox Protestantism an (aprioristic) faith in the Bible
> corresponds to this faith in dogma. The Biblical concept of faith which the

---

[77] Ibid.
[78] Ibid.
[79] Brunner, p. 162; cf. p. 181: "In fact the 'accidental fact of history', Jesus, who has caused offence
to the philosophers of all times, is the centre of Christian faith, and not the 'Christ idea' that is
championed against Him. If the Church had not early forgotten this, in spite of its fight against
gnosis and docetism, then the disastrous transformation of faith which made Church history so
tragic would never have occurred".
[80] Ibid., p. 185.
[81] Cf. ibid., pp. 185-89.

Reformers had rediscovered was replaced in the post-Reformation period by
a 'faith' in the Bible backed by an equally formal authority, namely the
authority of the Holy Book whose divine inspiration has to be believed
'from the first'.

Buber's problem with two types of faith is actually a modern problem of
Jewish-Christian relationships, as he himself makes clear in his
concluding remarks.[82] As a result, much of what he claims about the two
types of faith is based more upon his modern situation than upon biblical
and exegetical considerations. G. Ebeling makes a similar observation in
his critique of Buber's two types of faith:

> 'Glauben' ist also von Haus aus kein allgemeiner religiöser Begriff. Aber
> obwohl auf alttestamentlichem Boden erwachsen, hat er doch aus dieser
> Herkunft erst im Neuen Testament intensive Verwendung gefunden. Der
> Christ weist zurück auf das Alte Testament als den mit dem Judentum
> gemeinsamen Wurzelboden, wenn ihm 'Glauben' das Grundwort seiner
> Existenz ist. Der Jude aber verrät seine Begegnung mit dem Neuen
> Testament, wenn er, wie Buber, alles auf den Glaubensbegriff konzentriert
> sein läßt.[83]

From this modern perspective it is indeed easier to see how Buber can
build such a strong argument for a kind of Christian faith that is much
different from Jewish faith. And even Buber is at least partially willing to
admit that the problem of two types of faith must be viewed in a modern
context.[84] Nevertheless Buber's proposal that these two types of faith
have their roots in antiquity is also an accurate assessment.

    We have shown above in Chapter One that even from the Classical
period of Greek literature there were two types of faith, representing respectively an element of *Verbindlichkeit* and an element of
Unverbindlichkeit. The element of *Verbindlichkeit* was taken up by the
LXX translators in their equation of the πιστ- group with the Hebrew אמן
group. The element of *Unverbindlichkeit,* however, became
predominant in the Hellenistic use of the πιστ- group where πιστεύειν in
its religious usage became more or less synonymous with νομίζειν. And
so it is clear that even before NT times there were two distinct trends, two
distinct kinds of faith, and *both kinds* were expressed by the πιστ- word
group.

---

82   Buber, pp. 170ff.
83   G. Ebeling, "Jesus und Glaube", p. 239.
84   Buber, p. 170: *"The crisis of our time* is also the crisis of the two types of faith, Emunah and
Pistis" (italics mine).

Buber's categories are therefore useful, but they must be modified. It is not the Christian faith, as represented by πίστις in the NT (including use by Paul and John), which is essentially different from Jewish faith, as represented by אֱמוּנָה in the OT, but rather another kind of faith. G. Ebeling tries to emend the language of Buber and explain the difference between faith in the NT and faith in the OT in terms of 'two epochs of faith' rather than 'two types of faith'.

> Statt zweier Glaubens*weisen* handelt es sich um die Ansage zweier Glaubens*zeiten*: der vorläufigen Glaubenszeit und der endgültigen Glaubenszeit, *der* Zeit des Glaubens, die die Juden Juden und die Heiden Heiden sein ließ, und *der* Zeit des Glaubens, die Juden und Heiden eins sein läßt in Christus Jesus.[85]

This explanation, however, represents a side-stepping of the issue and suggests that there is more of a difference between faith in the OT and faith in the NT than is acutally the case.

The NT understanding of faith is firmly founded upon and represents a unity with the OT, whether one is considering the faith of Jesus or the faith of Paul. In contrast to Buber, it is indeed proper to speak of *one* kind of faith, which is *biblical faith*, incorporating as a unity *both* the OT אֱמוּנָה and the NT πίστις.

What, then, is the other kind of faith? I have already alluded to it above, and Buber himself gives an indication of what I would consider the more proper distinction between the two types of faith:

> The boundary line is drawn again in such a way that, having regard to the type of faith, Israel and the original Christian Community, in so far as we know about it from the synoptics,[86] stand on the one side, and Hellenistic Christianity on the other (whereas Hellenistic Judaism, with its effacements of the boundaries, has only rarely been equal to the earnestness of the religious process; *compare the vacillations in the conception of faith in Josephus and even Philo, who it is true does rise in a few places to a genuine philosophic expression of Israel's life of faith*).[87]

The other kind of faith is Greek faith. And the proper distinction between two types of faith is not Jewish faith versus Christian faith, but much rather Biblical faith versus Greek faith. Josephus' use of πιστ- as faith terminology provides us with an excellent case in point of this latter dis-tinction.

---

[85] G. Ebeling, "Jesus und Glaube", p. 244.
[86] Naturally, I would include at this point also Paul and John.
[87] Buber, pp. 33f (italics mine).

2 FLAVIUS JOSEPHUS: BIBLICAL FAITH VERSUS GREEK FAITH

2.1 Development of the Πιστ- Word Group as Faith Terminology

2.11 Two Trends

As we have repeatedly pointed out, πιστεύειν as faith terminology in Classical Greek implicitly possessed both the element of *Verbindlichkeit* and the element of *Unverbindlichkeit*.[88]   By the Hellenistic period, however, two distinct concepts of faith can be identified, both represented by the πιστ- word group.   The one trend, represented primarily by the equation of the πιστ- group with the Hebrew ˆma root in the LXX, remains generally consistent with the close connection of both elements of *Verbindlichkeit* and *Unverbindlichkeit*.   Through this association with the Hebrew concept of faith, the religious understanding of faith represented by the Greek πιστ- word group underwent a process of expansion and enrichment.   This development would not likely have been possible had the πιστ- group not already been understood in light of the two basic components of *Verbindlichkeit* and *Unverbindlichkeit*.

The other trend of religious use of the πιστ- group is identified in its association with and in its assimilation of the Greek faith terminology: νομίζειν θεοὺς εἶναι.   In this formula the element of *Unverbindlichkeit* is emphasized, often to the exclusion of the element of *Verbindlichkeit*.   Faith, then, is purely a 'belief that [such and such is the case]', and the element of personal commitment is lost.   Πιστεύειν ὅτι... and πιστεύειν with indirect discourse come to signify faith as an intellectual assent, and πίστις represents the fact or facts which comprise the content of this intellectual assent.   'Faith' in this sense is obviously a purely human act and not a divine gift.   This development took place within the Greek language itself and was not necessarily due to the influence of a foreign language tradition.[89]

---

88   In contrast to νομίζειν which was primarily *unverbindlich*.

89   This is not unlike the development of faith terminology even in modern languages, where an earlier integration of both elements of *Verbindlichkeit* and *Unverbindlichkeit* is lost in a later understanding of faith as simply belief in [a set of] facts.   A good example is the German term *Glauben*.   Karl Heinz Goll, a good friend of mine who is well-versed German etymology, has brought to my attention that 'Glaube, glauben' in Mittelhochdeutsch ('G(e)loube, gelouben') and in Althochdeutsch ('Giloubo, gelouben') was very closely related to earlier forms of the words: 'lieben, loben' and even 'erlauben'.   The common stem of all these terms was 'lub' which had the base meaning 'gutheißen, Vertrauen haben, sich etwas lieb, vertraut machen'.

2.12 Hellenistic Judaism

Both trends can be found within the broad spectrum of Hellenistic Judaism. As already noted, the LXX is by far the most consistent representative of the first trend with its understanding of πιστ- in connection with the Hebrew root אמן. It is quite clear, particularly from statements such as Ex. 4,5[90] and Ps. 27(26),13,[91] that the πιστ- words as faith terminology in the Greek OT encompass *both elements* of believing the truth of a fact (*Unverbindlichkeit*) and the personal commitment of trust (*Verbindlichkeit*). Of course, even here the πιστ- group as faith terminology cannot be fully appreciated outside of the context of the Hebrew root אמן and the concept of faith which it represents.

The Greek translation of Jesus Sirach further takes up and confirms this first trend. Greek Sirach expands the concept of πιστ- in some instances to encompass relationships expressed by Hebrew roots other than אמן, but nowhere is the element of personal commitment lacking. Even when the Law or the word [of God] are explicit objects of πιστεύειν,[92] Sirach is not singling out an element of *Unverbindlichkeit,* but rather urges personal commitment and faithfulness.

In later apocryphal writings there is evidence of a stronger influence of secular Greek. In certain passages in 4 Macc., for example, πιστεύειν has much more the 'flavor' of an intellectual (*unverbindliche*) belief which is characteristic of the secular Hellenistic trend.[93] And in other instances a purely profane use of both πιστεύειν and πίστις are the norm.[94] But as a rule, where the πιστ- group appears throughout the LXX (including the Apocrypha) as faith terminology, it is consistent with the OT concept of faith and an incorporation of both elements of *Verbindlichkeit* and *Unverbindlichkeit*.

In Philo's use of the πιστ- group there is a more pronounced distinction from the OT understanding of faith. Philo does indeed use the OT faith terminology as a point of departure for his concept of faith. The faith of Abraham in Gen. 15,6 is especially important for Philo. But this is purely a point of departure. With the exception of the terminology itself, Philo's concept of faith actually has very little in common with

---

[90]   ἵνα πιστεύσωσίν σοι ὅτι ὦπταί σοι κύριος ὁ θεὸς τῶν πατέρων αὐτῶν.

[91]   πιστεύω τοῦ ἰδεῖν τὰ ἀγαθὰ κυρίου ἐν γῇ ζώντων.

[92]   E.g., Sir. 32,24; 33,3.

[93]   Cf. 4 Macc. 5,25; 7,18-19. Nonetheless, it is important that, even in these instances, πιστεύειν appears in a context where there is a strong emphasis upon personal commitment. In this sense the heritage of the Hebrew אמן is still quite evident.

[94]   E.g., 1 Macc. 8,16; 10,27. 46; 3 Macc. 3,10.

that of the OT. Rather Philo's 'philosophical' faith is conceptually much closer to the kind of faith which had been evolving in secular Hellenism; i.e., it is a more intellectual faith, with little or no emphasis upon personal commitment. This is particularly clear in passages such as *leg. alleg.* 3,164 where faith[fulness] is explained in terms of believing that God rewards those who are worthy with good gifts, or *leg. al leg.* 3,229, where trust in God is 'the true doctrine'.[95] Also in Philo's use of epithets for God in connection with faith terminology, we have noted a subtle move, whereby Philo practically creates doctrinal (one could even say 'creedal') statements from the epithets themselves.[96]

This does not mean that the Philonic concept of faith displays no traces of the OT concept; it obviously does. On the other hand, the influence of the Greek concept of faith upon Philo's concept of faith is particularly pronounced. The utilitarian faith of Philo, whereby those who possess such faith stand to gain from God all of the good things in life, stems also from the Greek concept of faith, which emphasizes an intellectual process rather than an integrated act of faith and faithfulness (*Verbindlichkeit*). The opposite of this kind of faith is the 'heroic faith' of the patriarchs and martyrs in Heb. 11.

2.2 Πιστ- as Faith Terminology in Josephus and the NT

2.21 Two Types of Faith in Josephus

The final question to be addressed, then, is: Where do Josephus and the NT fit into this larger picture in their respective uses of the πιστ- word group as faith terminology? Josephus the Jew, writing primarily for a Hellenistic audience, was aware of two kinds of faith and employed the πιστ- word group in reference to both. Josephus, like Philo, represents a mixture of traditional Jewish and popular Greek influences. Yet there is an important difference. Unlike Philo, Josephus was neither a philosopher nor speculative theologian. He was primarily an [apologetic] historian. His account of the Jewish antiquities is no theological innovation, but rather a reflection upon tradition. His account of the Jewish war is primarily a historical reflection, not a religious one. The *Vita* and *Contra Apionem* are primarily apologetic. Of the latter two, *Contra Apionem* is indeed more religious in nature, but it by no means represents an attempt to systematize a theology.

---

[95] ἀληθὲς δόγμα.
[96] E.g., *de vita Mosis* 1,284; *quis rer. div. heres* 99; *de virt.* 218; et al.

The non-religious nature of Josephus' writings finds confirmation in his use of the πιστ- word group. Πίστις and πιστεύειν are predominantly non-religious vocabulary for him. Where the πιστ- words do in fact occur in a religious sense, the mode of employment is already fixed and determined by whichever tradition[97] Josephus follows at one point or the other. In other words, the continuing development of the πιστ- group as faith terminology which appears in two trends from the Classical period up to the Hellenistic period and is witnessed in the LXX, in Sirach, in Philo, as well as in secular Hellenistic writings,[98] is not continued in Josephus. It is not his aim to develop a further religious use of πιστ-; rather he employs categories of meaning for the word group which are already at hand.

For this reason also a clearer distinction between the two types of faith can be identified in Josephus' writings than, for instance, in the writings of Philo. Josephus does not 'mix and match' Jewish and Greek elements of πίστις as Philo does. Although Josephus does not rigidly follow the LXX pattern in employing the πιστ- group in connection with certain narrative events,[99] it is obvious that his religious understanding of the verb πιστεύειν within the context of the Jewish antiquities is very much influenced by the LXX use and understanding of πιστεύειν. He does not reduce faith to an intellectual or philosophical category, divorced from faithfulness and personal commitment.

The influence of biblical faith upon Josephus' concept of faith is particularly evident in passages where he refers to faith in God,[100] faith in the [OT] prophets[101] and faith in connection with signs and wonders.[102] Especially Josephus' use of πιστ- in connection with Moses reveals his heritage from the tradition of Ex. 4, Ex. 14,31 and Num. 14,11.[103] There is also evidence that Josephus understood the noun πίστις in the sense of the Hebrew אֱמוּנָה when referring to 'the faithfulness of God'.[104]

Josephus was also quite familiar with a kind of faith which is more intellectual than it is committal. He employed the πιστ- word group in this sense in a (Jewish) religious setting as well. This Hellenistic influence is more recognizable in Josephus' use of the substantive πίστις

---

[97] I.e., Jewish or Greek.
[98] And also in the NT!
[99] The word group is lacking, for instance, in Josephus in connection with the Abraham narratives.
[100] E.g., *Ant.* 2,117. 333; 3,309.
[101] E.g., *Ant.* 9,12. 72; 10,124; 11,96.
[102] E.g., *Ant.* 2,274. 276; 8,232.
[103] Cf. *Ant.* 2,274; 4,179.
[104] *Ant.* 17,179. 284.

as the content of what is believed; e.g., the Pharisaic creed in *Ant.* 18,14 or πίστις as the 'most correct faith about God' in *Ap.* 2,163.[105] In *Bel.* 2,135 πίστις appears as a religious term[106] but much more in the sense of a 'virtue' of personal fidelity. Πίστις commonly refers to 'loyalty, faithfulness' in Josephus but, with the exception of two references to the faithfulness of God, exclusively on a profane level. For Josephus, the substantive does not signify the proper relationship of men and women to God,[107] but rather the proper belief or the proper doctrine about God.

Josephus' use of the verb πιστεύειν also displays evidence of Greek influence. In some of the creedal formulas[108] faith appears as a non-committal, intellectual assent to a doctrine or set of doctrines. Along this line Josephus also speaks of a 'faith in the Bible'.[109] In some instances faith for Josephus has the 'utilitarian' character which is also present in the Philonic concept of faith[110] as a means to the 'good things' in life. In *Ant.* 8,279 πιστεύειν as religious faith has even a 'superstitious' character, referring to faith in idols. This is totally foreign to the OT use of πιστ- as the equivalent of אמן.

But the greatest influence of the Greek concept of faith upon Josephus is apparent in the fact that many [biblical] uses of the πιστ- group for faith are missing in Josephus. Πίστις (= אֱמוּנָה = 'faithfulness') never appears in Josephus, expressing the proper relationship of humankind toward God. Likewise, Josephus never uses the substantival participle ὁ πιστεύων to refer to 'the believer, the faithful one' in the sense of Isa. 28,16.[111] Also significant is the complete lack of religious use of the adjective πιστός in Josephus' writings, referring either to 'faithfulness' as a religious attribute (of God or of humankind) or, substantivally, to 'the faithful one, the believer' (= ὁ πιστεύων). The fact that such important expressions of the element of personal commitment—an element which is self-evident in the biblical concept of faith—are missing in Josephus, is evidence that Josephus' concept of faith was strongly influenced by the Greek concept of faith.

---

[105]   Cf. *Ap.* 2,169.

[106]   Referring to the πίστις of the Essene sect.

[107]   As, for example, in Hab. 2,4.

[108]   I.e., πιστεύειν ὅτι or πιστεύειν plus indirect discourse; cf. *Ant.* 4,60; 6,263; 10,267.

[109]   *Ap.* 1,38. This faith in the 'Bible' is something much different than the 'biblical faith' in our present discussion!

[110]   Cf. *Ap.* 2,218; Josephus differs from Philo here, however, in that he views the rewards of faith eschatologically, whereas for Philo the good things in life are to be experienced as present realities.

[111]   And much more often in the NT!

2.22 One Kind of Faith in the NT

In contrast to Josephus, the NT knows only one kind of faith: the faith of the OT. The NT employs the πιστ- word group as faith terminology only in reference to this one kind of faith. The πιστ- group also plays a much greater role as faith terminology in the NT than it does in Josephus. While the NT employs only a couple of profane uses of the group, πιστ- in Josephus occurs primarily in a profane sense and only in a minority of instances as religious faith. In other words, πίστις and πιστεύειν in Josephus by no means represent the central theological concept of faith which they do in the NT.

Yet the occasional parallelism between the religious use of the πιστ- group in Josephus and in the NT is very significant for the NT understanding of faith. Where parallelism exists, it exists in the context of Jewish and Hebrew usage, a heritage shared by both the NT and Josephus. Conversely, when Josephus deviates from the OT concept of faith in his use of πιστ- and displays more Greek influence, there are are no direct parallels in the NT. The indication in these instances is that the NT is not influenced by the Greek concept of faith to the degree that Josephus is. Moreover, the additional religious uses of the πιστ- group in the NT which do not appear in Josephus are directly parallel to, or derived from, similar uses of the group in the LXX.

The NT clearly represents a further development in the use of the πιστ- word group as faith terminology; and this, once again, is in contrast to Josephus. The mere frequency of appearance of the πιστ- words in the NT over against the lesser frequency of occurrence in the OT is an indication that the word group has developed beyond the OT in terms of be coming the *key theological terminology for religious faith*.. This development naturally took place as a result of the Christ event.

There are indeed two types of faith which can be identified within Hellenistic Judaism of the first century C.E. But the line of distinction between the two types of faith should not be drawn between the OT of the Jews and the NT of the Christians. The comparison of πιστ- as faith terminology in the writings of Flavius Josephus and in the NT has shown that this is in fact not the case. Rather, the line of distinction should be properly seen between the biblical kind of faith and the secular Greek kind of faith.

Josephus knew both kinds of faith, but the NT knows only the former. Building upon the foundation laid in the LXX (i.e., πιστ- = אמן)

and utilizing elements of biblical theology (not elements of non-Jewish Hellenistic religion), the NT authors further developed from the words of the πιστ- group the theological terminology to express the proper relationship of humankind to God.

HEBREW EQUIVALENTS FOR ΠΙΣΤ- IN JESUS BEN SIRACH

Key: LXX = Septuagint
KG = Kairo Geniza Fragments
Seg = Segal's "Back-translation"

1,14   (LXX) μετὰ πιστῶν ἐν μήτρᾳ συνεκτίσθη αὐτοῖς
(KG) . . .
(Seg) ועם נאמנים ברחם נוצרה

1,15   (LXX) μετὰ τοῦ σπέρματος αὐτῶν ἐμπιστευθήσεται
(KG) . . .
(Seg) ועם זרעם תאמן

1,27   (LXX) ἡ εὐδοκία αὐτοῦ πίστις καὶ πραΰτης
(KG) . . .
(Seg) ורצונו אמונה וענוה

2,6   (LXX) πίστευσον αὐτῷ
(KG) . . .
(Seg) האמן בו ועזרך בטח בו

2,8   (LXX) οἱ φοβούμενοι κύριον, πιστεύσατε αὐτῷ
(KG) . . .
(Seg) יראי יי האמינו בו

2,10   (LXX) τίς ἐνεπίστευσεν κυρίῳ
(KG) . . .
(Seg) מי האמין ביי ויבוש

2,13   (LXX) οὐαὶ καρδίᾳ παρειμένῃ, ὅτι οὐ πιστεύει
(KG) . . .
(Seg) אוי למוג לב כי לא יאמין

4,16   (LXX) ἐὰν ἐμπιστεύσῃ
(KG) . . .
(Seg) אם יאמין לי יירשני

4,17   (LXX) ἕως οὗ ἐμπιστεύσῃ τῇ ψυχῇ αὐτοῦ
(KG) ועד עת ימלא לבו בי
(Seg) ועד עת ימלא לבו בי

6,7   (LXX) μὴ ταχὺ ἐμπιστεύσῃς αὐτῷ
        (KG) ואל תמהר לבטח עליו
        (Seg) ואל תמהר לבטח עליו

6,14   (LXX) φίλος πιστός[1] σκέπη κραταιά
        (KG) אוהב אמונה אוהב תקוף
        (Seg) אוהב אמונה אוהב תקוף

6,15   (LXX) φίλου πιστοῦ οὐκ ἔστιν ἀντάλλαγμα
        (KG) לאוהב אמונה אין מחיר
        (Seg) לאוהב אמונה אין מחיר

6,16   (LXX) φίλος πιστὸς φάρμακον ζωῆς
        (KG) צרור חיים אוהב אמונה
        (Seg) צרור חיים אוהב אמונה

7,26   (LXX) μισουμένῃ μὴ ἐμπιστεύσῃς σεαυτόν
        (KG) ושנואה אל תאמן בה
        (Seg) ושנואה אל תאמן בה

11,21   (LXX) πίστευε δὲ κυρίῳ καὶ ἔμμενε τῷ πόνῳ σου
        (KG) רוץ לייי וקוה לאו[ו]רו ..
        (Seg) האמן לייי וקוה לארו

12,10   (LXX) μὴ πιστεύσῃς τῷ ἐχθρῷ σου εἰς τὸν αἰῶνα
        (KG) אל תאמין בשונא לעד
        (Seg) אל תאמין בשונא לעד

13,11   (LXX) μὴ πίστευε τοῖς πλείοσιν λόγοις αὐτοῦ
        (KG) ואל תאמן לרב שׂיחו
        (Seg) ואל תאמן לרב שׂיחו

15,15   (LXX) καὶ πίστιν ποιῆσαι εὐδοκίας
        (KG) ואמונה לעשׂות רצון אל
        (Seg) ותשבונה לעשׂות רצונו
               אם תאמין בו גם אתה תחיה

16,3   (LXX) μὴ ἐμπιστεύσῃς τῇ ζωῇ αὐτῶν
        (KG) אל תאמין בחייהם
        (Seg) אל תאמין בחייהם

19,4   (LXX) ὁ ταχὺ ἐμπιστεύων κοῦφος καρδίᾳ
        (KG) . . .
        (Seg) ממהר להאמין חסר לב

19,15   (LXX) μὴ παντὶ λόγῳ πίστευε
        (KG) . . .
        (Seg) ולכל דבר אל תאמן

---

[1] From the Greek one would expect the Hebrew equivalent to be נאמן; cf. also 6,15.

22,23   (LXX) πίστιν κτῆσαι ἐν πτωχείᾳ μετὰ τοῦ πλησίου
        (KG) . . .
        (Seg) ²האמן לרעך בעניו

27,16   (LXX) ὁ ἀποκαλύπτων μυστήρια ἀπώλεσεν πίστιν
        (KG) . . .
        (Seg) מגלה סוד יאבד אמונה

31,28³ (LXX) ἡ μαρτυρία τῆς καλλονῆς αὐτοῦ πιστή
        (KG) עדות טובו נאמנה
        (Seg) עדות טובו נאמנה

31,29⁴ (LXX) ἡ μαρτυρία τῆς πονηρίας αὐτοῦ ἀκριβής
        (KG) דעת רועו נאמנה
        (Seg) דעת רועו נאמנה

32,21⁵ (LXX) μὴ πιστεύσῃς ἐν ὁδῷ ἀπροσκόπῳ
        (KG) אל תבטח בדרך מחתף
        (Seg) אל תבטח בדרך מחתף

32,27⁶ (LXX) ἐν παντὶ ἔργῳ πίστευε τῇ ψυχῇ σου
        (KG) בכל מעשיך שמור נפשך
        (Seg) בכל מעשיך שמור נפשך

32,28⁷ (LXX) ὁ πιστεύων νόμῳ προσέχει ἐντολαῖς
        (KG) שומר תורה נוצר נפשו
        (Seg) נוצר תורה שומר נפשו

33,3a   (LXX) ἄνθρωπος συνετὸς ἐμπιστεύσει λόγῳ
        (KG) איש נבון יבין דבר ייי
        (Seg) איש נבון יבין דבר

33,3b   (LXX) καὶ ὁ νόμος αὐτῷ πιστός
        (KG) . . .
        (Seg) [. . .] ותורתו

34,8   (LXX) σοφία στόματι πιστῷ τελείωσις
        (KG) . . .
        (Seg) וחכמה לפי נאמן כליל

36,21   (LXX) οἱ προφῆταί σου ἐμπιστευθήτωσαν
        (KG) ונביאיך יאמינו
        (Seg) ונביאיך יאמינו

---

2 Imperative!
3 (= 34,23).
4 (= 34,24).
5 (= 35,21).
6 (= 35,23).
7 (= 35,24).

36,31   (LXX) τίς γὰρ πιστεύσει εὐζώνῳ λῃστῇ;
      (KG) מי יאמין בצבא גדוד
      (Seg) מי יאמין בגדוד צבא

37,13   (LXX) οὐ γὰρ ἔστιν σοι πιστότερος αὐτῆς[8]
      (KG) כי אם אמון ממנו
      (Seg) מי יאמין לך אמן ממנו

37,23   (LXX) οἱ καρποὶ τῆς συνέσεως αὐτοῦ πιστοί
      (KG) פרי דעתו בגויתם
      (Seg) פרי דעתו בגויתם

38,31   (LXX) πάντες οὗτοι εἰς χεῖρας αὐτῶν ἐνεπίστευσαν
      (KG) . . .
      (Seg) כל אלה בידידם יאמנו

40,12   (LXX) πίστις εἰς τὸν αἰῶνα στήσεται
      (KG) . . .
      (Seg) ואמונה לעולם תעמד

41,16   (LXX) οὐ πάντα πᾶσιν ἐν πίστει εὐδοκιμεῖται
      (KG) ולא כל הכלם נבחר
      (Seg) ולא כל הכלם נבחר

44,20   (LXX) ἐν πειρασμῷ εὑρέθη πιστός
      (KG) ובניסוי נמצא נאמן
      (Seg) ובניסוי נמצא נאמן

45,4   (LXX) ἐν πίστει καὶ πραΰτητι αὐτὸν ἡγίασεν[9]
      (KG) באמונתו ובענותו בחר בו מכל [בשׂר]
      (Seg) באמונתו ובענותו בחר בו מכל [בשׂר]

46,15a   (LXX) ἐν πίστει αὐτοῦ ἠκριβάσθη προφήτης
      (KG) ב[... ...]שׂ חזה
      (Seg) באמונתו נדרש חזה

46,15b   (LXX) καὶ ἐγνώσθη ἐν ῥήμασιν αὐτοῦ πιστὸς ὁράσεως
      (KG) וגם בדברו נאמן רועה
      (Seg) וגם בדברו נאמן רועה

48,22   (LXX) ὁ προφήτης ὁ μέγας καὶ πιστὸς ἐν ὁράσει αὐτοῦ
      (KG) . . .
      (Seg) הנביא הגדול והנאמן בחזיונו

---

8 I.e., βουλὴ καρδίας.
9 Hebrew: 'chosen.'

49,10   (LXX) ἐλυτρώσαντο αὐτοὺς¹⁰ ἐν πίστει ἐλπίδος
     (KG) [. . .ב] וישעוהו
     (Seg) וישעוהו באמונת תקוה

50,24   (LXX) ἐμπιστεύσαι μεθ' ἡμῶν τὸ ἔλεος αὐτοῦ
     (KG) יאמן עם שמעון חסדו
     (Seg) יאמן עם שמעון חסדו

---

¹⁰ [αὐτόν].

BIBLIOGRAPHY

1 PRIMARY SOURCES

1.1 Biblical Sources

Biblia Hebraica Stuttgartensia. Ed. K. Elliger and W. Rudolph. Stuttgart: Deutsche Bibelgesellschaft, 1983.
Die Bibel. According to Martin Luther's Translation. With Apokryphen. Stuttgart: Deutsche Bibelgesellschaft, 1984.
Novum Testamentum Graece. Ed. Eberhard Nestle and Kurt Aland. 26th ed. Stuttgart: Deutsche Bibelstiftung, 1979.
The Greek New Testament. Ed. Kurt Aland et al. 3rd ed. New York: United Bible Societies, 1968.
The Holy Bible. Revised Standard Version. Philadelphia: A. J. Holman Company, 1962.
The Septuagint with Apocrypha: Greek and English. Ed. Charles Lee Brenton. Reprint. Grand Rapids, MI: Zondervan Publishing House, 1978.
Septuaginta. Ed. Alfred Rahlfs. 2 vols. in one. Stuttgart: Deutsche Bibelgesellschaft, 1979.

1.2 Apocrypha and Pseudepigrapha

Die Apokryphen und Pseudepigraphen des Alten Testaments. 2 vols. in one. Ed. and trans. E. Kautzsch. Tübingen: J. C. B. Mohr (Paul Siebeck), 1900.
The Old Testament Pseudepigrapha. Ed. James A. Charlesworth. 2 vols. London: Darton, Longman & Todd, 1983.
Das vollständige Buch Ben Sira (hebräisch). Ed. M. Z. Segal. Jerusalem, 1958.
The Book of Ben Sira: Text, Concordance and Analysis of the Vocabulary. Jerusalem: Academy of the Hebrew Language and the Shrine of the Book, 1973.
Ecclesiastico: Testo ebraico con apparato critico e versioni greca, latina e siriaca. Ed. Francesco Vattioni. Napoli: Istituto Orientale, 1968.
Sapientia Iesu Filii Sirach. Ed. Joseph Ziegler. *Vetus Testamentum Graecum,* vol. 12,2. Göttingen: Vandenhoeck & Ruprecht, 1965.

1.3 Qumran

Die Texte aus Qumran: Hebräisch und Deutsch. Ed. Eduard Lohse. 4th ed. München: Kösel-Verlag, 1986.

1.4 Josephus and Philo

Flavii Iosephi Opera. Ed. Benedictus Niese. 7 vols. Berlin: Weidmann, 1955.

Flavius Josephus. *De Bello Judaico; Der jüdische Krieg: Griechisch und Deutsch.*
    Ed. Otto Michel and Otto Bauernfeind. 3 vols. Darmstadt: Wissenschaftliche
    Buchgesellschaft, 1969.
Flavius Josephus. *Jüdische Altertümer.* Trans. Heinrich Clementz. 2 vols. in one.
    Wiesbaden: Fourier Verlag (no date).
Josephus. 10 vols. Ed. and trans. J. Thackeray et al. *The Loeb Classical Library.*
    Cambridge, MA: Harvard University Press, 1965.
Philonis Alexandrini Opera quae supersunt. Ed. Leopold Cohn and Paul Wendland.
    6 vols. Berlin: Walter de Gruyter, 1962.
Philo von Alexandria. *Die Werke in deutscher Übersetzung.* Ed. Leopold Cohn et
    al. 7 vols. Berlin: Walter de Gruyter, 1964.
Philo. 10 vols. with 2 supplemental vols. Ed. and trans F. H. Colson et al. *The
    Loeb Classical Library.* Cambridge, MA: Harvard University Press, 1962.
"Philo: Selections". Ed. Hans Lewy. *Three Jewish Philosophers: Philo; Saadya
    Gaon; Jehuda Halevi.* New York: Atheneum, 1977.

1.5 Other Ancient Greek Authors

Aeschines: Oriatones. Ed. F. Blass. Stuttgart: B. G. Teubner, 1978.
Aeschyli Septem quae supersunt Tragoedias. Ed. Denys Page. Oxford: Clarendon
    Press, 1972.
Aristophanes. 3 vols. English trans. B. B. Rogers. *The Loeb Classical Library.*
    Cambridge, MA: Harvard University Press, 1963.
Euripides. 4 vols. English trans. Arthur S. Way. *The Loeb Classical Library.*
    Cambridge, MA: Harvard University Press, 1971.
Inscriptiones Graecae IV: Inscriptiones Epidaurii. Ed. Fredericus Hiller de
    Gaertringen. Berlin: Walter de Gruyter, 1929.
Lucian. 8 vols. English trans. M. C. Macleod. *The Loeb Classical Library.*
    Cambridge, MA: Harvard University Press, 1967.
Platon: Werke in acht Bänder; Griechisch und Deutsch. Ed. Gunther Eigler.
    Darmstadt: Wissenschaftliche Buchgesellschaft, 1970.
Polybius: The Histories. 6 vols. English trans. W. R. Paton. *The Loeb Classical
    Library.* Cambridge, MA: Harvard University Press, 1968.
Porphyrii Philosophi Platonici Opuscula Selecta. Ed. Augustus Nauck. Leipzig,
    1886.
Sophocles. 2 vols. English trans. F. Storr. *The Loeb Classical Library.*
    Cambridge, MA: Harvard University Press, 1968.
Sophoclis Fabulae. Ed. A. C. Pearson. Oxford: Clarendon Press, 1971.
Thukydides. 8 vols. Ed. J. Classen. 3rd ed. Berlin: Weidmann, 1912.
Xenophon. 7 vols. English trans. E. C. Marchant, u. a. *The Loeb Classical
    Library.* Cambridge, MA: Harvard University Press, 1968.
Xenophontis Commentarii. Ed. Carolus Hude. Stuttgart: B. G. Teubner, 1985.

2 REFERENCE WORKS

Autenrieth, Georg. *A Homeric Dictionary.* Trans. Robert P. Keep. Norman, OK: University of Oklahoma Press, 1982.

Barthelemy, D., and O. Rickenbacher, eds. *Konkordanz zum hebräischen Sirach.* Göttingen: Vandenhoeck & Ruprecht, 1973.

Bauer, Walter. *Greek Lexicon of New Testament and Other Early Christian Literature.* Trans. William F. Arndt and F. Wilbur Gingrich. Chicago: University of Chicago Press, 1957.

Blass, F., and A. Debrunner. *A Greek Grammar of the New Testament and Other Early Christian Literature.* Trans. Robert W. Funk. Chicago: University of Chicago Press, 1961.

Brown, Francis, S. R. Driver and C. A. Briggs. *Hebrew and English Lexicon of the Old Testament.* Oxford: Clarendon Press, 1906.

Dos Santos, Elmar Camilo. *An Expanded Hebrew Index for the Hatch-Redpath Concordance to the Septuagint.* Jerusalem: Baptist House, Dugith Publishers (no date).

Feldman, L. H. *Josephus and Modern Scholarship 1937-1980.* Berlin: Walter de Gruyter, 1984.

Fraenkel, Ernst. *Griechische Denominativa in ihrer geschichtlichen Entwicklung und Verbreitung.* Göttingen: Vandenhoeck & Ruprecht, 1906.

Kautzsch, E., ed. *Gesenius' Hebrew Grammar.* 2nd English ed. A. E. Cowley. Oxford: Clarendon Press, 1976 = 1910.

Goetchius, Eugene van Ness. *The Language of the New Testament.* New York: Charles Scribner's Sons, 1965.

Hatch, Edwin, and Henry A. Redpath. *A Concordance to the Septuagint.* Graz, Austria: Akademische Druck- und Verlagsanstalt, 1954.

Holladay, William L. *A Concise Hebrew and Aramaic Lexicon of the Old Testament.* Grand Rapids, MI: William B. Eerdmans Publishing Company, 1971.

Lampe, Geoffrey W. H. *A Patristic Greek Lexicon.* Oxford: Clarendon Press, 1968.

Liddell, Henry George, and Robert Scott. *A Greek-English Lexicon.* 9th ed. (Reprint). Oxford: Clarendon Press, 1958.

Mandelkern, Solomon. *Veteris Testamenti Concordiantiae.* Reprint. Graz, Austria: Akademische Druck- und Verlagsanstalt, 1955.

Menge, Hermann. *Langenscheidts Taschenwörterbuch der griechischen und deutschen Sprache. Erster Teil: Altgriechisch-Deutsch.* 42nd ed. Berlin: Langenscheidt, 1985.

Moulton, James Hope, and George Milligan. *The Vocabulary of the Greek Testament.* Reprint. Grand Rapids, MI: William B. Eerdmans Publishing Company, 1980.

Moulton, W. F., and A. S. Geden, eds. *A Concordance to the Greek Testament.* 5th ed. Edinburgh: T & T Clark, 1978.

Rengstorf, K. H. *A Complete Concordance to Flavius Josephus.* Leiden: Brill, 1973.

Robertson, A. T. *A Grammar of the Greek New Testament in the Light of Historical Research.* Nashville, TN: Broadman Press, 1934.

Rüger, Hans Peter. *Text und Textform im hebräischen Sirach.* Berlin: Walter de Gruyter, 1970.

Smend, Rudolf. *Griechisch-Syrisch-Hebräischer Index zur Weisheit des Jesus Sirach.* Berlin: Georg Reimer Verlag, 1907.

Smyth, Herbert W. *Greek Grammar.* Cambridge, MA: Harvard University Press, 1984.

Stephanus, Henricus. *Thesaurus Graecae Linguae.* Vol. 6. Paris, 1829.

Weingreen, J. *A Practical Grammar for Classical Hebrew.* 2nd ed. Oxford: Clarendon Press, 1975 = 1959.

3 SECONDARY SOURCES

Attridge, Harold W. *The Interpretation of Biblical History in the Antiquitates Judaicae of Flavius Josephus.* Harvard Theological Review, Harvard Dissertations in Religion, No. 7. Missoula, MT: Scholars Press, 1976.

Baillie, D. M. *Faith in God and Its Christian Consummation.* London: Faber and Faber, 1964.

Barth, Gerhard. "πίστις". *Evangelisches Wörterbuch zum Neuen Testament.* Vol. 3 (1983): 216-231.

——. "*Pistis* in hellenistischer Religiosität". *Zeitschrift für die Neutestamentliche Wissenschaft* 73 (1982): 110-126.

Baur, L. "Philo v. Alexandria". *Lexikon für Theologie und Kirche.* Vol. 8. Ed. Michael Buchberger. Freiburg: Herder & Co., 1936. Pp. 242-243.

Betz, Otto. "Die Geschichtsbezogenheit des Glaubens im Alten und Neuen Testament". *Glaube und Geschichte: Heilsgeschichte als Thema der Theologie.* Ed. Helge Stadelmann. Giesen/Basel: Brunnen Verlag, 1986.

——. "Die Gestalt des Glaubens im Alten Testament und im frühen Judentum". (Unpublished lecture.)

——. "Jesu Evangelium vom Gottesreich". *Das Evangelium und die Evangelien.* Ed. Peter Stuhlmacher. Tübingen: J. C. B. Mohr (Paul Siebeck), 1983. Pp. 55-77.

——. *Jesus: Der Herr der Kirche.* Tübingen: J.C.B. Mohr (Paul Siebeck), 1990.

——. *Jesus: Der Messias Israels.* Tübingen: J.C.B. Mohr (Paul Siebeck), 1987.

——. *Wie verstehen wir das Neue Testament?* Wuppertal: Aussaat Verlag, 1981.

——. "Zwei Wesen der Geschichtsbetrachtung". (Unpublished lecture.)

Bousset, D. W. *Die Religion des Judentums im neutestamentlichen Zeitalter.* 1st ed. Berlin: Verlag v. Reuther & Reichard, 1903.

Brandenburger, Egon. "Pistis und Soteria. Zum Verstehenshorizont von 'Glaube' im Urchristentum". *Zeitschrift für Theologie und Kirche* 85 (1988): 165-198.

Brunner, Emil. *The Christian Doctrine of the Church, Faith, and the Consummation; Dogmatics: Vol III.* Trans. David Cairns. Philadelphia: The Westminster Press, 1962.

Buber, Martin. *Two Types of Faith.* Trans. Norman P. Goldhawk. New York: Macmillan Publishing Company, 1951.

Bultmann, Rudolf. "πιστεύειν, κτλ." *Theological Dictionary of the New Testament.* Vol. 6. Ed. Gerhard Friedrich. Grand Rapids, MI: Wm. B. Eerdmans Publishing Co., 1968.

——. *Theologie des Neuen Testaments.* 9th ed. Tübingen: J. C. B. Mohr (Paul Siebeck), 1984.

Di Lella, Alexander. *The Hebrew Text of Sirach.* London: Mouton & Co., 1966.

Dobbeler, Axel von. *Glaube als Teilhabe.* Tübingen: J. C. B. Mohr (Paul Siebeck), 1987.

Ebeling, Gerhard. "Jesus und Glaube". *Wort und Glaube.* 3 vols. Tübingen: J. C. B. Mohr (Paul Siebeck). Vol. 3 (1975): 203-254.

——. "Was heißt Glauben?" *Sammlung gemeinverständlicher Vorträge und Schriften aus dem Gebiet der Theologie und Religionsgeschichte* 216, 1958.

Fahr, Wilhelm. "ΘΕΟΥΣ ΝΟΜΙΖΕΙΝ: Zum Problem der Anfänge des Atheismus bei den Griechen". *Spoudasmata* 26. Hildesheim: Georg Olms Verlag, 1969.

Feldman, L. H. "Josephus as a Biblical Interpreter". *Jewish Quarterly Review* 75 (1985): 212-252.

——. "Josephus' Portrait of Saul". *Hebrew Union College Annual* 53 (1982): 45-99.

Friedländer, Paul. "Platon". Vol. 2: *Die Platonischen Schriften: Erste Periode.* 2nd ed. Berlin: Walter de Gruyter, 1957.

Grässer, Erich. *Der Glaube im Hebräerbrief.* Marburg: N. G. Elwert Verlag, 1965.

Haaker, Claus. "Glaube II. Altes und Neues Testament". *Theologische Realenzyklopädie* 13 (1984): 277-304.

Hackforth, R. *The Composition of Plato's Apology.* London: Cambridge University Press, 1933.

Hamm, Dennis. "Faith in the Epistle to the Hebrews: The Jesus Factor". *Catholic Biblical Quarterly* 52,2 (April, 1990): 270-291.

Hay, David M. "Pistis as 'Ground for Faith' in Hellenized Judaism and Paul". *Journal of Biblical Literature* 108,3 (1989): 461-476.

——. "The Psychology of Faith in Hellenistic Judaism". *Aufstieg und Niedergang der Römischen Welt.* Part II: Principat. Vol. 20.2. Ed. Wolfgang Haase. Berlin: Walter de Gruyter, 1977. Pp. 881-925

Hays, Richard B. *The Faith of Jesus Christ.* Chico, CA: Scholars Press, 1983

Hermisson, Hans-Jürgen, and Lohse, Eduard. *Glauben.* Stuttgart: Kohlhammer Taschenbücher Reihe, Vol. 1005, 1978.

Hooker, Morna D. "ΠΙΣΤΙΣ ΧΡΙΣΤΟΥ". *New Testament Studies* 35 (1989): 321-342.

Hultgren, Arland J. "The *Pistis Christou* Formula in Paul". *Novum Testamentum* 22,3 (Juli 1980): 248-263.

Jepsen, A. "אמן". *Theological Dictionary of the Old Testament.* Vol. 1. Ed. G. Johannes Botterweck and Helmer Ringgren. Grand Rapids, MI: Wm. B. Eerdmans Publishing Co., 1974.

Johnson, Timothy Luke. "Rom. 3:21-26 and the Faith of Jesus". *The Catholic Biblical Quarterly* 44 (1982): 77-90.

Kaiser, Otto. "Die Bedeutung des Alten Testaments für den christlichen Glauben". *Zeitschrift für Theologie und Kirche* 86 (1988): 1-17.

Keller, C. A. "Glaube in der *Weisheit Salomos*". *Festschrift für W. Eichrodt* (*Abhandlungen zur Theologie des Alten und Neuen Testaments* 59, 1970): 11-20.

Kerényi, Karl. *Die antike Religion.* Düsseldorf/Köln: Eugen Diederichs Verlag, 1952.

Kinneavy, James L. *Greek Rhetorical Origins of Christian Faith. An Inquiry.* New York/Oxford: Oxford University Press, 1987.

Latte, Kurt. Review of: *I. G. IV²1: Inscriptiones Epidauri* (ed. Hiller de Gaertingen). *Gnomon* 7 (1931): 113-135.

Lee, T. R. *Studies in the Form of Sirach 44 - 50.* Society of Biblical Literature Dissertation Series, 75. Atlanta: Scholars Press, 1986.

Lohse, Eduard. "Emuna und Pistis—Jüdisches und urchristliches Verständnis des Glaubens". *Zeitschrift für die neutestamentliche Wissenschaft* 68 (1977): 147-163.

Lührmann, Dieter. "Glaube". *Reallexikon für Antikum und Christentum.* Vol. 11, Col. 51.

———. *Glaube im frühen Christentum.* Gütersloh: Verlagshaus Gerd Mohn, 1976.

———. "Pistis in Judentum". *Zeitschrift für die neutestamentliche Wissenschaft* 64 (1973): 19-38.

Oh, Sung-Jeung. *Der Gerechte wird durch den Glauben leben.* Tübingen Dissertation, 1992.

Peisker, M. *Der Glaubensbegriff bei Philon.* Dissertation. Breslau, 1936.

Perry, Edmund. "The Meaning of *'emuna* in the Old Testament". *The Journal of Bible and Religion* 21 (1953): 252-256.

von Rad, Gerhard. "Die Anrechnung des Glaubens zur Gerechtigkeit". *Gesammelte Studien zum Alten Testament* (Th. B. 8, 1963): 130-135.

———. *Theologie des Alten Testaments.* 2 vols. 8th ed. München: Kaiser, 1982-1984.

Reitzenstein, R. *Die hellenistischen Mysterienreligionen nach ihren Grundgedanken und Wirkungen.* 3rd ed. Leipzig: 1927.

Schlatter, Adolf. *Der Glaube im Neuen Testament.* 6th ed. (with Introduction by Peter Stuhlmacher). Stuttgart: Calwer Verlag, 1927=1982.

———. "Wie Sprach Josephus von Gott?" *Beiträge zur Förderung christlicher Theologie.* Ed. A. Schlatter and D. W. Lütgart. Gütersloh, 1910.

Schmitz, W. *Ἡ Πίστις in den Papyri.* Dissertation. Köln, 1964.

Seidl, E. *Πίστις in der griechischen Literatur bis zur Zeit des Peripatos.* Dissertation. Innsbruck, 1952.

Smend, Rudolf. "Zur Geschichte von האמין". *Festschrift für Walter Bauer: Hebräische Wortforschung.* Suppl. *Vetus Testamentum* 16. Leiden: E. J. Brill, 1967. Pp. 284-290.

Snell, Bruno. *Die Entdeckung des Geistes.* 4th ed. Göttingen: Vandenhoeck & Ruprecht, 1975.

Spicq, C. *L'Épître á Hebreaux.* 2 vols. Paris, 1952.

Stuhlmacher, Peter. *Jesus von Nazareth—Christus des Glaubens.* Stuttgart: Calwer Verlag, 1988.

Tate, J. "Greek for Atheism". *The Classical Review* 50 (1936): 3-5.

——. "More Greek for Atheism". *The Classical Review* 51 (1937): 3-6.

Weiser, Artur. "πιστεύειν, κτλ." *Theological Dictionary of the New Testament.* Vol. 6. ed. Gerhard Friedrich. Grand Rapids, MI: Wm. B. Eerdmans Publishing Co., 1968.

Wildberger, H. "אמן". *Theologisches Handbuch zum Alten Testament* 1(1971): 177-209.

——. "Glauben im Alten Testament". *Zeitschrift für Theologie und Kirche* 65(1968): 129-159.

——. "Glauben—Erwägungen zu האמין". *Festschrift für Walter Baumgartner: Hebräische Wortforschung.* Suppl. *Vetus Testamentum* 16(1967): 372-386.

Williams, Sam K. "Again *Pistis Christou*". *The Catholic Biblical Quarterly* 49 (1987): 431-447.

Williamson, Ronald. *Philo and the Epistle to the Hebrews.* Leiden: E. J. Brill, 1970.

Windisch, Hans. *Die Frömmigkeit Philos und ihre Bedeutung für das Christentum.* Leipzig: J. C. Hinrichs'sche Buchhandlung, 1909.

Wißmann, E. "Das Verhältnis von ΠΙΣΤΙΣ und Christusfrömmigkeit bei Paulus". *Forschungen zur Religion und Literatur des Alten und Neuen Testaments* 40(1926): 43-47.

Wolfson, Harry Austryn. *Philo. Foundations of Religious Philosophy in Judaism, Christianity, and Islam.* 2 vols. Cambridge, MA: Harvard University Press, 1948.

INDEX OF PASSAGES CITED

OLD TESTAMENT

OLD TESTAMENT APOCRYPHA & PSEUDEPIGRAPHA

PHILO OF ALEXANDRIA

1 M. Hengel. *Die Zeloten*. Untersuchungen zur jüdischen Freiheitsbewegung in der Zeit von Herodes I. bis 70 n. Chr. 2. verbesserte und erweiterte Auflage. 1976. ISBN 9004043276

2 O. Betz. *Der Paraklet*. Fürsprecher im häretischen Spätjudentum, im Johannes-Evangelium und in neu gefundenen gnostischen Schriften. 1963. ISBN 9004001093

5 O. Betz. *Abraham unser Vater*. Juden und Christen im Gespräch über die Bibel. Festschrift für Otto Michel zum 60. Geburtstag. Herausgegeben von O. Betz, M. Hengel, P. Schmidt. 1963. ISBN 9004001107

6 A. Böhlig. *Mysterion und Wahrheit*. Gesammelte Beiträge zur spätantiken Religionsgeschichte. 1968. ISBN 9004001115

7 B. J. Malina. *The Palestinian Manna Tradition*. The Manna Tradition in the Palestinian Targums and its Relationship to the New Testament Writings. 1968. ISBN 9004001123

8 J. Becker. *Untersuchungen zur Entstehungsgeschichte der Testamente der zwölf Patriarchen*. 1970. ISBN 9004001131

9 E. Bickerman. *Studies in Jewish and Christian History*.
    1. 1976. ISBN 9004043969
    2. 1980. ISBN 9004060154
    3. 1986. ISBN 9004074805

11 Z. W. Falk. *Introduction to Jewish Law of the Second Commonwealth*.
    1. 1972. ISBN 9004035370
    2. 1978. ISBN 9004052496

12 H. Lindner. *Die Geschichtsauffassung des Flavius Josephus im Bellum Judaicum*. Gleichzeitig ein Beitrag zur Quellenfrage. 1972. ISBN 9004035028

13 P. Kuhn. *Gottes Trauer und Klage in der rabbinischen Überlieferung*. Talmud und Midrasch. 1978. ISBN 9004056998

14 I. Gruenwald. *Apocalyptic and Merkavah Mysticism*. 1980. ISBN 9004059598

15 P. Schäfer. *Studien zur Geschichte und Theologie des rabbinischen Judentums*. 1978. ISBN 9004058389

16 M. Niehoff. *The Figure of Joseph in Post-Biblical Jewish Literature*. 1992. ISBN 900409556X

17 W. C. van Unnik. *Das Selbstverständnis der jüdischen Diaspora in der hellenistisch-römischen Zeit*. Aus dem Nachlaß herausgegeben und bearbeitet von P. W. van der Horst. 1993. ISBN 9004096930

18 A. D. Clarke. *Secular and Christian Leadership in Corinth*. A Socio-Historical and Exegetical Study of 1 Corinthians 1-6. 1993. ISBN 9004098623

19 D. R. Lindsay. *Josephus and Faith*. Πίστις and πιστεύειν as Faith Terminology in the Writings of Flavius Josephus and in the New Testament. 1993. ISBN 9004098585